THE
CENTER
CANNOT
HOLD

THE CENTER CANNOT HOLD

The 1960
Presidential
Election
and the Rise
of Modern
Conservatism

LAURA JANE GIFFORD

ᵐ

Northern
Illinois
University
Press
DeKalb

© 2009 by Northern Illinois University Press

Published by the Northern Illinois University Press, DeKalb, Illinois   60115

Manufactured in the United States using postconsumer-recycled, acid-free paper.

All Rights Reserved

Design by Shaun Allshouse

Library of Congress Cataloging-in-Publication Data

Gifford, Laura Jane.

The center cannot hold : the 1960 presidential election and the rise of modern conservatism / Laura Jane Gifford.

p.   cm.

Includes bibliographical references and index.

ISBN 978-0-87580-404-0 (clothbound : alk. paper)

1. Republican Party (U.S. : 1854-)—History—20th century. 2. Conservatism—
United States—History—20th century. 3. Presidents—United States—Election—1960.
4. United States—Politics and government—1953–1961. I. Title.

JK2356.G53 2009

324.973′0921—dc22

2009007479

For Geoff

Contents

Acknowledgments

I owe debts of gratitude to many people who helped make this book a reality. Thanks to archivists at a variety of institutions, including Kate Moore and the archival staff at the University of South Carolina; archivists at Clemson University; Linda Whitaker and the staff of the Arizona Historical Foundation; Amy Fitch and the staff of the Rockefeller Archive Center; archivists at Yale University; Genie Guerard in the University of California, Los Angeles Department of Special Collections; Kirsten Julian and the staff of the Richard M. Nixon Library and Birthplace; and above all, Paul Wormser, Lisa Gezelter, and the fine folks of the National Archives and Records Administration Pacific Southwest Branch repository at Laguna Niguel, California, who dealt with my many, many visits and endless paging requests. Special thanks to the late William F. Buckley, Jr. for providing access to his papers at Yale and for his kind approval of their use, to Christopher Buckley for later permissions, and to Gregory D. Shorey for sharing his time and memories with me. Thanks also to Max Kravtsov for Russian translation services. A version of chapter 5 was originally published in the *Journal of Policy History* (19:2), Pennsylvania State University Press.

I appreciate the assistance I received from so many people at UCLA and above all from my supportive and understanding adviser, Jessica Wang (now of the University of British Columbia), committee members Robert A. Hill, Scott C. James, and Geoffrey Robinson, and graduate advisers Barbara Bernstein and Jinny Oh, who kept so many logistical wheels running smoothly. Thanks especially to Bobby Hill for offering me a research job before I even began at UCLA. Thanks to the UCLA interlibrary loan department for tracking down innumerable obscure references. Thanks also to the professors and staff who guided me and nurtured my understanding of the relationship between education and social responsibility at Pacific Lutheran University in Tacoma, Washington.

Editor Sara Hoerdeman and the rest of the staff and board at Northern Illinois University Press have been immensely helpful in moving this project from dissertation to published book. Thanks to them and to the thoughtful anonymous readers who offered such helpful recommendations. Conference audiences, commentators, and others, including Anthony Chen, Kirsten Fermaglich, Irv Gellman, and Gigi Peterson, offered insight and advice that have strengthened this volume in many places. Any errors of fact or interpretation are my own.

To the women of the "study group"—Erin Brown, Amy Cox Klug, and Marissa DeSiena McDaniels—many, many thanks for your years of support and friendship. I suspect none of us understood exactly how deep the bonding experience of three months of studying for written comprehensive exams would be. You've all been there for me then and ever since, and I hope I can always do the same for you. Thanks to Whitney Strub for his friendship, teaching assistant camaraderie, and many insightful responses to my chapter drafts. Thank you, Julie and Rhett Luedtke, for hour upon hour of much-needed and appreciated babysitting (and for listening to me vent!). Thanks to the Joyful Servant community and to all our friends who lift me up—and to my youth group kids, who keep me grounded. Thanks also to Chapters Books and Coffee in Newberg, Oregon, which offered a friendly place to write when I needed to hear other human voices.

Last, but very far from least, thank you to the many wonderful members of my family. You have all helped me in ways ranging from interest and prayers to mail delivery (thanks, Marcia!). Thanks to my grandparents, Edwin F. and Joye Ritchie, Thelma Ingalsbe Kurilo, the late Paul Ingalsbe, and the late Roger Kurilo, who have provided me with love, support, fantastic parents, and the foundation on which I stand. Thanks to my parents, Michael and Sally Ritchie, for raising me to believe I am capable of great things—and bear a responsibility to use these gifts in a way that will help others. Thanks to my sister, Sara—I am thrilled Mom and Dad gave me a "Sara without an H" with whom to share my life. Thanks to my beautiful daughter, Meredith, and thanks above all to Geoff, who has loved me, supported me, listened to me, comforted me, and been even more patient and understanding than I could possibly have imagined. You've been on the front lines throughout this process—the least I can do in return is to dedicate this book to you.

Thank you, Lord, for my many blessings.

THE CENTER CANNOT HOLD

Introduction

Cracks in the Consensus

"I don't know what can be done between now and 1960, but it will never be done by tiptoeing through the tulip bed. Somebody has to speak out in the forthright manner that Teddy Roosevelt employed. Who will it be?"—Robert Humphreys, Republican National Committee Campaign Director, December 31, 1958[1]

Arizona senator Barry Goldwater was a Renaissance man. He was a pilot and a legislator, a photographer and a retailer—and in the summer of 1959, a flight from his arid home state east to Washington, D.C. made him a philosopher. Waxing rhapsodic, he spoke of the thrill of cross-country flight and the emotions it unleashed: "I have always thought the spiritual feeling of seeing my America unrolled below me to be the strongest; the greenness of the valleys of California, the better known and loved beauties and canyons of my Arizona; the Rockies, the flat Middle West, the streams and farms of the East, the hills that keep the East from the West." Such emotions were tied to the people of each region—"the aircraft worker of California, the cowboy of my state, the miner in the Rockies, the farmer in Indiana . . . the automobile worker in Detroit, and the tobacco man of the South, the banker of New York and the professor in Princeton." What did each of these citizens think of his country? What did he view as his responsibility? Did he know that his freedom could only be preserved by his own actions and decisions or that Benjamin Franklin and Thomas Jefferson had warned of the importance and difficulty of preserving the republic? "Does he know, as he sits in his comfortable home, the lights flickering across the snow covered yards, signaling his happiness to me above, that government cannot be the provider without being the master?"[2]

The political universe of the 1950s was fundamentally moderate. As comedian Mort Sahl quipped when discussing voters' options in 1956, "Eisenhower stands for 'gradualism.' Stevenson stands for 'moderation.' Between these two extremes, we the people must choose!"[3] Goldwater was one of a few often-dismissed conservative Republican mavericks who, along with southern Democratic segregationists, marked the only real exceptions to centrist political leadership in both parties.[4] Changes, however, were afoot. Goldwater offered principled independence in a Cold War world marked by uncertainty and massive change. More significant to long-term success, conservative leaders understood the importance of cultivating grassroots support, while their more liberal party compatriots failed to connect to that cowboy in Arizona or even the banker in New York. A growing number of American conservatives were becoming disenchanted with the perceived "me-tooism" of liberal Republicanism, and the organizations they established in 1960 would forge the groundwork for a new GOP.

Americans generally regard the 1960 presidential election as the inauguration of "Camelot" and John F. Kennedy's New Frontier, a time when the nation threw off the bonds of parochialism to elect a Catholic president and endorse a moderate, statist government. Kennedy would take Americans to the moon and ask what they could do for their country, establish the Peace Corps to reach out to the world, and take a tough line against Soviet Premier Nikita Khrushchev when he attempted to extend Soviet influence to Cuba. Dominant perceptions aside, however, contemporary Americans' views of 1960 were quite different, and the election's lasting legacy has been remarkably different as well. In the election of 1960, less than 50 percent of the American population endorsed Kennedy and his program, a reality that fractures rosy portrayals of a county united behind the young president. Furthermore, 1960 also marked the consolidation of forces within the Republican Party that would eventually garner the support of well over half the electorate, taking the country in a conservative direction very different from the vision Kennedy projected.

The 1958 midterm elections were a nearly unqualified debacle for the Republican Party. The GOP was absolutely trounced at the polls, where Democrats gained thirteen Senate seats, a record victory, and 47 seats in the House of Representatives for the largest gain in ten years. Traditionally Republican farm states in the Midwest, frustrated by the policies of Eisenhower's agriculture secretary Ezra Taft Benson, ousted nineteen Republicans from the House of Representatives and elected two Democratic senators and three governors. In his sixth year as the Republicans' chief campaigner, Vice President Richard M. Nixon's vote-getting strength appeared to be at an all-time low. Dwight Eisenhower's second in command was unable to overcome the burdens of recessionary economic conditions and Ike's increasingly disturbing legacy of party neglect. Even so, most commentators continued to predict that, given his position and his long history of relationship building at all levels of the party, Nixon was the clear front-runner for the GOP presidential nomination in 1960. In the midst of the wreckage, two Republicans pulled out victories that would become enormously important for the future of the party. One went largely unheralded at the time, while the other was hailed as a sign of the party's future. Ironically, the former would become the pioneer of a massive sea change in American politics, while the latter faded into memory as a symbol of the road not chosen. The first of these men was the fiery young Goldwater, who won reelection to a second term on an anti-labor platform. The second was liberal Republican and Standard Oil heir Nelson A. Rockefeller, who, in a year of overwhelming Republican defeats won a massive victory in his first electoral campaign, displacing incumbent Democrat Averell Harriman. Rockefeller's election instantly propelled him into consideration for the 1960 presidential nomination, and liberal Republicanism appeared to many to be the way of the future.[5] Ultimately, of course, Nixon did become the Republican nominee in 1960—and he lost to Massachusetts Senator John F. Kennedy by the smallest of margins. Barry Goldwater, the object of an attempted draft in 1960 by conservative idealists, gained the nomination in 1964 and went down in flames as incumbent Lyndon B. Johnson and the Democrats successfully painted him as a dangerous extremist— a designation with which many liberal Republicans quietly agreed. One man's disaster, however, proved a movement's triumph, as the grassroots organizations Goldwater supporters had begun to build in 1960 continued to mature and develop into the strongest mobilizing force on the right side of the American political spectrum. Nixon ran to the right in 1968, and while some historians have argued that he governed toward the center, the events of Watergate effectively destroyed Nixon's chances of directing the party's future in a centrist direction.[6] The ultimate consolidation of conservative gains came with the Reagan Revolution of 1980.

The events that set this historical process in motion began in 1960, as a Goldwater-supporter-led challenge from the right and a Rockefeller challenge from the left buffeted Nixon on both sides. The way these forces played out over the course of the campaign determined the future of the Republican Party, even as Nixon struggled to gain the presidency. Political campaigns are essentially a series of appeals to constituent groups as a politician strives to cobble together sufficient support to win with a majority of the electorate. The ways in which constituent groups interact with and respond to candidates, therefore, tell historians a great deal about the manner in which a candidate is reaching out, being received, the relative success of various approaches, and the possibility for victory in the present or increasing support in the future. The success or failure of a given constituent group in affecting the direction of political events also demonstrates its relative power within the party and the country at large.

Constituent groups are the building blocks from which political actors construct governments, and as such are instrumental to any coherent explanation of partisan change. By the end of the 1960 election, analysis of the responses and activities of six key constituent groups—party liberals, African Americans, the conservative intelligentsia, youth, Southerners, and ethnic groups—reveals that conservatives within the Republican Party had gained sufficient momentum to direct the party's future. At the very point in American history when liberalism appeared to be most dominant, the underpinnings of the liberal consensus were disintegrating beneath the surface. Conservatives made far more effective use of grassroots organization to develop networks that could push the Republican Party in a rightward direction. Vital developments in these grassroots organizations took place over the course of the 1960 election. Furthermore, conservatives like Goldwater responded to their supporters more effectively than did liberal and moderate leaders like Rockefeller and Nixon. The 1960 election demonstrates the agency individuals and groups possess within a highly structured political framework like the American party system. Liberals scored individual victories in the 1960s and even the 1970s, but the future course of the Republican Party had been charted.

Realignment?

Over the past several decades, realignment theory has held a dominant position in the historiography of electoral politics and party change. Political scientist Walter Dean Burnham, perhaps the most prominent scholar in this field, argued in 1967 that the American party system had seen "critical realignments" about once per generation, with the most recent stable system reflecting a New Deal political order.[7] Each system was characterized by a high degree of political stability and a dominant political culture that favored a particular partisan arrangement, whether of one-party dominance or of an ongoing split. "Critical realignments" were the result of political crises brought on by what Burnham characterized as a basic flaw in the organization of American party institutions. The parties, he contended, have a chronic tendency to ignore emerging mass political demands until a boiling point is reached that results in the formation of third-party insurgent groups.[8] Subsequent stresses on the party system lead to "short, sharp reorganizations of the mass coalitional basis of the major parties."[9]

Burnham speculated in 1970 that, provided the party system was still strong enough in an era of personality politics and split tickets, a sixth party system might be in the making. He viewed the 1964 election as having some characteristics of a realigning election and was particularly interested in the impact of Alabama Governor George Wallace's 1964 and 1968 third-party campaigns upon the electorate. He even pondered the possibility of a semisocialist versus semifascist party alignment coming out of the tumultuous 1960s.[10]

In recent years, realignment theory has come under challenge. Some scholars contend that realignment theory is excessively stringent in its categories or that it fails to explain American politics after the 1930s. Others believe the theory as a whole should be discarded; it is not an adequate guide to American electoral, party, or policy history, and its continued presence is hobbling the course of academic inquiry.[11] Despite these cautions, however, evidence demonstrates that while Burnham's theories about socialist and fascist developments were exaggerated, his suggestion that the 1960s marked a "critical realignment" are borne out by the subsequent ascendance of conservatives to power in the Republican Party and eventually to dominance in the nation as a whole.[12]

The idea of a realignment is implicit in the works of scholars like Thomas and Mary Edsall, who contend that since the 1960s, conservatives have capitalized on a set of barriers arising between former members of the New Deal coalition. These barriers include race, taxes, the "rights revolution," and rights-related political reform movements. Combined, they have generated a "chain reaction" forcing the realignment of the presidential electorate.[13] E.J. Dionne also argues for the lasting impact of the 1960s upon American politics, stating that "liberalism and conservatism are framing political issues as a series of false choices." In essence, he argues that the major parties are still fighting the "cultural civil war of the 1960s," with both parties expressing the interests of upper-middle-class Americans and not the public as a whole.[14]

The theory of "critical realignment," then, continues to have significant merit in considering political trends of the 1950s and 1960s and the ideological polarization of political parties that resulted. Analysis of the constituencies profiled in this book demonstrates the extent to which the dominant consensus liberalism of the day focused upon the advice of experts and the continuing strength of the status quo rather than recognizing the growing power of a variety of insurgent groups. Burnham and the realignment theorists, however, overlook the complicated story of electoral campaigns in their efforts to impose an overarching theory. The analytical framework of realignment theory elides many of the specific historical realities of political mobilization—how parties operate, how constituents respond to party leaders, and how individuals and groups influence the political process. The earlier shifts Burnham cites are readily apparent, and any American living in a post-Reagan world can hardly deny that politics have changed significantly since the 1960s. Missing from all of the above analyses, however, is the answer to a key question: how, exactly, did all of the forces these theorists discuss affect the process of choosing a presidential candidate? Burnham and other realignment theorists have attempted to build a theory without paying attention to the discrete components from which American government is built. This book aims to reclaim the history of the electoral campaign itself by studying the dynamics of electoral change on the ground. In so doing, we gain a fuller understanding of how the "critical realignment" of which Burnham speaks might have begun. A constituent-based focus will provide the groundwork upon which overarching theories might stand.

A Note on Terminology

American political parties have traditionally been peculiarly non-ideological organizations. With pragmatic goals of victory and patronage in mind, the long-lived Democratic and Republican parties, in particular, have been characterized by "remarkable social pluralism."[15] Machine politics and the presence of unified voting blocks in regions like the South meant that the national Democratic Party, for example, contained both working-class Irish American urbanites and the southern gentry. Traditional patronage structures began to disintegrate as early as the turn of the twentieth century, but long-standing partisan loyalties and notions of party competitiveness based upon a perceived need for ideological heterogeneity meant that the old system persisted. In 1960, for example, politicians as diverse in ideological sympathies as Barry Goldwater and Nelson Rockefeller could call the Republican Party home.

Goldwater was the party's—and, indeed, the country's—signal representative of the conservative vision. Goldwater described conservative politics as "the art of achieving the maximum amount of freedom for individuals that is consistent with the maintenance of the social order."[16] For Goldwater, this conservative vision translated into support for states' rights, local jurisdiction over policies like education and civil rights, and the Cold War fight against the Sino-Soviet menace, a war that could only be won if the

United States did not subordinate itself to institutions such as the United Nations. The senator opposed a large federal government, legislation increasing union power, and foreign alliances and foreign aid programs. Goldwater was also an early example of a Republican politician who forthrightly stated that an uncompromising conservative platform was the key to the GOP's future success. The Arizona senator's beliefs represented a departure from traditional partisan politics and as such became a rallying point for conservative Americans determined to create a more ideologically coherent party—and nation.

Rockefeller, on the other hand, was one of the leading proponents of Republican liberalism. The governor advocated federal aid for education and federal action to further the cause of civil rights. He argued that the government had a positive role to play in stimulating economic growth, and while he favored reforms in labor practices, he was more supportive of union rights and advocated similar checks on corporate power. Like Goldwater, Rockefeller was a Cold War hawk, but, unlike the senator, he believed in international organizations, even going so far in 1962 as to suggest that the federal idea could be applied to the world of nations as well as to the United States.[17]

The similarities between Rockefeller's political beliefs and the liberal consensus politics of the 1950s are immediately apparent. Consensus theory taught that in the form of the liberal, New Deal system, the United States had established an ideal compromise between free market capitalism and a social welfare state. As historian Arthur Schlesinger, Jr. wrote in 1949, "the center is vital; the center must hold. The object of the new radicalism is to restore the center, to reunite individual and community in fruitful union. The spirit of the new radicalism is the spirit of the center— the spirit of human decency, opposing the extremes of tyranny."[18] While Republican and Democratic adherents might have articulated the details of consensus liberalism—this "new radicalism," as Schlesinger termed it—a bit differently, with Rockefeller Republicans placing more faith in capitalism than Democrats such as Hubert Humphrey, the fundamental principles were the same. Once asked why he remained a member of the Republican Party, Rockefeller argued that he felt he was more temperamentally suited to pushing the Republicans forward as a liberal Republican than to holding the Democrats back as a moderate Democrat.[19]

Rockefeller, then, represented the continuation of the liberal consensus politics of the 1950s. Eisenhower, while personally more conservative than this political mainstream, recognized the limits on his power when six of his eight years in office saw Democratic majorities in the House and Senate. As political scientist Stephen Skowronek put it, he was content to "prune the radical edge off New Deal liberalism," despite his own preferences for fiscally conservative economic policies and hesitancy in the realm of civil rights.[20] Nixon, while personally more liberal than Eisenhower, represented the former general's political legacy. The vice president was less hesitant about using government power and resources to aid the economy, or even, at least in private, to further civil rights. He read the trends that were beginning to emerge within the Republican Party, however, as Goldwater and his followers became increasingly restive. He desired to reach out to these new potential constituents but was forever linked to Eisenhower's "Modern Republican" legacy. In the end, Nixon's personal politics were less important than his organizational ties to the Republican hierarchy as the Eisenhower administration's chief campaigner, which were a bane to Rockefeller's chances, and his attempts to reach out to the growing right wing, which spelled his doom among traditional constituencies.

Conservatism grew in prominence during the 1960s thanks to admirably well-organized grassroots efforts, changes in party politics like the growth of a primary system that privileged ideological fidelity over crossover appeal, and increasing domestic and foreign unrest. These trends marked the development of a more ideological American party system.[21] Increasing conservative control over the Republican Party meant liberals began to leave for safer harbors among the Democrats—and conservative Democrats began to switch their own party registrations. Today, Americans rarely see a Goldwater and a Rockefeller appearing under the same political banner. In the twenty-first century, Rockefeller would have been a Democrat—and a conservative like South Carolina Senator Strom Thurmond would have begun his political career as a Republican.

It is important to mention that "liberal" and "conservative" have not always borne the same meanings that they carried in the 1950s and 1960s. In the nineteenth and early twentieth centuries, liberal generally indicated an individual who adhered to the principles of classical liberalism—laissez-faire capitalism. Even mid-century figures such as Herbert Hoover and Ohio Senator Robert Taft insisted on being called liberals, despite being two of the more right-wing figures of their day. "Right" and "conservative," then, were not always synonymous. Before World War II, conservative was a term generally used to refer to fringe groups like the southern agrarians or the leadership of the isolationist Liberty League. Postwar, scholars such as historian and poet Peter Viereck popularized the idea of conservatism as an ideology based upon Judeo-Christian values and an understanding of "the inner unremovable nature of man as the ultimate source of evil."[22] These ideals, generally labeled "traditionalism," were combined with the ideals of classical liberalism to develop a conception of conservatism in sync with Goldwater's agenda.[23] Meanwhile, over the course of the New Deal years, liberalism came to be used as a term referring to politics just left of center, with an emphasis on the role of government in maintaining the economy and furthering social goals. When "conservative" and "liberal" are utilized in this book, the post–World War II meanings are intended. Even within these umbrella terms, of course, regional and individual variations exist and must be accounted for—"conservative" in the South, for example, might denote racial conservatism, while in the Sunbelt cities of the Southwest, "conservatism" might be expressed first and foremost in economic terms. Overall, however, by relying on the ideological philosophies of such figureheads as Goldwater and Rockefeller some general assumptions are obtainable.

A final note: opposition to Communism was an ideal shared by liberals and conservatives alike in both political parties. Conservatives' conceptions of anti-Communism tended to be more narrowly focused, with participation in international organizations or summit meetings regarded as caving in to Communist pressure. Conservative tendencies to claim anti-Communism as their own special preserve, however, should not obscure the reality that Nelson Rockefeller and Richard Nixon—as well as John F. Kennedy and Hubert Humphrey—were equally committed to winning the Cold War.[24]

Reading the Right

Most scholars writing in the 1950s dismissed conservatives as reflecting the status anxieties of a series of marginalized individuals—"soured patricians," the "new rich," a rising middle-class strata of ethnic groups, and a small group of intellectuals composed largely of "cankered ex-Communists," to borrow the colorful phrasing of Daniel Bell.[25] *The New American Right*, a 1955 collection of writing edited by Bell, provides the best glimpse of this older interpretation. Conservatives were suffering, Richard Hofstadter wrote, from factors including the loss of the "built-in status elevator" ensured by the frontier and immigration; the growth of mass media, which, by bringing politics closer to the people, encouraged the transference of personal problems and emotions onto politics; the long reign of liberalism from the New Deal years onward; and the presence of the Cold War, which inhibited the ability of Americans to return to their traditional peacetime preoccupations.[26] Preoccupied themselves by Senator Joseph McCarthy's rise and fall, most of these scholars believed it was "extremely doubtful" that the "Radical Right" would grow in influence beyond McCarthy's high-water mark in 1953–1954.[27] Overall, their interpretations of the right resembled nothing so much, in the words of Godfrey Hodgson, as "a topology of the pet hates of New York intellectuals at the time."[28] Given to describing conservatives as "more than ordinarily incoherent about politics," or as lacking enough "material and psychic security, and considerable sophistication" to be tolerant toward others, the prejudices of the authors come streaming through.[29] Conservatives represented the last vestiges of the unenlightened past, unable to understand the new, postwar world. With the passage of time they would eventually disappear from the spectrum of American politics.

These scholars' outlook was emblematic of the liberal consensus view placing those outside the perceived political mainstream on the ideological fringes. By assuming that all conservatives were members of a lunatic fringe, Bell, Hofstadter, and others ignored the growing body of conservative scholarship and organization simmering just below the political horizon. By assuming that the liberal consensus would continue, they failed to take conservative challengers seriously and neglected to shore up their own ideological defenses. Even more moderate scholars fell under this consensus-era spell. Political scientist and historian Clinton Rossiter, for example, is regarded in some circles as a conservative for his close association with Peter Viereck and his skepticism when faced with some of the period's liberal ideas. Even so, Rossiter concluded in his 1960 book *Parties and Politics in America* that "barring a nuclear catastrophe that would leave anarchy or autocracy in its wake, American politics in 1984 will look much like American politics in 1960."[30]

Many political players of the time failed to note the growth of a conservative movement heading into the 1960 election. Liberal Republicans were one of these groups—although in all fairness, the party was coming off eight years of a decidedly unpartisan Eisenhower administration. Eisenhower administration cheerleader Arthur Larson gave party liberals the name "New Republicans" in his buoyantly enthusiastic 1956 book *A Republican Looks at His Party*. Larson, who was an undersecretary of labor at the time, argued that Eisenhower and his associates had discovered and established the "Authentic American Center in Politics." "It is a safe bet," he proclaimed, "that nine out of ten Americans agree with nine-tenths of what is said and proposed in the 1955 and 1956 State of the Union Messages." This consensus— "the distinctive mark of the American party system"—was the result of a variety of factors, including a common American background; the moving together of interests; the rise of the Communist threat; and, most central to Larson's discussion, the rise of the Eisenhower administration to define, give voice to, and put consensus positions into practice.[31] This ideology of consensus had gained the name "Modern Republicanism" by 1960.

The past ten to twenty years, however, have seen the development of a substantial body of literature on the rise of the modern, post–World War II conservative movement in the United States. This collection of scholarship acknowledges the strength, adaptability, lasting power, and diversity of conservatism beginning in the late 1950s and early 1960s. The move-ment is generally characterized as a broad, multifaceted collection of forces that have worked together to successfully advocate a turn toward economi-cally and socially conservative ideological dominance in the United States. Taking a longer view, newer scholarship tends not to adopt the antagonis-tic outlook of earlier scholars such as those in Bell's collection. In a post–Reagan Revolution world, it is difficult to avoid the reality that modern conservatism became a dominant force, and the historiography demon-strates this shift. Moving beyond the liberalism-as-normative approach that has plagued scholarship as recently as a 1994 essay by Alan Brinkley, these scholars have attempted to approach the conservative movement on its own terms.[32] Post–World War II conservatism is now acknowledged to be a vibrant, independent development rather than a simple reaction on the part of social misfits to a world they no longer understood. Conservatives might have drawn upon the lessons of the past, but they have done so in the context of looking toward the future.

George H. Nash's *The Conservative Intellectual Movement in America Since 1945* anticipated the new movement in conservative scholarship and remains the standard interpretation of intellectual trends in the conservative move-ment. Nash is especially helpful in clarifying three parallel developments of the late 1940s and early 1950s: libertarianism; a "traditionalism" that rejected moral relativism; and "militant, evangelistic anti-communism."[33] By way of comparison, historian Whitney Strub has defined the consensus liberalism of the day as entailing

> . . . a general acceptance of capitalism, along with an active federal govern-ment that provided a basic social welfare safety net; a belief that social con-flict could be solved through economic progress; internationalism in foreign policy; support for civil rights, at least to a limited extent; and a broad prefer-ence for personal choice over governmental intrusion in matters of culture and morality.[34]

Nash argues that the three major strains of conservatism were consolidated in the mid- to late-1950s through journals like the *National Review* and the *Modern Age*, although tensions reasserted themselves by the early 1960s. Eventually, the right was "pragmatized" by these rifts, with some fringe members of the coalition dropping out of the picture and the movement realigning toward the photogenic conservatism of Ronald Reagan and away from mavericks like Goldwater.[35]

Several scholars have written in general terms about the rise of the con-servative movement in the United States, including Godfrey Hodgson,

Jerome L. Himmelstein, Donald T. Critchlow, Mary C. Brennan, William C. Berman, Lisa McGirr, Jonathan M. Schoenwald, and Donald T. Critchlow.[36] Their works differ somewhat in terms of periodization. Himmelstein, for example, contends that the conservative movement failed to have a decisive impact upon American politics before the end of the 1970s—a curious argument in light of Goldwater's candidacy in 1964 and Nixon's appeal to the "silent majority" in 1968. Critchlow goes so far as to contend that although the "defining moment" for development of self-confident conservatism came with Goldwater's nomination, conservative triumph within the Republican Party was not complete until 2000.[37] Most historians of the period, however, argue for the development of a strong conservative movement by at least the early 1960s. Brennan argues most strongly for the significance of 1960 as a watershed in the movement's development. Her overview does not, however, analyze the diverse range of factors impacting this election, as she focuses primarily upon later developments.

Hodgson's *The World Turned Right Side Up: A History of the Conservative Ascendancy in America* provides a strong overview of the movement from the late 1940s into the 1990s. While much of his analysis seems to borrow heavily from Nash, the length of his survey enables him to make two helpful insights. First, he argues, the rising prominence of conservative doctrines, which he describes in terms similar to Nash, resulted in the partial "Southernization" of American politics. Second, American politics have become more European, based upon ideological differences to a previously unimagined degree. Where the Democratic and Republican parties once included individuals of widely divergent views under the same party labels, conservative Democrats and liberal Republicans are increasingly endangered species.[38] This circumstance, of course, represents a significant change from the 1950s-era scholars who proclaimed "the end of ideology." McGirr makes an important contribution to the literature by explaining how the focus of conservatives' attention shifted over time from concerns about the enemy without (Communism) to the enemy within (moral issues like abortion or school curricula). She also demonstrates the importance of grassroots organizing in transforming conservatism from a marginal force preoccupied with the threat of internal Communist subversion to a "viable electoral contender."[39]

Finally, where most scholars have followed Nash's lead and argued for a unification of diverse conservative elements in the late 1950s and early 1960s leading to growing pains and realignment in the 1960s, Schoenwald contends that there were two distinct, although overlapping, movement cultures until after the 1964 election. One strain focused on party and electoral solutions, the other upon private organizations; the latter was more cordial toward extremist elements. Goldwater's defeat in 1964 marked the end of the legitimacy of extremist elements within the movement, and as subsequent candidates—most notably Reagan in his 1966 campaign for the California governorship—sought office, they learned from the mistakes of the '64 campaign.[40]

The terms "social movement" and "movement culture" crop up often in the literature of the conservative movement, especially in the work of scholars such as McGirr and Schoenwald who describe the actions of specific groups and grassroots organizing efforts. Despite some interpretive deficiencies, social movement theory offers helpful perspective into the growth of the conservative movement with regard to differences between social movements and interest groups.[41] Theorists often differentiate the two, with interest groups regarded as legitimate actors within a political arena who pursue their objectives through institutionalized means like lobbying, while social movements typically exist outside the polity and use primarily non-institutional means like boycotts, marches, or sit-ins.[42] Using this framework, the conservative movement moved quickly in many cases from a social movement toward interest group politics, with the petitions, meetings, and demonstrations of extra-party attempts to draft Goldwater for the presidency in 1960 and 1964, for example, giving way to working through the GOP to secure Goldwater's nomination. A straightforward boundary is difficult to draw; petitions and demonstrations often coexisted with organized attempts to elect conservative convention delegates or support conservative platform planks. Even so, a transition is apparent over the course of the 1960s, with origins in the primarily movement-oriented conservatism of the 1960 campaign.[43]

Conservatism was already gaining significant strength in the Republican Party at the time of Nixon's 1960 campaign, but "modern Republicans"— the liberal wing of the Republican Party—were not about to give up the fight for the soul of their party. As such, GOP liberals are an integral part of the story of 1960. The clarity of hindsight should not obscure the reality of a perceived liberal consensus faced by political actors of the period. Ultimately, conservatives triumphed through their long-term emphasis on building effective mass organizations and coalitions. In his second presidential race, Nixon recognized the growing strength of conservatives within the Republican Party and switched his focus almost entirely to them. In 1960, however, Nixon's attempts to conciliate everyone spelled his short-term doom in an America where liberal Republicans and Democrats still held the balance of power.

By 1968, of course, that would no longer be the case. As Nicol C. Rae puts it in his chronicle of liberal decline, Republican liberals suffered from tactical ineptitude, lack of discipline, lack of foresight, and failure to construct the type of political organization required by reforms in the nominating process during the 1960s and 1970s. Nixon began as a perfect choice for the Republicans: his anti-Communist credentials made him popular with the right, and his Modern Republican stances on domestic matters made him acceptable to liberals. However, "by trying to appease both Rockefeller and the conservatives, Nixon succeeded in displeasing both."[44] Rae contends that 1960 was the last presidential election year in which the Republican Party's liberal and conservative wings were roughly equivalent in strength.[45] Nixon attempted to straddle the fence—and was hit from both sides. The 1960 campaign is an important bellwether for understanding what would come later.

Putting the People Back into the Process

Examining the dynamics of the 1960 election "on the ground" requires a careful consideration of key constituent groups. How did Nixon, Goldwater, and Rockefeller—and their supporters—interact with these groups? How do studies of specific constituencies reveal the relative successes and failures of these men, whom we can safely use as representations of center, right, and left within the Republican Party? To examine these questions, this volume focuses upon the six key constituencies introduced above: liberal Republican activists; African Americans; the conservative intelligentsia; youth; Southerners; and ethnic groups. Each of these groups is important either for its historical ties to the GOP or for the increasing influence it would have upon Republican politics in the future. In one way or another, each constituency is transitional, and the events of 1960 marked a turning point for each. The conclusions drawn from this ground-level examination of specific constituencies should prove helpful to scholars interested in how individuals affect political party development, as well those studying the histories of the Republican Party and of the post–World War II conservative movement. In essence, this is a story of how constituent groups, operating from the bottom up, interact with and affect a political establishment geared toward operating from the top downward. Both action and reaction are important if we are to gain a full understanding of the dynamics at work.

Chapters 1 and 2 deal with liberal Republicans' failures in 1960. In Chapter 1, Nelson Rockefeller's abortive presidential campaign demonstrates liberals' misplaced faith in expert studies and a mythic "vital center" in American society that would rally around a liberal consensus candidate. Rather than devoting his time and resources to mobilizing a mass following, Rockefeller relied on the advice of a small circle of advisers. His refusal to relinquish his position of stature on the party's left wing, even as he refused to pursue an active campaign, spelled doom for liberal Republicanism more swiftly than a more dedicated party liberal in a similar position might have done. Chapter 2 demonstrates the failure of the Republican Party to regain the allegiance of its traditional, and traditionally liberal, African American constituency.

Chapters 3, 4, and 5, on the other hand, showcase the many ways in which conservatives successfully mobilized support and established grass-roots networks over the course of the 1960 election. In chapter 3, analysis of *National Review*, the leading journal of conservative opinion, provides insight into the conservative intellectual climate in 1960, demonstrating how movement intellectuals guided their followers and interacted with the Republican Party, as well as the freedom, in a certain sense, that Nixon's defeat offered conservatives. Chapter 4 provides a more hybrid look at youth organization in 1960, offering insight into both liberal failures and conservative successes in youth mobilization. Conservative youth would exit 1960 in the more powerful position. Chapter 5 moves Republicanism into a new region of the country, exploring the origins of the post–World War II GOP in South Carolina and demonstrating the party's growing strength in the South, as well as the motivations behind partisan change in this former Democratic stronghold.

Finally, chapter 6 discusses the failure of liberal Republicanism's last, best hope of mobilizing behind a liberal anti-Communist agenda. Anti-Communism could have been the salvation of a big-tent GOP in 1960, but party leaders failed to encourage the kinds of solid grassroots ethnic networks that conservatives were constructing with such success in other arenas. Liberals failed to inspire their traditional constituencies, and with the failure of the party's ethnic outreach campaign in 1960, they demonstrated their inability to reach out to new groups along liberal lines.

Overall, three primary conclusions are argued for in this book. First, conservatives demonstrably gained the upper hand in organizational terms during the 1960 election. Rockefeller and Nixon forces were simply unable to mobilize supporters and satisfy their constituents to the same degree as conservative activists. Here, the resources and political establishment of party elites failed to address constituent needs as well as the grassroots organizations that conservative groups built for their own constituents. Rockefeller's failure to actually enter the presidential race deprived his liberal constituents of a legitimate voice in the political process. Nixon's attempts to bridge the gap between liberals and conservatives led him to straddle the ideological fence without giving either side a compelling reason to give him their enthusiastic support. In the general election, Kennedy made much more effective use of television and the new, image-based world of campaigning that had emerged by 1960.[46] More successful conservative organizers, on the other hand, enthusiastically entered the political fray, constructed responsive networks of supporters, and presented an ideologically coherent conservative alternative to establishment Republicanism. In so doing, they established beachheads that would evolve into primary sources of support, while moderates and liberals were left lacking significant electoral resources.

Second, 1960 marks the boundary between success in appealing to voters on anti-Communist grounds and the transfer of constituents' concerns to new fronts: civil rights, social disorder, the war in Vietnam, and the first falterings of the post–World War II economy. Nixon, Rockefeller, and Goldwater shared impeccable anti-Communist credentials. They differed, however, in how they would deal with domestic problems, the Third World, international cooperation, and other concerns. While 1960 might have offered the last opportunity for a Nixon or a Rockefeller to mobilize support on liberal anti-Communist grounds, Rockefeller's reticence about entering the race and Nixon's reluctance to alienate conservatives meant that they failed to grasp that chance. Again, those at the top failed to utilize their resources effectively. Kennedy's assassination placed the Republican Party in an extremely weak position in 1964, regardless of whomever the candidate might have been. By 1968, with the nation fragmented by struggles over war abroad and rights at home, it was too late. Combined, these conclusions spelled the doom of liberal Republicanism as a dominant force in party politics and the rise of modern conservatism.

Finally, and most importantly, a ground-level examination of the 1960 campaign demonstrates the importance of individuals and groups in directing the future of a political party. This point is related to the first two in that it helps explain the catalysts for these developments. Certainly structural forces ranging from the changing economy of the South to the societal pressure resultant from the maturation of the baby boom generation influenced the American political system throughout the 1950s and 1960s. Even so, the effects of individuals and groups upon the 1960 campaign demonstrate the inadequacy of structural arguments in determining electoral outcomes. These effects were manifested from both the top down and the bottom up, as, for example, responsive ideological leaders motivated their grassroots supporters and effective grassroots organizers furthered the causes of their chosen standard-bearers.

Eisenhower, for example, was an abysmal party leader who preferred to cast himself as above partisan bickering and refused to invest the time and energy necessary to mobilize Republicans for electoral action, believing that the political outcomes he desired should be achieved simply upon the basis of their objective qualities.[47] Furthermore, his lack of enthusiasm for Nixon was apparent from at least 1956, when he suggested to the incumbent vice president that he might consider stepping down from the number-two slot to gain a little "administrative experience" in a cabinet secretarial position. Leading up to and during the 1960 campaign, Eisenhower made a number of comments that, whether unintentional gaffes or intentional slights, did little to establish Nixon as the war hero's successor. Most notable among these comments was an August 1960 press conference response to a question about Nixon's major contributions to the Eisenhower administration: "If you give me a week, I might think of one," the president said.[48]

Goldwater, Nixon, and Rockefeller all made personal marks on the 1960 election as well. Goldwater's uncompromising public persona made him a hero for millions of conservative followers, even though he remained a loyal party adherent. The distrust of outsiders and obsession with organizational control that would become so sadly destructive during Nixon's presidency were already apparent in his actions during the 1960 campaign. Time and time again, the archival record preserves examples of his followers and enthusiasts urging the vice president to address a certain constituency's needs or take a set of ideas into consideration, only to express frustrated disappointment after the election that his or her words had not been heeded. To be sure, as Nixon himself pointed out in his 1962 memoir, in such a close election everyone felt they knew the reason for his loss, even if opinions directly conflicted—"I should have been more 'liberal' . . . I should have been more 'conservative . . .'"[49] Even so, his closed-off attitude toward most groups surely cost Nixon sympathy and votes. Rockefeller's inability to decide whether he should risk a candidacy in 1960 wasted liberals' resources and time. While he raised serious issues through his criticism of Nixon and of the party, the New York governor's refusal to seek either the presidency or the vice presidency prevented him from offering constructive alternatives to what he viewed as mistaken policies.

Meanwhile, activists such as Gregory D. Shorey of the South Carolina GOP and the youthful founders of Young Americans for Freedom laid the groundwork for a transformation of the Republican Party. Their hard work and dedication transformed a party seeking direction into a conservative vanguard, and Goldwater and other leading conservatives greeted grassroots organizers' efforts with open arms and encouragement. Had liberals motivated, mobilized, and responded to their followers in a similar fashion, late twentieth century party politics might look very different. Conservative activists in 1960 took the GOP up the first of two steps toward the party we know today. Twenty years would pass before Ronald Reagan consolidated the conservative movement with his 1980 election to the presidency. By December 1960, however, conservatives had effectively taken control of the Republican Party. They might not have been aware of this control at the time—and party liberals were certainly not yet willing to relinquish their traditional home. Never again, however, would a liberal Republican be able to mobilize sufficient support through a liberal campaign to win the party's presidential nomination. Even presidents who governed toward the center, such as Nixon after 1968, motivated voters through conservative appeals. The days of Modern Republicanism were over.

1 A Rocky Course for Liberalism

Nelson Rockefeller and the Failure of
the Modern Republicans

"Don't sit in your rock-ing chair,

And let folks call you a 'square.'

Latch on-to your hat and coat,

And get to the polls and vote . . .

Let's ROCK WITH ROCK-E-FEL-LER,

And give him all the votes we can.

He's sure to be the winner,

Three cheers for 'Rock-y,' He's our man."

—"Rocking With Rockefeller," 1958[1]

The mainstream, national Republican Party of the 1950s was not an ideological organization. As mentioned in the introduction, Eisenhower administration official Arthur Larson described his boss as having tapped into
the essential balance of the American people, a position from which only
a "rather small minority," one that was "out of tune with the feelings of
the overwhelming majority of Americans," would deviate. Arguing that
the sources of conflict in government came from two ideologies—the pro-
business, anti-labor, limited-government ideology of "1896" and the anti-
business, pro-labor, big-government ideology of "1936"—Larson proposed
that Eisenhower had found a solution to this fundamental disagreement.

The former general was simply pro-*both*—for labor and for business, trusting of full roles for both the federal government and for the states. In a country free of depression, war, or significant unemployment, with an industrialized corporate economy in all fields and tremendous Cold War responsibilities, governmental strife was a relic from the past. Eisenhower's politics of balance would move the United States into a new era of cooperation and consensus.[2]

The president, a man for whom partisanship never came easily, no doubt welcomed Larson's optimistic analysis of his administration. Over the course of his two terms in office, Eisenhower held himself above party conflict, preferring to send his second in command into the fray of electoral squabbles and partisan contests. The negative legacy he bequeathed to Nixon, then, included an image as a hardscrabble campaigner in addition to the questions Eisenhower's actions and comments raised about the vice president's credentials. Beyond any personal distaste for partisan conflict, however, Eisenhower harbored dreams of creating a new, third force in American politics. In 1954, for example, irritated by the Republican right wing's recriminations following congressional election defeats, he contemplated founding a new party of the center. Such a party would, in the words of Eisenhower biographer Piers Brendon, "appeal to the majority of people in America who were middle-class and believed in common sense." Beyond this vague definition, the president never defined exactly what he thought was the "center," although given his own ideological predilections it seems safe to assume that it was a variation on Arthur Schlesinger's "vital center" involving fewer fetters on capitalism and less strident advocacy of civil rights. Eisenhower got as far as considering names for his new party, an unsuccessful pursuit. While he later denied such flirtations with party unorthodoxy, he returned to these dreams during times of frustration throughout his presidency.[3]

On the whole, Eisenhower's presidential legacy was one of moderation much akin to the liberal consensus politics described earlier. In political scientist Stephen Skowronek's words, Eisenhower's program of "moderation, sensibility and accommodation" gave Republicanism a new sense of respectability in the wake of Hoover and the party's Depression legacy.[4] In general he was a fiscal conservative, favoring a balanced budget and worrying about inflation during a time when the dominant thinking in American economics deemed inflation favorable for growth, although his administration's policy decisions sometimes deviated from his own more conservative preferences. He was not averse, however, to social programs. His administration created the Department of Health, Education and Welfare and expanded Social Security, among other ventures. While Secretary of State John Foster Dulles might speak of "brinksmanship," the Eisenhower administration participated in summit meetings and invited Soviet Premier

Nikita Khrushchev to the United States. Unfortunately, to the chagrin of Republicans of all political stripes, Eisenhower's lack of interest in partisan concerns atrophied the party during his eight-year reign as head of the GOP. Furthermore, his moderation, while successful as far as his own administration was concerned, stimulated a simmering undercurrent of discontent among conservatives. Mobilized by this disaffection, conservatives would organize to redirect the future of Republicanism, a development with dangerous consequences for Eisenhower's moderate successors.

Despite underlying problems, Eisenhower's Modern Republicanism was still at the top of the nation's political radar screen in 1958, and liberal Republican Nelson Rockefeller's gubernatorial victory in New York instantly propelled him into consideration for bigger and better things. Rockefeller's home state had long been seen as a launching pad for presidential aspirations, with Franklin Roosevelt and Thomas Dewey serving as recent examples. As such, it was no surprise that the new governor's admirers often mentioned a presidential run in the same letters in which they offered him congratulations on his gubernatorial triumph. While Nixon remained in the lead as far as poll numbers and Republican Party workers were concerned, the national media immediately latched onto Rockefeller as the Republicans' "liberal" possibility in 1960. "An important Republican" told *U.S. News and World Report* that easterners now wanted Rockefeller in 1960, just as they had wanted Wendell Willkie in 1940. *Newsweek* described Eisenhower as plotting a course of "strict neutrality" between Nixon and Rockefeller, and in New York City, the Legislative Correspondents Association's spring 1959 dinner featured a skit portraying Rockefeller as Snow White and Nixon as the Wicked Queen. Thomas Dewey as Prince Charming would wake one of the men in 1960, according to "King Ike," and send him to Washington, D.C.[5] Rockefeller demurely disavowed any intention of running for national office, affirming his desire to serve the people of New York. Behind the scenes, however, the enormous machinery of the Rockefeller operation swung into action.

Rockefeller never actually ran for the presidency in 1960. He gave tacit approval to fact-finding missions that attempted to gauge support for a potential run, and he made speaking tours around the United States in the fall of 1959 to measure public response to his persona and programs. His organization assisted, and even played key roles in organizing, ostensibly independent groups to advocate a Rockefeller candidacy, and throughout the 1960 pre-convention season he indicated his willingness to accept a draft for the nomination. The governor spoke out forcefully on a number of occasions in late spring and early summer 1960 but failed to parlay these statements into an active run for the presidency.

Rockefeller's actions resulted in a multi-pronged dilemma for the GOP. As governor of the most populous and influential state in the union, the governor's outspoken advocacy of liberal Republican positions effectively established him as the party's liberal spokesman—even as he refused to give Republican voters the option of approving or disapproving his stands in primary elections or caucus deliberations. Other leading party liberals of the 1960s, such as George Romney of Michigan or William Scranton of Pennsylvania, were not sufficiently prominent in 1960 to challenge the New York governor.[6] Although fall 1959 polls indicated that Nixon was the choice of most Republicans, liberal and conservative alike, Rockefeller's many critiques of the vice president's positions jeopardized Nixon's ability to present himself as a big-tent candidate. As a result, Rockefeller's non-candidacy was perhaps the single most frustrating event of the pre-convention campaign for the GOP leadership. Without offering a true alternative, Rockefeller disrupted appearances of party unity. By contrast, prior to the convention, Goldwater steadfastly maintained his support for the vice president, even as some of his conservative supporters desired that he make his own run for the presidential nomination.

Ultimately, Rockefeller's actions in June and July led Nixon to take steps in the name of unity that would play an essential role in mobilizing conservatives against Modern Republicanism. Rather than furthering the cause of liberal Republicanism, Rockefeller's disruptive failure to establish a true alternative, combined with Nixon's attempts to silence the governor and preserve party unity, stimulated conservatives' anger and sense of disenfranchisement. In the eyes of conservatives, Goldwater had played the role of loyal party man, only to have his views trampled upon by the Eastern Establishment. In response, conservatives strengthened extant networks and established new grassroots organizations to challenge what they perceived as liberal dominance. What looked like liberalism's pinnacle was actually the foundation of conservatives' triumph.

Rockefeller and his liberal supporters consistently displayed the types of faults typical of liberal Republicans from the late 1950s onward: tactical ineptitude, indiscipline, lack of foresight, and a failure to construct the type of political organization a reformed nominating process required.[7] Rockefeller failed to understand the degree to which Nixon, through eight years of dogged campaigning, had built his ranks of supporters at the state and local levels—where precinct leaders and convention delegates were selected. Political columnist Stewart Alsop once commented that one of the most commonly heard comments at any gathering of the party faithful in the late 1950s was "Nixon is our kind of guy."[8] While many Americans believed Rockefeller would be good for the United States, he failed to reach out on a personal level, relying instead upon the views of experts and on wide-ranging statements to articulate his political opinions.

In this sense, Rockefeller's almost-campaign exemplified the limitations of consensus liberalism, with its emphasis on expert opinion. The Rockefeller organization's perceptions of the American electorate simply did not hold true. Liberals remained confined by the conventions they had created—established economic and political practices, the perceived importance of leaders and experts, fixation upon the middle class, and concerns about the Cold War.[9] By the end of the decade, individuals from all sides of the political spectrum were beginning to regard the current system as bankrupt. The problems of race, Cold War, economic growth, and regulation seemed too complex to be solved within a politics of liberal consensus.

Furthermore, liberals' focus on expert opinion placed them at a remove from their constituents. While Rockefeller sponsored position papers and waited for a "draft" to materialize, conservative activists frustrated by Eisenhower Republicanism's lack of ideological vigor organized grassroots organizations to challenge the GOP establishment. From 1958 onward, Barry Goldwater warned the Republican hierarchy that he felt a strong conservative stance would garner them more votes. "The reason we lost elections [in 1958] in the main," he wrote to Nixon following that election, "was because our candidates were trying to hedge on to the spots occupied by the opposition." Republicans and Democrats alike were looking for the GOP to reassert its claim as the United States' conservative party. Party liberals should have been wary from the start, given conservatives' astonishing fund-raising capabilities. In early 1959, a GOP senator commented on Goldwater's reappointment as chairman of the Senate Republican Campaign Committee that "Barry Goldwater can raise 10 times as much money for the party as any 'liberal' Republican could raise."[10]

Rockefeller envisioned a grand coalition of the center at a period in history when the right and the left were poised to take control. The seeming strength of the liberal consensus would encounter a series of obstacles in the 1960s from which it would never recover, and even in 1960, the absence of a truly viable liberal Republican option demonstrated the problems lurking beneath the surface of this supposedly robust system. John F. Kennedy and Lyndon Johnson might perpetuate the appearance of consensus a few years longer, but all the while, conservatives would be organizing—and young liberals would begin to abandon their insufficiently ideological elders through such organizations as Students for a Democratic Society. Perhaps a liberal Republican with sufficient idealism, enthusiasm, organizational understanding, and, above all, the dedication to put his (given the year) future on the line might have rescued and recuperated Modern Republicanism. Nelson Rockefeller, however, was not the man for the job in 1960.

Testing the Waters

Rockefeller's initial foray into electoral politics nearly came to naught. New York State Republican Committee Chairman L. Judson Morhouse locked onto Rockefeller as early as 1955 as the hope of the New York GOP, and he tried to get him to run for the Senate in 1956. The Standard Oil heir and veteran of three presidential administrations was not interested, however, in a legislative position; his ambitions were geared more toward executive administration. Morhouse shifted his entreaties to the 1958 gubernatorial race. As Rockefeller biographer Cary Reich has beautifully described his subject, Rockefeller was "plagued with a Hamlet-like indecision about his political career"—"a trait that would bedevil him time and time again in the future."[11] In 1958, this wavering resulted from concerns about the special circumstances of being a Rockefeller, grandson of the great—and sometimes infamous—John D., and running for public office. Further complicating matters, Rockefeller's wife at the time, Mary Todhunter Clark Rockefeller, hated politics. Once he made his decision, however, the candidate jumped in with both feet, engaging in a crash course in state administration and politics via his favorite mode of analysis, expert studies, and turning his famous charm on the populace.

Rockefeller's overwhelming victory in such a terrible year for Republicans made him the center of national attention. Letters poured into his offices from all over the nation in the months leading up to and after the election. Some writers recommended that he wait until 1964, either because GOP prospects in 1960 seemed so poor or so he could prove himself as a governor first.[12] Most of those sending their congratulations to the governor-elect, however, urged him to consider a presidential run. Joanne Collins of Chicago, for example, expressed her appreciation of Rockefeller as "one who has great riches and yet is understanding of those who are poor." Rockefeller's second-eldest son, Steven, married a Norwegian woman who served as a housekeeper in the Rockefeller household, and Collins was impressed by what this revealed: "For you must know that there are many fine persons who have strong character, high morals, and intelligence, and yet are without wealth. If you are warm and human enough to realize this, you are very capable of understanding the many other problems citizens are faced with today."[13]

Mrs. F.R. Edwards of Lafayette, California, asked what she could do personally to ensure Rockefeller's nomination, telling him that he was the only person who could beat any of the Democratic candidates. A.C. Harlander of San Francisco pledged that many Californians would support Rockefeller instead of Nixon, even though he was California's native son, and Cleveland attorney Richard B. Kay shared a newspaper clipping announcing the formation of the country's first "Rockefeller for President" organization. Eve Berkowitz of New York City was one of many Democrats who wrote to express their support for Rockefeller, commenting that she was beginning to think like Harry Truman when he said once, "the only thing wrong with Rockefeller is that he is a Republican." Berkowitz hoped he would reach his goals: "'Even the White House' it's O.K. by me."[14]

Whether Rockefeller had always intended a presidential run in 1960 is open for debate, but the positive response to his gubernatorial election, especially among self-described moderates who personified the "consensus" atmosphere of the late 1950s, was certainly encouraging. Many commentators remarked that his inaugural address, peppered with references to the problems facing the nation as a whole, sounded more like a declaration of a presidential candidacy than the kickoff to a gubernatorial administration. In the summer of 1959, Rockefeller associates took the first steps toward the development of a two-tiered organization that would characterize Rockefeller's presidential attempt. A group of the governor's friends and supporters, including staff associates R. Burdell Bixby, George L. Hinman, Roswell B. Perkins, Oren Root, and Oscar Reubhausen, state chairman Morhouse, and Alexander Halpern, met to develop a framework for what would become the Rockefeller for President Citizens' Information Center. Formally organized in September 1959, RFPCIC's offices opened in the Belmont Plaza Hotel in New York City in October, with Halpern serving as chairman. The organization acted as a distribution center for information about the governor and a clearinghouse for individuals and groups interested in supporting a Rockefeller candidacy.[15]

RFPCIC, however, was one level of a unique, two-tiered structure composed in a way that enabled Rockefeller to preserve some level of "deniability" regarding his presidential intentions even as subsidiary organizations carried on full-steam ahead. On one track, Rockefeller and his political and policy advisers quietly gathered information, formulated position papers, made "fact-finding" missions, and coordinated with Rockefeller advocates behind the scenes. On a second track, these advocates established RFPCIC and, in the weeks leading up to the 1960 convention, the Draft Rockefeller Committee.

Rockefeller and his organization, then, were able to collect information on supporters and forge the beginnings of a campaign while still allowing the governor to maintain a personal aura of noninvolvement in such a campaign and dedication to his present office. This aura wore thin, of course, on a number of occasions. Rockefeller's critics, especially, were skeptical of his claims that he was not a candidate for the presidency and that his many statements and speeches represented only his concerns about the future of American society. In theory, the RFPCIC might have been an effective clearinghouse for Rockefeller supporters, consolidating their efforts and feeding them needed financial and logistical support. In practice, it was barely functional, chronically short on cash, and finally bailed out via a series of contributions by various members of the Rockefeller clan. In principle, Rockefeller's preserved "deniability" could have strengthened his image, just as Eisenhower's nonpartisan persona made him a rallying figure for Americans from a variety of backgrounds. Had Rockefeller taken the plunge into a full-fledged candidacy, his statements might have served him better. As an "outside observer" unwilling to make a full commitment to a presidential race, however, they were the remarks of a gadfly.

Halpern's initial announcement of RFPCIC's formation demonstrated the Rockefeller organization's interest in keeping advocacy of a presidential run separate from the governor himself:

> As citizens of New York State, we are especially appreciative of Mr. Rockefeller's feeling of responsibility toward his state. But as citizens of the United States, we are equally determined to aid a growing grass roots movement that is seeking the presidential nomination for our governor from almost every state in the Union.[16]

Halpern declared his independence as a political actor, casting himself as a citizen of the state and of the nation rather than a member of Rockefeller's inner circle—whatever the hidden reality.

Halpern was correct in stating that many citizens around the country were eager to support a Rockefeller candidacy, although supporters often continued to write directly to Rockefeller, an indication that the subterfuge of RFPCIC was irrelevant from the start. Rockefeller Press Secretary Dick Amper expressed his frustration with requests coming to his office for biographical information. He was finding it difficult to comply with the requests because implicit in such compliance was an acknowledgment that the governor was interested in a presidential run.[17] College students in several states expressed interest in Rockefeller, and the New York governor had considerable support among Californians, despite Nixon's own southern Californian heritage. Much of this support came from politically liberal northern California. Hunter and Staples, Inc., a consulting firm based in San Francisco and Sacramento, compiled a detailed report on how a northern California campaign might be waged. Local officials like F. Clinton Murphy, a member of the Yolo County Republican Central Committee just north of Sacramento, emphasized that while the GOP organization in California might largely be in Nixon's hands, this did not necessarily mean rank-and-file voters were committed to the vice president.[18]

Even in southern California, though, indications of Rockefeller support surfaced. Albert Otis of Los Angeles, for example, wrote that many citizens were frustrated by California's 1958 electoral debacle, when Governor Goodwin Knight and Senator Bill Knowland were essentially forced to switch political positions, with Knight running for senator and Knowland for governor. The men lost their campaigns in both cases. The state had also experienced a disastrous fight over a "right to work" proposition outlawing closed union shops that went down in flames in November. Nixon was seen by many Californians as having been ineffective in mediating intraparty conflict. Democrats expressed interest in the New York governor, as well. In October, Richard R. Rogan, Los Angeles County's chief deputy attorney general, called to ask if he could give a cocktail party for Rockefeller while the governor was in Los Angeles. Rogan was a Democrat, but he disliked Nixon intensely and wanted "to do anything he can to be of assistance to NAR." He had personal connections to Rockefeller, having served as an assistant to John Hay Whitney in the Roosevelt administration's Latin American Affairs office from 1941 to 1943, when Rockefeller was Coordinator of Inter-American Affairs. Rockefeller's bipartisan history of government service was standing him in good stead.[19]

Citizens elsewhere in the country were similarly interested in Rockefeller. Ray Bengert of Denver, Colorado, wrote to Halpern on October 20, describing a "People for Rockefeller" movement he and four other enthusiasts had organized. Drawing on Colorado's "Rush to the Rockies" Centennial celebrations, Bengert and his compatriots had adopted the slogan "Rush for Rocky," and they claimed to have commitments from 5,000 voters.[20] The Adair County Citizens for Rockefeller from Adair County, Kansas, announced their organization in November. Reasoning that the Republicans needed a candidate who could receive Democratic and independent votes in addition to Republican votes, the Adair County Citizens planned to lobby their state committee to attend the convention pledged to Rockefeller.[21]

Most exciting for RFPCIC were indications that some celebrities—including known Democrats—might be willing to support a Rockefeller candidacy. In early December, for example, Mrs. Rockefeller reported that she had lunched with New York Secretary of State Caroline Simon and Mrs. Richard Rodgers, of Rodgers and Hammerstein. Mrs. Rodgers had shown great interest in Rockefeller, and said she and other independent Democrats she knew were quite enthusiastic about the governor. Later in the month,

Simon reported to George Hinman that she'd also been informed of play-wright Edna Ferber's interest in supporting Rockefeller. "This name and the Rodgers are all known as Democrats," she reported, "and I feel evidence a trend."[22] Halpern's brainstorming memos of suggested names for a National Citizens Executive Committee—memos passed along to Rockefeller person-ally, demonstrating his awareness of RFPCIC's activities—included Henry Ford (II, presumably), Marshall Field, Jr., Mrs. Odgen Reid, John Gardner, John McCloy, Lester Granger, and Helen Hayes.[23]

Although indications of liberal Republican and Democratic support for the governor were encouraging, many of those who wrote to RFPCIC were less than thrilled by its activities. Halpern sent out a mass mailing on RFPCIC letterhead, enclosing a copy of a recent Rockefeller address before the Eco-nomic Club of New York. Several irritated recipients voiced their opinion on handwritten scrawls across returned copies of Halpern's letters. Tom Cole of Lockport, New York, conceded that Rockefeller was a "nice person, but one who apparently believes in 'Tax and Spend—inflate and try to win election.'" Cole was against that way of life, he wrote. A man named John from Bayside, New York, was less charitable, ranting, "This is utterly ridicu-lous! Not even Governor of N.Y. for a full year and he's running for President. He has to prove himself first," he wrote, "and one year or one term is not enough to judge his capabilities for this office." New York needed a full-time governor—and this was the feeling of many Republicans with whom John of Bayside had spoken. Another respondent anonymously expressed his frustra-tion with a recent tax hike in New York, proclaiming, "Nuts to Nels!"[24]

Two arguments were common among letter writers opposed to a Rocke-feller candidacy. The first was John of Bayside's concern—although often expressed in kinder terms—that the governor could use a bit more season-ing. Others, while they might like Rockefeller, believed Nixon was the best choice for the presidency in 1960. A respondent from Fort Wayne, Indiana, argued that while Rockefeller was a "fine man," Nixon was "the best man for now."[25] George S. Cluff of Pittsford, New York, liked Rockefeller but felt that in 1960, Nixon was best qualified in terms of both administrative abil-ity and experience. If he aspired to the presidency, perhaps the governor would submit to taking the number-two spot on the national ticket.[26]

The arguments pro-Nixon respondents made to RFPCIC were typical of the arguments in favor of Nixon in the Republican Party at large. RFPCIC, however, attempted to turn the very same arguments on their heads, con-tending that in fact it was Rockefeller who had superior administrative experience and was better suited for the presidency. In August planning sessions, Roswell Perkins recommended that Rockefeller's campaign biogra-phy be keyed to counter the contention that Nixon had greater experience, pointing out that the vice president had had no real opportunity to take on administrative roles beyond his personal offices as congressman, senator, and vice president. By contrast, Rockefeller had administered a major governmental unit, the office of Inter-American Affairs, during World War II and had served as assistant secretary of state in charge of Latin American relations for over a year. During the early years of the Eisenhower administration, he ran day-to-day operations in the Department of Health, Education and Welfare as the department's first undersecretary. Currently, he supervised the entire executive branch of what was then the largest and most important state in the union. Nixon had carried out many ceremonial duties in the foreign policy field and traveled extensively, but he had no substantive responsibility in the conduct of foreign relations. Rockefeller, on the other hand, had experience dealing with intensive, substantive diplomatic negotiations from the Chapultepec and United Nations organizing conferences in 1945 to his participation in the Geneva Conference of 1955 as a special assistant to Eisenhower.[27]

The final drafts of RFPCIC's campaign literature used the foundations of Perkins' ideas. Pamphlets like "The Rockefeller Record" and "Nelson Rockefeller: Man With a Mission" catalogued a litany of achievements to demonstrate that "Nelson Rockefeller's whole life furnishes superb training for the Presidency." Boldly printed subheadings in "The Rockefeller Record," for example, introduced paragraphs explaining how Rockefeller had held "the good will for Latin America for the free world" during World War II. He had laid the groundwork for alliances like NATO and SEATO through his advocacy of a regional security pact clause in the United Nations charter and had chaired the International Development Advisory Board committee that developed Point Four during the Truman administration. He "was instrumental in extending Social Security to 10 million more workers" as undersecretary in Health, Education and Welfare and had saved the state of New York from financial ruin during one short year in office. Farmers, workers, businessmen, educators, women, youth, and minorities all loved Rockefeller. The governor was a winner, a man with "courage, dynamic drive, an ability to understand people, to analyze issues, to meet problems, to organize, and *to get things done!*"[28]

Organizational Lapses and Strategic Failures

Unfortunately, however, Rockefeller's understanding of people and his ability to get things done did not extend to an accurate reading of the political situation in fall 1959. In 1960, convention delegates were chosen by primary votes in sixteen states, with all others selecting representatives through party conventions and caucuses.[29] As a result, appeals to the party's state and local leadership were of paramount importance. Such leaders might be receptive to arguments that a candidate with bipartisan appeal would be most helpful to the party's electoral chances, a window that would close over the years as the proliferation of closed presidential primaries encouraged nomination of ideological candidates appealing to active party minorities; however, party officials were also cognizant of Nixon's long years of activity on the campaign trail as vice president.

Furthermore, polling trends seemed to indicate that Nixon's support among Republican voters—and voters in general—was growing. In July, the *Minneapolis Tribune*'s Minnesota Poll found that 54 percent of Minnesota Republicans favored the vice president, while only 40 percent were for Rockefeller. Even among independents, 10 percent more voters preferred Nixon. This represented a major switch from January 1959, when Minnesota independents preferred Rockefeller over Nixon, 38 to 24 percent. In mid-September, Gallup reported that for the first time Nixon had outpolled Kennedy, 51 to 49 percent. In October, a *Miami Daily News* poll in Democratic Dade County, Florida, found that 48 percent of respondents favored Nixon, compared to 13 percent for Rockefeller and just 11 percent for Kennedy.[30] In part, these numbers reflected the wide-open Democratic field, where Kennedy, Hubert Humphrey, Lyndon Johnson, Adlai Stevenson, and Stuart Symington were all regarded as potential candidates. It was also clear, however, that among Republicans there was no such wide-open field.

By mid-October, private Republican Party polls indicated that the party's 1956 convention delegates favored Nixon over Rockefeller, 89 to 8 percent. A full 90 percent of those polled felt Nixon would win the nomination.[31] Nixon's organizational strength might still have left Rockefeller with the possibility of gambling on primary victories, despite primaries' tendency to reward ideological fealty. As late as 1960, some states, including Wisconsin, maintained "open primaries" in which voters of either party could vote for any primary candidate. A strong Rockefeller showing could have demonstrated the governor's strength among Democrats and independents at a time when only 30 percent of the electorate considered itself Republican, while 47 percent of Americans identified themselves as Democrats and 23 percent as independents.[32] Even closed primaries would have given Rockefeller an opportunity to test his suspicions about the presence of a liberal ideological consensus in the country, contrary to naysayers' opinions. As it turned out, however, he refused to give his putative supporters a chance.

While RFPCIC undertook an active role in encouraging the governor's presidential aspirations, Rockefeller himself remained coy about his intentions. Letters coming out of Rockefeller's office were extremely noncommittal. Comments Rockefeller made at a governor's conference in Puerto Rico in summer 1959 indicated that he would base a decision on whether to run on what poll figures looked like by November. In later statements, however, he disavowed this timetable—a decision with which staffer Harry O'Donnell was mightily pleased, as non-campaign news stories ranging from Eisenhower's coming tour of Western Europe to the World Series would mean poll figures were unlikely to change much through late fall. Rockefeller's advisers urged the governor to delay declaring his candidacy. O'Donnell felt any formal announcement could be withheld until January or even February 1960. Meanwhile, the governor should "'concentrate' on state matters, designed to improve the 'image' in New York state" and make a few well-selected national television appearances.[33] Curiously, even evidence that would favor an opposite strategy did not sway Rockefeller's team. Sharing the contents of a mid-September conversation with a close Nixon observer, Morhouse reported that Nixon forces believed that every day they could prevent Rockefeller from announcing his candidacy was a day gained for Nixon. Nixonites felt the vice president had the GOP organization tied up, but they feared a Rockefeller announcement might cause the rank and file to begin to shift toward the governor. "The warmth of the Rockefeller smile, charm and personality makes the Nixon group cringe."[34]

An open declaration of candidacy, then, could be a tremendous boon to Rockefeller's presidential chances—but Morhouse and the Rockefeller organization chose not to take it that way. Rather than capitalize upon what would seem to be favorable signs and jump into the partisan fray, Morhouse continued to counsel the Rockefeller staff to follow a strategy outline asserting that the governor was not a candidate. His travels were based only upon a desire to reinforce the Republican Party and the two-party system through espousal of a liberal Republican philosophy and should even include, on one appropriate occasion, a plea for party unity that might disassociate the governor from others' criticism of Nixon. He urged the Rockefeller staff to alert friends and supporters working in other states to this strategy. The governor put off a group of New Hampshire citizens seeking to enter his name in their primary by telling them that at this point "my first responsibility is to the people of New York who elected me Governor last year." He needed to work on legislative proposals for 1960 before he could divert his attention from state affairs. Morhouse's goal was to develop Rockefeller as a man who told people the facts and got things done.[35]

While the governor's advisers put highest priority upon maintaining a nonpartisan persona in keeping with the politics of the "vital center," poll figures demonstrated that Rockefeller was failing to connect with local party adherents. Eisenhower had been successful because he was seen as a unifying candidate. His heroic military background effectively placed him above the fray of partisan politics. Rockefeller lacked these qualities. Rather than encouraging him to reach out on a practical level and demonstrate his personal dedication to the party and the presidential campaign, Morhouse indulged Rockefeller's "Hamlet-like indecision," validating the idea that the governor could somehow remain above politics.

Under the radar, Rockefeller associates carefully compiled information on possible bases of support. George Hinman, who was also a member of the Republican National Committee, recorded in August that a few state delegations appeared to be leaning in Rockefeller's direction. Rhode Island's governor was for Rockefeller, as was the district chairman from the District of Columbia. New Hampshire had a good, active group of supporters, and there were a few friendly faces in North Dakota, Illinois, Iowa, and possibly Indiana. National committeeman Robert Mautz would likely control Oregon's delegation, but Governor Mark Hatfield, at least, was privately for Rockefeller. Even Arizona—where Goldwater was not yet on the radar screen as a presidential option—might have possibilities. State Chairman Richard Kleindienst was friendly toward Rockefeller, although the state as a whole remained stubbornly pro-Nixon.[36]

Meanwhile, Rockefeller spent part of fall 1959 on the road, touring western and midwestern states in what an objective observer could refer to only as campaign appearances. The governor was a man possessed by research reports, and his staff files contained reams of material outlining state issues, party leaders, and potentially helpful contacts. As early as July 1959, DNA staff members prepared news summaries outlining Rockefeller coverage around the nation and compared it to that of Nixon and the Democratic hopefuls.[37] The governor's organization also commissioned a survey on "presidential images" to gauge public reaction to Rockefeller and Nixon in California, Ohio, Illinois, Pennsylvania, New York, and New Hampshire. The survey interviews were conducted just before Soviet Premier Nikita Khrushchev's arrival in the United States, when pollsters anticipated Nixon's ratings would reach their highest peak. On average, the survey found that 46 percent of respondents ranked Nixon's potential presidential performance as "outstanding or above average," while only 32 percent awarded Rockefeller the highest rating. Significantly, however, New Yorkers ranked Rockefeller higher in terms of leadership ability than the six states as a whole, indicating that increased knowledge of the governor might help his numbers.[38] Furthermore, Rockefeller's weak points appeared to be in areas he could remedy—informing the public of his extensive experience, showing he was for the common people and not biased toward big business, and making himself known throughout the country. Nixon's weakest points, on the other hand, were in areas concerning personality and character—things the pro-Rockefeller pollsters believed the vice president could not fix.[39]

Accordingly, Rockefeller set out to make his name and his qualifications known—but without actually declaring his candidacy, in a climate where state and local party leaders were already overwhelmingly pledged to Nixon. Although the vice president suffered in some circles for his role as the Eisenhower administration's chief campaigner, his long years of work on behalf of congressional candidates and gubernatorial hopefuls around the country left him with a long, long list of political chits to collect. As a result, even Rockefeller's most adoring crowds often represented little in the way of concrete, organizational support among the people who formed convention delegations. As Rockefeller activist Bill Brinton reported of the governor's November visit to California, "the visit here was an enormous personal success but a qualified political success. It was qualified politically because I doubt very much that more than a handful of the so-called organization people have changed their minds."[40]

Rockefeller's DNA research team continued its newspaper analyses throughout the fall, reporting in mid-November, for example, that overall newspapers gave much more coverage to Rockefeller than to Nixon, with Rockefeller's stories in larger, more prominent locations. Two weeks later, the DNA staff conceded that in most mid- and far west newspapers, Gallup poll stories on Nixon's lead over Rockefeller figured prominently, and more newspapers in these regions carried columnists like Westbrook Pegler, Fulton Lewis, Jr., and Raymond Moley, who were generally anti-Rockefeller. Still, Rockefeller received more coverage around the country than Nixon, although DNA saw growing evidence of a campaign to build up human interest in the vice president and his family through feature stories and photographs. By mid-December, despite wide coverage awarded to Rockefeller's midwestern tour, Nixon's coverage was growing in both space and prominence. Some papers in the South, in New England, and even in upper New York State could be characterized as developing a pro-Nixon slant, at least in terms of allotted space.[41] Given the stagnation of the Rockefeller "campaign," with no formal declaration or even implicit avowal of interest in actually running for the presidency, the news media were likely beginning to lose interest.

By the end of December, the RFPCIC card file included organizations of varying size in 21 states, although none were south of Tennessee and Kentucky.[42] Rockefeller's liberality on civil rights made him eternally unpopular in Dixie. Both the parent organization and its subsidiary groups, however, were seriously short of funds. Brinton, the San Franciso activist, suggested a "Dimes for Rockefeller" campaign, drawing upon the legend of John D.

Rockefeller, Jr. building Standard Oil and the Rockefeller fortune from a single dime, as well as his famous distribution of dimes to youngsters on the street. Rockefeller staffers, however, were aghast at the idea for a number of reasons, most notably the possibility that such a campaign would appear to be piggybacking on the "March of Dimes" campaign held to combat infantile paralysis each January. No doubt they were also less than thrilled by the idea of drawing attention to Rockefeller's immense family fortune and monopolist history, although the governor, a loyal grandson, defended his grandfather throughout his life.[43]

RFPCIC's primary financial stumbling block was likely the governor's immense family fortune. Even wealthy supporters might well have felt that Rockefeller could use his own resources to fund his campaign. Besides, a contender not serious enough to declare his candidacy hardly merited contributions. In the end, family funds did come through to pay off the debts incurred by RFPCIC. The organization's account book, in addition to a paltry list of small donations made primarily by staff members each month, included $3,000 donations from the governor's father, mother, each of his siblings, and Nelson himself following suspension of operations in January.[44] Several Rockefeller biographers have noted that this was a common family habit—all the family members would be called upon to bail out whomever (often Nelson) needed financial assistance. Beyond the vast number of people he employed to run his DNA research department, however, the governor never seemed sufficiently committed to his presidential run to throw large quantities of money into a campaign. The Rockefellers' $21,000 and a couple of hundred dollars in small donations appear to have represented the sum total of RFPCIC's operation, excluding the governor's self-funded trips.

With the Christmas season came an understanding among Rockefeller's political advisers that his chances of victory in the New Hampshire primary were slim. Victor Borella reported that, having started from an 80–20 pro-Nixon position, the situation in New Hampshire was currently somewhere between 75–25 and 65–35 pro-Nixon. Given national polls strongly favoring Nixon—in mid-November, Nixon led nationally by 68 percent to Rockefeller's 18—this was better than expected.[45] A good cross section of hardworking people were actively fighting for the governor throughout the state, keeping many Republican voters uncommitted. All this had been accomplished despite the fact that the Rockefeller organization had no "machine" in the state and that both senators and the most prominent newspaper, as well as most prominent GOP contributors, were pro-Nixon. On the negative side, however, Rockefeller's image in the state remained blurred, with many voters believing Nixon had "earned" the nomination as Eisenhower's "right hand man," while the governor was suspected of being a high-tax New Dealer. Furthermore, the Rockefeller organization could not proceed at full speed until or unless the governor announced his candidacy—and provided more funds.

In theory, the nature of the New Hampshire primary held promise. It was dominated by the kind of off-the-cuff, person-to-person campaigning at which Rockefeller had proven so skilled. Rockefeller was a Dartmouth graduate, and despite the prominence of conservative Republican senator Styles Bridges, New England was traditionally a friendly place for party liberals. However, given the campaign's numerous disadvantages, Borella believed Rockefeller had only a "very long shot chance" at victory. A loss in New Hampshire would hamper Rockefeller's ability to make a serious fight in important primaries like Wisconsin and Oregon. Furthermore, even in the unlikely event that the governor won, primary victories were of questionable importance given the "closed shop" for Nixon attitude held by Republican machines in most non-primary states. Rockefeller's most prudent course, Borella concluded, was to withdraw gracefully—a move made easier by the fact that he was not a declared candidate—and preserve his future as a GOP leader. "He could still lead the New York delegation to Chicago," Borella concluded, "and if the political winds have turned by then (as they so often have done), might not there still be a chance to do something?"[46]

In Borella's analysis of the New Hampshire situation we see the first appearance of the "draft" philosophy, the idea that without actually campaigning Rockefeller might still be able to maneuver himself into position as the choice of the Republican Party. Confidentially, Borella advised the governor to adopt a hybrid strategy. Rockefeller should announce to the public that given his activities and travel, it was implausible for the governor to say he was *not* a candidate. He would not be entering any primaries, however, because he felt that the results of primary elections were not a faithful reflection of the sentiment of most voters. Rather, "while a number of very conscientious people do turn out for primaries, a disproportional [sic] number of voters in primaries represent the established, entrenched party interests in either party"—in other words, Nixon supporters. Rockefeller, on the other hand, was concerned with *all* voters—Republicans, independents, and even Democrats who might choose to favor Rockefeller once given an opportunity to understand what the governor stood for. In 1960, when primary voters selected a minority of convention delegates, it was still feasible—barely—to stand for nomination without participating in the primaries.

Borella believed Rockefeller should state that he was "only human and would of course be honored to be considered as a possible candidate—and you hope to be so considered." But he should not actively campaign. Rather, he should concentrate on his activities as governor and on developing the notion of a "Bill of Responsibilities" as an umbrella strategy for talking about national and international issues: responsibility to oneself, to the community, to the nation, and to the world. Meanwhile, behind the scenes, Rockefeller should hire two nationally known Republicans with intimate knowledge of party organization, one to travel on the governor's behalf and the other to organize operations at "headquarters." Through his regular speeches Rockefeller could transmit his views to the American people.[47]

Borella seemed to ignore, however, his own observation that the party officials selecting the balance of convention delegates would be just as "established and entrenched," if not more so, as primary voters. Given Nixon's support and Rockefeller's reluctance to reach out to the state and local officials composing most conventions and party caucuses, primary campaigns could really have been Rockefeller's greatest opportunity. Furthermore, Borella's strategy of relying on subordinates to reach out to the people rather than reaching out and adopting Nixon's strategy of collecting party chits reflects the elitist attitude that plagued liberal Republicans. Again, Rockefeller's handlers appear to have given him advice that hurt both the governor's chances and chances for liberalism in general within the Republican Party. Rockefeller would not be able to sell himself and his programs openly, but he would stand in the path of anyone, including Nixon, who strove to articulate liberal Republican principles.

Out of the Race—But Not Off the Radar

Rockefeller ultimately took some of Borella's advice, choosing to follow much of his behind-the-scenes program while opting for a more deceptive public approach. Rather than making an open-ended statement, Rockefeller appeared to close the door on a presidential run:

> . . . only by meeting and talking with many citizens of many states could I form a reasoned conclusion as to how I may best serve both the State of New York and the nation.
>
> These trips have made it clear to me, as I believe they have to others, that the great majority of those who will control the Republican Convention stand opposed to any contest for the nomination. Therefore any quest of the nomination on my part would entail a massive struggle—in primary elections throughout the nation—demanding so greatly of my time and energy that it would make impossible the fulfillment of my obligations as Governor of New York.
>
> My conclusion, therefore, is that I am not, and shall not be, a candidate for nomination for the Presidency.
>
> This decision is definite and final.

Rockefeller also explicitly refused consideration of the vice presidency, arguing that doing so would run counter to the considerations motivating his decision not to run for the presidency. He did, however, assert that the nation had entered a time when national and world issues held the "omen of both menace and hope, both danger and opportunity" as never before. Such a time required a "profound and continuous act of national self-examination." Rockefeller proclaimed he would "contribute all I can to this political act. I shall speak with full freedom and vigor on these issues that confront our nation and the world."[48]

Here, then, was Rockefeller's window into continued involvement. He essentially manufactured for himself an ongoing role in national politics. Disingenuous though it proved to be, a complete withdrawal did legitimate this "nonpartisan" course of continuing to speak out on important issues. The governor was a savvy operator when it came to preserving all his options for the future, although the lengths to which he routinely went to preserve these options served to make him appear slippery and noncommittal to many outside his circle of support. While his "statesmanship" approach did mean Rockefeller could pursue his pet project—reaching out to voters across the political spectrum—it would prove worthless in gaining the concrete delegate support he needed to win the nomination. Meanwhile, the visible machinery of a potential national Rockefeller candidacy faded away. RFPCIC closed up shop and instructed its subsidiary organizations to do likewise. Many local supporters, however, were not so easily diverted from their goal of seeing Rockefeller become president.

On January 5, Alexander Halpern told Rockefeller that "on the grass root level your supporters have increased rather than lessened since your considered announcement." RFPCIC had received daily communications reflecting supporters' disappointment with Rockefeller's withdrawal and belief that "with your great ability and integrity, [you] should be on the national scene as the President of the United States for the next four years."[49] Seymour Blum of Plymouth, Massachusetts, for example, wrote to RFPCIC to lament that "in my opinion, the 'organization' Republicans don't control a damn thing except the court house workers. Nobody I know except that gang wants Nixon."[50] Over the next few months, Rockefeller organizations in several states would transfer their efforts to attempts to "draft" Rockefeller for the presidency. Actively encouraging such efforts might have placed the governor in a position to declare his candidacy later in the spring, but the Rockefeller organization was more interested in information gathering than in stimulating the "grassroots." Unlike their conservative counterparts on the opposite end of the Republican spectrum, liberal

Rockefeller adherents could not count on the support of more influential backers at higher financial and organizational levels.

In typical Rockefeller fashion, the first clue that the governor's campaign was not truly over was the DNA research staff's continuing interest in press reaction. Researcher Mary Boland reported that editorials and columns immediately following the statement generally praised Rockefeller for his "realistic approach to an impossible situation." Some criticized the governor for not specifically stating that he would support Nixon, and a few took exception to Rockefeller's implied accusation of GOP "bossism." In the main, however, the image projected of the governor was "one of a man of keen, honest and realistic viewpoint." More encouragingly, as news of the withdrawal began to sink in, columnists had begun speculating as to Nixon's real chances, moving beyond initial comments that Rockefeller had given the vice president a wonderful Christmas present. Most "reputable columnists," Boland reported, concluded that "although Nixon gains great prestige by being identified with Eisenhower, Nixon has grown in office, Nixon has matured from his Helen Gahagan Douglas-Jerry Voorhees [*sic*] days, he still does not have the stature, warmth and bi-partisan appeal that is Eisenhower's strength."[51]

Even many of Rockefeller's rank-and-file employees had no indication that the governor intended anything different than full withdrawal. Not only did the governor's office fail to mobilize grassroots support, therefore, but top-level staffers failed even to consolidate the assistance of loyal employees. Boland wrote to George Hinman, begging him, "Cannot something be done to salvage the enthusiasm shown by the country?" Attaching a list of prominent Rockefeller supporters in eighteen states and the District of Columbia, she suggested that some of these figures be used as "focal points for an underground campaign." "The pros have to be for Nixon in case Ike dies before his term expires," she noted—a savvy observation, and one many historians have commented upon given Eisenhower's checkered health history from 1955 onward. Rockefeller, however, had been the target of far greater newspaper coverage and, she contended, voter interest, especially among independents and Eisenhower Democrats. "I just cannot believe anyone, much less Governor Rockefeller, would give up so easily," she lamented, "when the real battle has not begun and the country is just beginning to know him." Apologizing for her forwardness, Boland asked Hinman to "Please excuse my despondency and disappointment. If there is anything at all, however, that I can do at this end to help the Governor change his mind, please let me know."[52]

However Hinman decided to respond to Boland, his actions throughout the month of January indicated that Rockefeller's declaration of withdrawal was far from final. Early in the month, Hinman worked with Pennsylvania State Republican Chairman George Bloom to secure a speaking invitation at the Lincoln Day dinner of one Pennsylvania county near Harrisburg. This first meeting would likely lead to an appearance at the party's statewide finance dinner later in the spring—a gathering at which all of Pennsylvania's 67 counties would be represented. "While George's meeting of course would be political," Hinman related to fellow staffer Oren Root,

> . . . it seems to me that the Governor can help himself by appearing to be laboring in the political vineyard for the good of the party and that there should be no trouble in so handling these matters that it will not have any appearance of continued interest in candidacy. It has always seemed to me to be of the highest importance that the Governor get acquainted with the leading Republicans in Pennsylvania.[53]

Hinman also worked to arrange trips to North and South Dakota so Rockefeller could maintain contacts with friendly state chairmen and supporters in those states.[54] Such trips would keep Rockefeller in the public eye and allow him to share his thoughts on the issues of the day without actually declaring candidacy. They also reflected a rare acknowledgment of the importance of state and local support.

Overall, however, the governor's staff used the bulk of its ample funding to commission studies laying out future options. One such report, made by Jack Platten of J.A. Ward, Inc., advised the Rockefeller organization that from a purely practical standpoint, Rockefeller's opportunities to reach the presidency were in 1960 and 1964. By 1968, he would face the obstacles of other new faces, two reelection cycles as governor, and advancing age. Accordingly, if Rockefeller was not nominated in 1960—an option he returned to later in his report—"his main avenue to the Presidency now is one where Nixon is nominated in 1960 but loses the election." Platten admitted this put Rockefeller in the unfortunate position "of mixed emotions; like the man who watches his mother-in-law drive his new Cadillac off the cliff," but it also meant that the governor needed to pay very close attention to how he conducted himself during the general campaign. Three options presented themselves: either Nixon could lose, despite holding New York State; Nixon could lose, unless he won New York State; or Nixon could win, even without New York State.

In the first scenario, it was essential that Rockefeller make every effort to put his state in the Republican column, thereby proving he still had voter appeal and could be a better choice for the GOP in 1964. In the third scenario, Rockefeller was more or less out of luck. The second scenario, however, presented a dilemma for the governor that Platten suggested could be solved by offering his full support to Nixon strategists—and letting *them* call the shots. That way, Rockefeller's dedication to the cause would be unimpeachable, but he could blame the loss on the Nixon campaign's poor decisions. Platten further recommended that Rockefeller continue to refuse the vice presidency unless it appeared that a Nixon-Rockefeller ticket would lose nationally but win New York State. Accordingly, it would be necessary to know such a ticket's odds of victory immediately after the Democratic convention had chosen its ticket and before Rockefeller needed to make a commitment either way.

Finally, however, Platten concluded his analysis with a discussion of the possibility of a Rockefeller "draft" in 1960. "I think there is a political truism in the statement that there is never a genuine draft," he wrote. "Drafts have to be organized, and so there has to be an organization somewhere." He believed that the governor would not object to efforts being made on his behalf to stimulate such a draft and laid out a variety of steps he deemed necessary to create favorable conditions. The governor should focus upon his present activities, firm rejection of the vice presidency, and travel to potentially favorable states, especially non-primary states where he could not be accused of campaigning. Meanwhile, word should go out that while Rockefeller was completely sincere in his pledge that he was not a candidate, some members of his staff and leaders within the party continued to believe that he was the GOP's best hope in 1960. Former Rockefeller volunteers in states like New Hampshire, Wisconsin, and Oregon should be encouraged to continue their primary campaign activities on a wildcat basis. Like Borella, Platten felt that the Rockefeller team needed an experienced GOP organizer. He suggested liberal Pennsylvania Senator Hugh Scott. Finally, Rockefeller staffers should carefully mine voting trends for information they could use as "cloak-room material" in Chicago.

As in the past, the governor and his staff acted upon some of these proposals, most notably the ones regarding Rockefeller's personal behavior. Platten's travel recommendations, however, were largely ignored, and these were the steps that might have provided the governor with a true base of support upon which to "organize" an ostensibly spontaneous draft. The consultant had recommended Colorado, Illinois, Iowa, Indiana, Michigan, and Minnesota as good targets for visits. By mid-April, at the end of the New York legislative session, Rockefeller had only one trip planned to any of these states—a trip to dedicate a new law center at the University of Chicago, a school largely funded by his grandfather.[55] If Rockefeller staffers followed Platten's recommendation to mobilize Rockefeller supporters in key primary states like New Hampshire, Wisconsin, and Oregon, their efforts garnered little success. New Hampshire's March contest marked the high point of Rockefeller's primary support, with 2,890 citizens writing in his name versus 65,077 votes for Nixon. Rockefeller was completely ignored by Wisconsin voters in April and won only an inconsequential number of write-in ballots in Oregon's May primary.[56] Bringing Hugh Scott onto the team also proved impracticable; the senator remained a loyal Nixon supporter.

In short, the studies his staff commissioned and the advice his advisers dispensed indicate that Rockefeller wanted to be drafted for the presidency in 1960. The governor's actions betrayed his belief that despite Platten's warnings, a truly spontaneous draft was a possibility. As a result, Rockefeller rested on his laurels through the spring as Nixon crisscrossed the country and the Democrats waged battle in the primary elections. The governor's organization continued to monitor the political situation within the GOP. A Morhouse contact with links to several key party figures reported in late February, for example, that longtime GOP Nationalities Director A.B. Hermann believed things were too good, too soon for Nixon, and Nixon campaign director Len Hall feared the same. The previous fall, Hall had believed that Nixon had only a fifty-fifty chance against Rockefeller—and Hall was not a Rockefeller pal, having clashed with the governor on numerous occasions. By mid-April, Hermann was said to believe an additional two-point drop in Nixon's already sagging poll numbers would cause RNC members to "press the panic button"—possibly bringing Rockefeller back into the picture. RNC publicity director Hal Short reported that the national committee was bending over backward to avoid being openly identified with Nixon.[57] These reports must have struck joy into the hearts of Rockefeller staff members. Even so, a May poll showed that Nixon was favored by 84 percent of Republicans, and Rockefeller and his associates remained uninterested in taking the time to reach out to the masses and present an active alternative to Nixon.[58]

In mid-May, the Rockefeller team finally kicked into gear in response to a proposal by Republican National Committee Chairman Thruston Morton. Interested in creating an atmosphere of Republican unity, Morton invited the governor to take on the convention leadership role of his choice: keynote speaker and temporary chairman or permanent convention chairman. Hinman reasoned to the governor that Nixon's collection of primary victories all but guaranteed him the nomination, and given the situation, party criticism of Rockefeller's failure to endorse Nixon was growing. On the other hand, Kennedy's win in overwhelmingly Protestant West Virginia and the recent U-2 spy plane incident would likely combine to send Nixon's poll numbers even farther south against the Massachusetts senator. This was likely, unfortunately, to redound primarily to the benefit of the Democrats.

Given the situation, it might have been prudent to accept the permanent chairmanship of the convention, once again renounce both the presidency and the vice presidency, and therefore present a team-player image in preparation for 1964. Jud Morhouse could announce the New York delegation's endorsement of Nixon, implying Rockefeller's support while still leaving him personally uncommitted in the event that lightning struck and the convention swung open. Such a course would only make the governor more desirable to independents, "enlightened Republicans," and even the party organization if things really got rough for Nixon. He still might take flak for refusing the vice presidency, which various party leaders had attempted to force upon Rockefeller all spring, but it would be far more harmful to wait and reject the office at the convention itself.[59]

Prudent though Hinman's suggestions might have been—after all, given Nixon's sagging overall poll numbers, Rockefeller might already be watching his mother-in-law drive his Cadillac off a cliff—the governor just could not abide the idea of biding his time until 1964. At this point, Rockefeller's traits as an individual become even more significant. Another person might have been able to stand aside. Rockefeller, however, frustrated by the path of Republican politics and no doubt irritated by the public's failure to spontaneously recognize him as their best option, began a course of speaking out that would seriously damage Nixon's ability to make a big-tent appeal to party liberals. As early as the previous fall, Rockefeller had spoken out on the need for the GOP to look to the future and stimulate a national discussion about vital issues. This in itself was nothing unusual among Republicans. Eisenhower had organized the Committee on Program and Progress in 1959 to forge a direction for the party of the future, and politicians including Nixon, Hugh Scott, and members of Eisenhower's cabinet had spoken out in similar terms. Now, however, Rockefeller's rhetoric took on a more explicitly challenging tone: he refused Morton's convention offer, stating that he would not attend the convention at all as it seemed the only way to keep his name out of contention for the vice presidency. His decision reflected both personal conviction and concern for party welfare, he argued, because the convention should not waste its time considering an unavailable candidate. "Frankly, I could not justify leaving the governorship of the state of New York to become the Vice President." Meanwhile, Morhouse, who had become something of a Rockefeller lieutenant, proclaimed that despite this statement, the governor "should not be ruled out of contention for the Presidency." The GOP was in danger of losing not only the presidency, but also many state and local offices, unless its national ticket "is headed by a candidate capable of the appeal that thrusts across and beyond Republican Party lines. . . . The place for that broad appeal, however, is at the head of the ticket. Its absence there cannot find or claim compensation elsewhere."[60] In other words, it was the presidency or bust for Rockefeller.

Back into the Fray

On May 23, Rockefeller delivered the first of his statements on "national issues of serious moment," as he had stated he would do in his December withdrawal. Focusing on the recent failure of a summit conference at Paris in the aftermath of the U-2 incident, Rockefeller argued that, "The people need to know what went wrong, where we are, and where we are going." Democrats should refrain from shallow partisan use of this breakdown in relations, but neither should Republicans try to disguise the present situation for partisan reasons. "National unity" did not mean that "debate threatens unity or that dissent suggests disloyalty—for true and honest unity only issues from honorable debate." Accordingly, Rockefeller outlined several areas in which he believed the summit conference failure posed serious questions. First, he suggested that the conference placed in "serious question some of the illusions, as well as the procedures, that led to the summit itself." However progressive Rockefeller might have been on many domestic issues, like most 1950s liberals he was an implacable cold warrior, gaining credit even from the overwhelmingly anti-Rockefeller staff of *National Review* for his outspoken opposition to the Soviets. Second, the governor argued that despite the crudity of the Soviets' response to the U-2 incident, the way the U.S. government dealt with the incident, coming as it did just before the conference, suggested that the "purpose and prudence" of American actions also required serious examination. Finally, he warned that the summit conference's failure created additional pressure upon friends and allies abroad. American bungling had serious consequences. The failure of the conference was not a "fatal debacle" but neither was it a "shining victory." The United States owed the world a thoughtful examination of its actions. "This is the way, and the only way, for a free people to act their age—and <u>for</u> their age," Rockefeller concluded.[61]

Two days after this statement, Rockefeller announced to a meeting of state Republican leaders that "in all candor" he would accept a draft for the presidential nomination, were it proffered. With his entry into the debate over issues and this declaration of continuing interest, he had jumped back into the presidential scrum—but once again, he did so without actually making himself a candidate. The governor also suggested that he might change his mind about attending the convention, were the GOP to accept his complete lack of interest in the vice presidential nomination.[62] Morton proclaimed his happy reaction to the news that Rockefeller might decide to attend the convention, calling his 1958 election "one of the few shining stars in the Republican scene in 1958," but behind the scenes, there were indications of nervousness among Nixon supporters.[63] The vice president's campaign staff carefully monitored press reaction to Rockefeller's statements, reporting to Nixon, for example, on a June 3 *Wall Street Journal* article in which columnist Alan Otten analyzed the governor's recent moves as evidence that he felt Nixon would lose the general election. Rockefeller was setting himself up to head the GOP ticket in 1964, and he wanted to stay clear of Nixon until forced to back him following the nomination. Even then, he would speak out on a consistently liberal line so if Nixon lost, it would be clear that Rockefeller had predicted it on the basis of Nixon's lack of sufficient liberalism.[64]

To at least some degree, this nervousness proved well founded. Not only did Otten predict exactly what the governor planned to do for the remainder of 1960, but reaction to Rockefeller's statements indicated that despite his failure to openly encourage such activity, the governor truly did continue to enjoy legitimate grassroots support. "Draft Rockefeller" clubs sprouted around the country, and many supporters who wrote to Rockefeller failed to distinguish between his recent statements and an open campaign for the presidential nomination. Some writers, like Glennoirre Blough of Arlington, Virginia, merely congratulated the governor on his statement of availability, saying she had been hoping to hear just that and would hope that he was nominated and elected.[65] Others, however, like Samuel Walker of New York City, expressed their "thanks for your decision to compete against Richard Nixon—it is extremely important for all red-blooded Americans to have your leadership and its national purpose."[66]

On June 8, Rockefeller let loose a fusillade of criticism against Nixon and Eisenhower, effectively opening the floodgates of controversy for the remainder of the pre-convention season. "I am deeply convinced, and deeply concerned," he said, "that those now assuming control of the Republican party have failed to make clear where this party is heading and where it proposes to lead the nation." He complimented Eisenhower's service as a general and a president but argued that "we cannot and we must not confuse taking pride in the past with taking measure of the future." The Democratic Party was bereft of leadership and hopelessly divided on the civil rights question, but this did not lessen the duty of the Republican Party to put forward a positive alternative, and "I cannot pretend to believe that the Republican party has fully met this duty." While Rockefeller acknowledged that it was not conventional to mention "lacks or lapses" in one's own party, "the times we live in are not conventional." Accordingly, he said, he felt compelled to state two things bluntly:

One: I find it unreasonable in these times—that the leading Republican candidate for the Presidential nomination has firmly insisted upon making known his program and his policies not before, but only after, nomination by his party.

Two: I find it reasonable—and urgently necessary—that the new spokesmen of the Republican party declare now, and not at some later date, precisely what they believe and what they propose, to meet the great matters before the nation.

He had been waiting for such a program, but at this late date he could no longer remain silent. "We cannot, as a nation or as a party, proceed—nor should any one presume to ask us to proceed—to march to meet the future with a banner aloft whose only emblem is a question-mark." In this spirit, Rockefeller went on to outline ten "concrete and crucial" problems on which he felt the leadership of the GOP should state its stances. First, he felt that the United States' position in the world was "dramatically weaker" in 1960 than in 1945, and the free world must be strengthened. Second, the national defense establishment had become inadequate and too well known to the Russians; it must be improved. Third, he recommended spending an additional $3 billion for immediate defense and another $500 million for civil defense programs. Fourth, the structure of the U.S. government required overhauling to deal effectively with modern needs and problems. Fifth, adequate and formal international control and inspection of arms was essential, but the United States lacked a formal position on the matter; this problem should be remedied. Sixth, the American economy needed strengthening, with revised tax laws to encourage investment, elimination of labor, and management excesses, and a coherent farm policy. Seventh, constant vigilance was necessary to combat inflation. Eighth, the federal government must allow no sabotage of the Supreme Court's *Brown v. Board* decision. Ninth, Rockefeller called for an increase in federal education aid and scholarship programs. Finally, he urged medical help for the elderly, not through a subsidy but through expansion of the already existent system of contributory social insurance.[67]

Despite his kind words for Eisenhower, then, Rockefeller's statement was both a challenge to Nixon and a critique of Eisenhower administration programs. Rockefeller was a Cold War hawk and a domestic liberal, unafraid to spend money in both realms to accomplish his goals. The fiscally conservative president and his middle-of-the-road deputy were simply too cautious for Rockefeller's tastes—and now the entire nation knew that. While he told the president in advance of his plans to make the statement, Eisenhower was reported as being less than thrilled with the tone of the governor's attack, not just on Nixon personally but also on the policies of his administration. The vice president initially avoided comment on the statement, although his supporters publicly welcomed a pre-convention debate on the issues.[68] Once Nixon did speak out, he attempted a statesmanlike response to this barrage of criticism threatening to destroy the GOP leadership's careful portrayal of a sterling Eisenhower legacy, with the vice president as heir.

"I've known the Governor for a good number of years," Nixon said, "and I know of his integrity and deep interest in the Republican party and its policies, and he is free to criticize, since it is motivated by his concern over some administrative policies." He did not share the views of some of his Republican colleagues, he said, that Rockefeller should not speak out critically about administration policies—a tacit suggestion that perhaps this *was* out of line, but Nixon was man enough to allow Rockefeller his fun. The vice president stated that he did not believe Rockefeller's statement would hurt his electoral chances, and he insisted that he had already set forth his policies "with greater precision and in much more detail than the candidates of either party."[69]

Emmet Hughes, the author of Rockefeller's ten-point statement, warned the governor prior to its release that he ran two risks by making such a belligerent move. First, he said, if Nixon's election in November was seen as doubtful, a more cautious approach might place Rockefeller in a better position to take over as benevolent leader of the GOP heading into 1964. Second, posing a challenge to Nixon ran the risk that the vice president would answer it with sensible and persuasive responses to the questions thrown at him. If he was able to do this, Rockefeller could not do much more than agree, removing the power of his challenge and possibly dragging him further into the Nixon organization than he intended. As Hughes pointed out, "the man you are addressing is a master of the I-am-so-glad-you-asked-that-question technique."[70]

Hughes's predictions proved true in the first instance and unfounded in the second. In the main, Nixon avoided answering Rockefeller's charges, although he did continue to aver that he had already stated and would continue to state his views on the issues of the day in detail. The campaign released a series of "Vice President Richard Nixon answers questions about . . ." publications, listing series of quotations from Nixon's spring speeches and television appearances on issues including foreign trade and aid, the economy, and civil rights. New elaboration of his in-depth thinking on key questions, however, had to wait until August, when Nixon met with his Policy Advisory Group and announced the forthcoming release of a series of papers outlining his thoughts on issues such as Communism, "national purpose," "the scientific revolution," and education.[71]

Rockefeller's outburst, however, mobilized Nixon backers against him, poisoning relations for the future. As Nixon supporter Walter Annenberg's *Philadelphia Inquirer* put it, if Rockefeller had concerns, he could have entered the primaries to compete against Nixon or come out openly as a candidate and debated the vice president all over the country, but instead, "Rockefeller preferred to stand in the wings. . . . Now, with his blast against Nixon and the Eisenhower Administration, his stance is one of re-entering the race without taking the risks."[72] The governor had created a controversy where a foregone conclusion once existed, destroying the Republicans' opportunity for a public display of unity in contrast to Democratic infighting. He also placed pressure on Nixon to demonstrate his liberal credentials, a situation that would in the next month create the conditions for conservatives to demonstrate their own political power. Rockefeller's disastrous combination of a desire to speak out and hesitancy about actually committing himself to a presidential run had pushed Modern Republicanism over a cliff. What would emerge at the base of the canyon looked nothing like Eisenhower—and it would become the dominant form of Republicanism into the early twenty-first century.

As Rockefeller took the high road of supposedly nonpartisan criticism, his supporters revitalized local organizations and created a national "Draft Rockefeller" committee under the auspices of San Francisco activist Bill Brinton. Letters poured into Rockefeller's offices, begging him to run openly and pledging their support. On June 11, Celia P. Fay of Fort Wayne, Indiana, offered her assistance and waxed poetic over Rockefeller's "vision, your forthrightness, your sound fiscal approach to our governmental matters which shine like beacons to those of us in search of our true American destiny at this desperate hour."[73] R.R. Greenbaum of Wichita, Kansas, wrote urging the governor to change his mind about an open run for the nomination:

> Frankly speaking, you <u>can not</u> be elected unless you are nominated—and you can not be nominated unless you are available, and in order for this country to have the kind of leadership that it deserves in these trying and crucial times, you must now change your stand and make yourself available. You must campaign vigorously for this nomination.[74]

Unfortunately, Fay, Greenbaum, and other supporters could take little solace from the form letter Rockefeller sent back to his eager acolytes. The letters stated only that he appreciated their interest and generous comments. "Although I am not a candidate for the Presidential nomination, I feel it is my duty to express my views on the grave issues confronting the country." It was essential that these issues be discussed within each party as well as between Republicans and Democrats.[75] The extent to which an active Rockefeller candidacy might have boosted the fortunes of liberal Republicanism in 1960 is evident in the levels of support he achieved even without offering voters a true choice. Despite his cold-fish attitude toward his supporters, at least twenty states established "Draft Rockefeller" committees, and the lists of chairmen and co-chairmen revealed many of the same names active in fall 1959 on the governor's behalf.[76]

Noncommittal platitudes aside, Rockefeller's staffers were as busy as ever, counting potential delegate votes and contemplating the possibility of a convention challenge. In detailed reports, staff members compiled delegate lists, collected press clippings, and outlined the possibility of support from various states—beginning in early May, well before Rockefeller began his round of prominent statements. Delaware, for example, was considered a bastion of Rockefeller support, with six of twelve delegates strong for the governor by May 2 and as many as four more remaining persuadable.[77] These already sympathetic delegations became even more interested in Rockefeller following his June statement; a Delaware activist, for example, invited the governor to come down to Wilmington for a "mammoth rally."[78] North Dakota reported on June 17 that there would be substantial support for the governor among state delegates if he were to declare himself a candidate, and Kentucky's national committeeman told Hinman there was sentiment for Rockefeller within his delegation as well.[79] Meanwhile, Rockefeller partisans made preparations for a presence at the Chicago convention, although as one supporter told New York Lieutenant Governor Malcolm Wilson, they faced some logistical hurdles in renting rooms and, once again, financing their activities.[80]

As the convention approached, Rockefeller focused his attentions upon influencing the Republican Party platform while his Draft Rockefeller supporters worked to further the notion that Nixon could not be elected. As the platform committee began its meetings, Rockefeller inundated delegates and the committee alike with his views on major issues. Appearances before the committee by key party figures were a regular feature of platform procedures, and Rockefeller, Barry Goldwater, and several other leading Republicans were invited to share their views. Rockefeller took the process further, however, by printing up flashy presentations of his views for distribution. Aides broadly distributed two major Rockefeller speeches, one on civil rights and one on foreign policy. The Rockefeller organization also produced a 32-page report titled "A Republican Approach to the Great Issues" for distribution to all convention delegates. Covering foreign policy, defense, government reorganization, arms control, economic growth, inflation control and labor management, civil rights, education, and medical care for the elderly, this publication was an expanded version of his June 8 statement. The governor proclaimed his hope that "this frank expression of a Republican's approach to the great issues may bring forth equally frank expressions from others."[81] He also, no doubt, hoped that delegates would like the report so much that they would simply nominate its author. Finally, Rockefeller had printed for distribution copies of his detailed statement to the platform committee on July 19, covering similar political ground.[82]

Unfortunately, many delegates did *not* like what they read, a problem that would come to a head when Nixon attempted to placate his liberal challenger. Meanwhile, however, Draft Rockefeller activists were busily fomenting the idea that Nixon was a sure loss for the Republicans in November. On July 21, the committee reported with typical Rockefellerite faith in expertise that a recent five-state survey showed "Republican defeat is certain unless Governor Rockefeller is nominated by delegates to the GOP National Convention next week." Adding legitimacy to the survey, Brinton reported that the survey firm, Political Analysis Associates, had done substantial work for the RNC, including work with Nixon campaign manager Len Hall, with the same kind of sampling techniques used to gauge voter response in 1952 and 1956. Draft Rockefeller's survey did not show that Kennedy had received a significant boost from the Democratic National Convention, but nonetheless Nixon was projected to lose in California, New York, Pennsylvania, Illinois, and Texas. The margin of "undecided" voters was at least 19 percent and as high as 25 percent in each state, but Brinton asserted that this represented significant falloff from Nixon support into the undecided column since the Democrats had met in Los Angeles. "Nixon's image is fixed. And it is not a winning image." Brinton did not extensively elaborate on how a Rockefeller candidacy would change the situation, but he did point out that in the five North Dakota counties where Rockefeller campaigned for the Republican candidate in a special election the previous spring, the Republican won four of five votes. In counties where Nixon campaigned, the GOP lost two out of every three votes.[83]

The Draft Rockefeller Committee continued to promote the results of its survey as delegates arrived at the convention, stating in a "Rockefeller Roll Call" publication to delegates that "to win in November, we must attract the independent vote. We must attract Democrats disgusted with the Kennedy-Johnson ticket." Nixon could do fine among Republicans, but they constituted a distinct minority of American voters. Only Rockefeller could win the loyalty of independents and Democrats.[84]

Behind the scenes, though, Draft Rockefeller was becoming increasingly concerned. Rockefeller needed to make a statement allowing his name to be placed in contention for the nomination or "the 'Draft Rockefeller' movement will die aborning [sic]." Furthermore, Rockefeller supporters made the surprising proposal that, "The only possible chance to electrify the convention lies in offering the nomination for Vice President to Senator Barry Goldwater." Evidently Arizona Representative John Rhodes had approached the senator to gauge his interest, and Goldwater had responded that "'Rockefeller and I are not nearly so far apart as you might think.'" Such a team would be a geographic and ideological coup for the governor, and Goldwater was a party player who could be counted upon to go along with the plan.[85]

The Compact of Fifth Avenue

Unfortunately, any possibility that this creative thinker's proposal might have had was torpedoed by Rockefeller's next moves. Not only did he fail to declare his availability for the nomination, but he consented to meet with none other than Vice President Nixon at Rockefeller's Fifth Avenue apartment. This meeting, held the Saturday before the convention opened in Chicago, was peculiar for a number of reasons. First, Nixon requested the conference and traveled to New York to meet with Rockefeller in Rockefeller's apartment. Furthermore, Rockefeller was allowed to release the results of their meeting. These conditions violated all the rules of political protocol requiring lower-ranking officials to defer to their superiors. Nixon was so concerned with placating the governor that he consented to these breaches in propriety, opening himself to charges of kowtowing. After several hours of late-night discussion, the two men agreed to a set of fourteen positions, seven domestic and seven foreign, which they believed should be reflected in the platform committee's final report. Rockefeller then issued their statement from his New York City office. The text of this statement became known as the "Compact of Fifth Avenue."

When news of Rockefeller and Nixon's agreement reached Chicago, the convention erupted in fury. Not only was this an affront to the platform committee, usurping its role in the development of party principles, but it represented a sellout on Nixon's part to his liberal challenger. Conservatives were outraged, with Goldwater referring to the decision as the "Munich of the Republican Party" and a robust movement developing to nominate the Arizona senator to the presidency. Nixon would later argue that his positions had never been dramatically distant from Rockefeller's on the fourteen issues they discussed. He later wrote that while it took the two men almost three hours to resolve one sticky issue, national security, most decisions were made fairly quickly—with the vice president rejecting any positions not in accord with Eisenhower's and his own, and Rockefeller acquiescing. "I knew I was in the stronger bargaining position and that Rockefeller was confronted with a very ticklish face-saving problem," Nixon recalled. "By going to see him in New York and working out differences that were more illusory than real, I was able to ensure his support for the Republican ticket."[86] Nixon's account likely represents a certain amount of bravado; the vice president was facing a gubernatorial election at the time he wrote his first volume of memoirs. The California Republican Party of the early 1960s was heading in an increasingly conservative direction, and, at the very least, Nixon needed to promote an image of Rockefeller caving to him, rather than vice versa. Even so, most commentators at the time argued that the vice president was more liberal on a number of fronts than Eisenhower, and was just waiting for the convention so he could be out from under the president's shadow and able to articulate a slightly different vision.[87]

Conservatives, however, would remember the Compact as a paramount example of the liberal establishment's high-handed assertion of authority from above. As such, it functioned as a rallying point for right-wing members of the GOP in formulating a coherent opposition to Modern Republicanism. The organizational framework conservatives established in 1960 helped them promote their cause effectively in the future. By contrast, Rockefeller's meeting with Nixon marked the end of his ability to serve as an advocate of liberal Republicanism—or even as a gadfly. As soon as Rockefeller metaphorically signed his name to the same sheet of principles as Nixon, the governor's ability to serve as a loyal Republican voice for liberalism dissolved. He was implicated in the Nixon campaign and its ideals. Regardless of how liberal Nixon might actually be—and many conservatives, of course, dismissed him following the Compact as hopelessly liberal—he would always be a member of the Republican class of 1946 that passed the Taft-Hartley labor law, which restricted union activities, and the man who brought down Alger Hiss. These realities would forever tarnish his appeal among some liberal voters, who, anti-Communist though they might have been, nonetheless deplored the tactics of the House Committee on Un-American Activities. Goldwater, on the other hand, loyally campaigned for Nixon, but he retained his independence as a conservative. This placed him and his supporters in a far stronger position post-November.

The General Election

With the Republican nomination decided, Rockefeller turned his attentions to New York State Republican races and to support of the Nixon-Lodge team. He and his staff continued to attempt to position himself as the liberal voice of the GOP, with George Hinman, for example, encouraging Rockefeller to campaign for a Republican congressional nominee in Seattle, as well as for specific candidates in Wisconsin and Kentucky. While he could also plug for Nixon-Lodge at these appearances, "this would be incidental to the main purpose." By supporting these particular candidates, Hinman explained, he could "underline again your alignment with the progressive elements of the party."[88] In early October, Emmet Hughes encouraged Rockefeller to consider writing a short book titled something like "What I Believe" or "This is Where I Stand." If Nixon was defeated, there would be obvious value in setting forth the governor's stands and promoting his beliefs among Democrats and independents as well as Republicans. If Nixon did win, regardless of Rockefeller's relation to a Nixon administration, "it would seem no less appropriate and effective a way for you, in so many words, to say publicly what you expect of such an administration."[89]

As the campaign progressed, New York's Republican leadership appeared confident that Nixon would win the state's electoral votes. Jud Morhouse informed the press on October 23 that all-time high voter registration levels in New York pointed toward a winning margin for Nixon-Lodge. Nixon's victory might not be as large as Eisenhower's in 1956, but it still appeared substantial.[90] Accordingly, Rod Perkins encouraged the governor to call specific attention to his efforts on behalf of Nixon-Lodge with comments such as "This is my 210th (?) speech for Dick Nixon in this campaign. And why have I been going all out for Vice President Nixon? . . ."[91]

Unfortunately for the Republican Party, Nixon won neither New York State nor the election. In contrast to Eisenhower's 60.3 percent of the New York vote, Nixon garnered only 46.6 percent.[92] Rockefeller and his advisers attempted to position the governor as heir apparent in the wake of Nixon's defeat. Just three days after the election, for example, Hinman reported his pleasure at learning that RNC Chairman Thruston Morton intended to stay on as chairman for a time at Nixon and Eisenhower's request, in order to allow time for stocktaking and decision-making within the party. "I think this is a good thing," Hinman said. "It gives us time to make our constructive purposes in regard to the party clear to our friends and to the world and to consolidate as broad a coalition within the party as we can."[93]

The RNC Research Division's preliminary reports on the election indicated that especially large declines were evident in cities and suburban areas surrounding the major cities of the East. Buffalo, Boston, and Newark, for example, had all seen drop-offs of over 20 percent compared to 1956, and Baltimore, Cleveland, and Chicago were not far behind with declines of 15 percent or more. Boston, Buffalo, Baltimore, New York, and Cleveland suburbs all recorded drops of 15 percent or greater since 1956.[94] These areas were the strongholds of Eastern Establishment liberalism and therefore boded well for Rockefeller in theory. As RNC Research Director Bill Prendergast commented, "[the Nixon campaign] found out there just weren't that many white southern Baptists." The vice president should have spent more time in northern, urban states like New York and "to hell with the south."[95] What they failed to note, however, were changing settlement patterns bringing ever more Americans to conservative Sunbelt cities in the South and Southwest. Their analysis also did not reflect the growing Republican vote in the South, which affected the quadrennial reapportionment of convention delegates. The nation might have *looked* liberal in 1960, but geographic and demographic trends both nationally and within the GOP would bring dire results for Rockefeller's brand of liberalism.

A Lesson in the Importance of Organization

Conservatives within and outside the GOP mobilized over the course of 1960, with new organizations and a new figurehead—Barry Goldwater— behind whom they could rally. By contrast, Rockefeller's expectation of a spontaneous "draft" exposed the absence of a widespread, politically active moderate coalition within the Republican Party. Given Nixon's control over much of the Republican Party organization in 1960, it was also bad politics. The majority of Americans might well have been moderates, as they generally are, but to forge a vibrant campaign, either an active candidate or a fresh set of ideas—and, preferably, both—is necessary. Effective organization is also essential. During the nomination process, the Nixon organization's popularity among state and local officials put it in a markedly superior position. While the vice president's campaign developed numerous problems, partly as a result of the "Compact" and especially during the general election campaign, his long years of service on behalf of Republican candidates had garnered him the support of state and local party leadership in most regions of the country. Just as importantly, adequate organizational strength was something conservatives were developing from the ground up.

Rockefeller's on-again, off-again "run" for the nomination offered neither. His failure to commit to the race and his reliance on expert studies, rather than upon the efforts and activities of his erstwhile supporters, failed to stimulate the organizational strength needed to mount an effective challenge. When party liberals tried to organize in support of the governor, Rockefeller discouraged their efforts by persistently denying his presidential intentions. His criticisms of Nixon from the left damaged the vice president's ability to cast himself as a politician with big-tent appeal and resulted in Nixon's disastrous attempt to regain control over his left flank with the "Compact of Fifth Avenue." While Nixon managed to consolidate support over the short term and retain the nomination, the long-term effect of the "Compact" was to mobilize conservatives in their attempt to take control of the Republican Party. Meanwhile, Goldwater's forthright stands and uncompromising persona made him a conservative folk hero.

A more active liberal Republican in 1960 might possibly have won the nomination and even the election, given the close outcome of the Nixon-Kennedy race; however, 1960 marked the last presidential election year in which the liberal and conservative wings of the GOP were roughly equivalent in strength in the national party.[96] Given the disastrous course of Republican electoral politics as a whole during the late 1950s, Rockefeller and Goldwater were rare stars. Goldwater and his supporters proved to be the wave of the future. The Rockefeller organization's tactical ineptitude and lack of discipline provided conservatives with a window through which they could enter to take control of the party machinery. By 1964, the organizations they had so diligently fostered from 1960 onward had become an unstoppable force.

Elephant on a Tight Rope

Republicans and the African American Vote

"An elephant does not make a pretty picture on a tight rope. This is especially true if a trip of the foot will send him crashing into an open sewer that empties into the dead sea of racial segregation."—Clarence Mitchell, Washington, D.C., NAACP, in the *Baltimore Afro-American*, July 30, 1960

Forged in the struggle over the future of American slavery and consolidated during the fratricidal battles of the Civil War, the Republican Party long stood symbolic of African Americans' hopes and dreams of full citizenship. Republican presidents signed the Emancipation Proclamation and the Thirteenth, Fourteenth, and Fifteenth Amendments, freeing African American slaves and granting, in theory, the rights to due process and the vote. Republican congressmen held out for stronger conditions during Reconstruction, aiming to punish the South for its acts of treason and ensure a better start for the formerly enslaved portion of its citizenry. Through World War II, southern states' Republican Party organizations were composed of and led largely by African Americans, although in the wake of late nineteenth-century Jim Crow legislation, many of these parties were relegated primarily to patronage-awarding skeletal structures.

In the 1930s, however, the history of African American political involvement in the United States took a sharp turn. Franklin Roosevelt's New Deal, while it might not have been a fair deal for most African Americans, offered far greater opportunity and assistance than minority populations had hitherto seen. By the 1940s and 1950s, Republicans could no longer consider

African Americans' loyalty a foregone conclusion. Even the nationally popular Eisenhower won only a minority of the African American vote in each of his electoral victories. Optimistic liberals within the GOP could point toward a slight increase in the former general's support between 1952 and 1956. The trends that have since placed African Americans firmly into the Democratic column had yet to fully develop. After all, despite the advances of the New Deal and the pro–civil rights policies of northern liberal Democrats like Hubert Humphrey, the Democratic Party remained the home of the segregationist South. In terms of African Americans' relationships to the two major political parties, then, as in so many other areas, the presidential election of 1960 provides an illuminating window into fundamental changes underway.

As late as 1960, various pundits predicted that the limited gains Eisenhower made among African American voters might accelerate with Nixon as a candidate. African Americans had become devoted members of the New Deal coalition, but their position was not cast in concrete. Nixon was well liked by many African American leaders, and some leading figures cast their support behind him publicly for a number of reasons, ranging from his civil rights record to his apparent awareness of the connections between the international struggle against Communism and the fight for civil rights at home. Still others indicated early support for the liberal policies of Nelson Rockefeller, and this challenge on Nixon's left flank led him to articulate more fully some of his own liberal feelings regarding civil rights. At the same time, however, Nixon was engaged in an unprecedented outreach to southern white voters. This outreach had unfortunate implications for African American voters. Primarily, it meant that Nixon was extremely cautious about the degree of support he gave to black leaders and their causes. Nixon's reluctance to engage fully with this important constituency may have cost him the election in several key states.

A full understanding of the relationship between African Americans and the Republican Party during this period requires examination of their interactions from two perspectives. First, the manner in which Nixon and the Republican Party dealt with—and often fumbled—their outreach to African Americans provides a window into party organization circa 1960. Even as they strove to maintain and develop black allegiance, party leaders like Nixon and his subordinates were often preoccupied with new, conservative constituencies, neglecting their traditional supporters and failing to speak out on even a symbolic level. John F. Kennedy and the Democrats, on the other hand, effectively used the politics of symbolism to reach out to African American voters. In short, Nixon and the Republicans chose the South in 1960, while Kennedy and the Democrats chose African American voters. African American party leaders and volunteers were overwhelmed by inadequate resources and support from Nixon and his cohorts and were demoralized by the campaign's failures.

Second, the choices and decisions African Americans made when faced with various political options illuminate the issues they felt were most important. The commentary of the black press provides insight into how African Americans reacted to the presidential race—and how they strove to influence the political process. Republicans' failure to respond adequately to black constituents cost them African American support, even as they gained the growing allegiance of other constituencies. Rockefeller's influence from the left was not sufficient, especially by the time of the general election campaign, to force Nixon to speak out more boldly throughout the race along themes that African Americans had long championed, such as the connection between civil rights at home and the Cold War struggle abroad.[1] The vice president's past support for such ideals was muted in his attempts to avoid alienating more conservative groups, even as Kennedy used symbolic action to convince many African Americans of his sincerity. A focus on symbolic action should not diminish the many concrete issues of importance to African American voters in 1960, including economic and foreign policy concerns. In the midst of the civil rights movement, however, outreach on this agenda was essential, and it is in the arena of symbolic action that Kennedy and Nixon made most of their successes—and failures. In the long run, of course, the GOP would benefit politically from the bridges it built to southern conservatives. In 1960, however, their lack of attention to the rickety old bridges still leading to traditional constituencies helped put Kennedy in the Oval Office.

A Party with Potential?

As early as 1928, the Republican Party hinted at outreach toward white southern conservatives by eliminating language from the party platform favoring enforcement of the Fourteenth and Fifteenth Amendments. The GOP in that year also alleged that New York Governor Al Smith, the Democratic candidate for the presidency, had encouraged interracial marriage in New York City, playing upon many white Americans' fears of miscegenation. While most black voters stayed with the party of Lincoln, some African American leaders became sufficiently disillusioned with Republican overtures to the South that they began to drift toward the Democrats.[2] This movement accelerated greatly with the coming of Franklin Roosevelt's New Deal and, perhaps just as important, his wife, Eleanor, as an outspoken advocate for improved racial relations.

Roosevelt's personal popularity, however, did not necessarily transfer into permanent gains for the Democratic Party. In 1940, for example, 67 percent of blacks supported the incumbent president despite Republican candidate Wendell Willkie's appeals, but only 42 percent of these voters considered themselves Democrats. Both Democrats and the GOP noted in 1944 that a shift in the black vote in eight states would have cost Roosevelt his fourth term in office. Republicans attempted to take advantage of this reality in 1948, including in their platform explicit opposition to racial segregation. The vast majority of black newspapers supported Thomas Dewey, the Republican candidate in 1948, but despite the wishes of their higher-status publishers, most lower-income readers of these newspapers voted for Harry Truman.[3] Socioeconomic factors seemingly trumped race considerations, although the Democrats no doubt benefited from Dixiecrats' abandonment of their party, which highlighted the civil rights advances the Truman administration had made.

Intending to reverse their losses of the past twenty years, Republicans formed the National Council of Negro Republicans in 1948 to lure back African American voters. Their efforts bore little fruit in 1952, however, as Democratic candidate Adlai Stevenson garnered 73 percent of the black vote against Dwight Eisenhower. The GOP's emphasis on "Korea, Communism and Corruption" left little time for discussion of race issues. Ike's emphasis on gradualism and persuasion over coercion and legal action cost him black support in states like Louisiana, South Carolina, Kentucky, and Arkansas, placing them in the Democratic column. In an about-face from 1948, nearly all black newspapers supported Stevenson.[4]

The first Eisenhower administration quickly established a pattern of federal response and a public expectation of civil rights advance within a framework of political moderation and consensus. Even sympathetic accounts of Eisenhower's civil rights efforts acknowledge that the president tended to focus on the federal level, where he had the most authority, and to take a "gradualist" stance—like most politicians of his era.[5] A 1953 executive order created the President's Committee on Government Contracts to investigate discriminatory behavior in the awarding of government contracts, but actual enforcement of the committee's recommendations was left to individual agencies. Eisenhower felt it was improper to bar members of a specific race from a given community, but as Housing and Home Finance Agency administrator Albert M. Cole put it in 1953, the administration felt "federal intervention is incompatible with our idea of political and economic freedom."[6]

Eisenhower's selection of California Governor Earl Warren to serve as Chief Justice of the Supreme Court, however, cast the battle for civil rights in an entirely new framework. While historians disagree about the president's enthusiasm regarding this decision, Warren engineered the landmark *Brown v. Board of Education* ruling in 1954, outlawing segregation in public schools and overturning *Plessy v. Ferguson*'s support for Jim Crow regulations. The *Brown* decision galvanized African Americans for action and was formative in the development of the civil rights movement. It also mobilized white Southerners behind a program of massive resistance. This development had paralytic effects on registration of new black voters in the South, but it resulted in significant electoral gains for the Republican Party. While African American leaders may not have been entirely enthusiastic about the GOP—as NAACP Chairman Roy Wilkins put it, "The Democratic plank smelled to heaven; the Republican plank just smelled"—Republicans were encouraged by the results. While Stevenson still won 60 to 65 percent of the black vote overall, Eisenhower's vote totals were up 5 percent nationwide from 1956 and rose substantially in key areas. In the South, for example, African American support for the Republican Party went up by 25 percent, resulting in wins in Tennessee and Kentucky. In northern urban regions, the Eisenhower-Nixon ticket was up 16.5 percent in Harlem precincts and 11 percent in Chicago.[7]

By 1960, additional factors increased the possibility that more African American voters might consider returning to the party of Lincoln. Chief among them was the 1957 passage of the first piece of civil rights legislation since Reconstruction. This legislation created the Commission on Civil Rights, upgraded the Civil Rights Section to a division of the Department of Justice, and empowered the attorney general to initiate civil proceedings to enforce voting rights. The original legislation also contained a provision enabling the attorney general to enforce school desegregation, but, faced with southern opposition that could sink the entire bill, Eisenhower withdrew his support from this provision. Voting rights were more in accordance with the president's philosophy of gradual change through established avenues. The elimination of the school desegregation enforcement clause, as well as the addition of provisions calling for jury trials in some voting rights cases, frustrated African American leaders.[8] Most, however, agreed that some legislation was better than nothing, and Eisenhower's vice president benefited in particular from passage of the legislation.

Nixon was a strong advocate of the civil rights bill, and he had taken a leading role in helping bypass delays in the Senate Judiciary Committee by placing the House-passed bill directly on the Senate's calendar.[9] Black leaders recognized both his interest in civil rights and his potential to be of further assistance. Martin Luther King, Jr., for example, expressed to Nixon his gratefulness for his "assiduous labor and dauntless courage in seeking to make the Civil Rights Bill a reality." While he did not refrain from expressing his disappointment at the extent of the bill, referring to it as "compromised," King told the vice president that his championing of the legislation had impressed Americans of all races. Deftly connecting civil rights to Nixon's presidential hopes, the black leader noted that Nixon's actions were also

> an expression of your political wisdom. More and more the Negro vote is becoming a decisive factor in national politics. The Negro vote is the balance of power in so many important big states that *one almost has to have the Negro vote to win a presidential election.* [emphasis added][10]

The vice president and his staff were thinking along similar lines, and they commissioned favorable comparisons of Nixon s civil rights credentials vis-à-vis his young upstart counterpart in the Democratic Party, John F. Kennedy.[11]

Even so, Nixon already recognized the potential pitfalls of appearing too devoted to the cause of civil rights. In October 1957, Nixon staffer Charlie McWhorter notified his boss that Kenneth Keating, a liberal Republican congressman from New York, was preparing to introduce another round of civil rights legislation in the wake of the school desegregation debacle in Little Rock that fall. McWhorter believed such an action would be "most unfortunate," as the administration needed some southern Democratic support to gain renewal of the reciprocal trade program and continuation of foreign aid. The GOP was already in a good position politically to gain African American voters' support. Rather than supporting additional legislation, educational campaigns "to gain a better climate for progress in this field" would be a better choice. Nixon agreed with his aide, proclaiming, "that will be the strategy unless it is changed at the W[hite] H[ouse]"— unlikely given Eisenhower's reluctance to expand federal power.[12]

As explained in the introduction, 1958 was a nearly unqualified disaster for the GOP. While Republicans suffered at all levels and among almost all groups, E. Frederic Morrow, the first African American appointed to the White House staff, expressed to Nixon and others his frustration with ongoing racism and lack of attention to black voters on the local level. He pointed out that in most of the states where the GOP was hammered, black voters held the balance of power in any close race. Despite their position of importance, however, party leaders were not friendly toward them, and the only time they expressed much interest in black support was during the closing days of an election.

Morrow became active in Republican Party politics after a childhood of watching the GOP control and often hoodwink African Americans in his hometown of Hackensack, New Jersey, with platitudes and appeals to Lincoln. Frustrated by this corruption of traditional Republican values, he vowed that "someday I would fight with all my might and mind within the Republican Party to beget respect and dignity for the Negro's position in American life."[13] Morrow's goal was to retake Lincoln's Republican legacy for true civil rights advocates. His rise to high position had not been an easy one. Following service in Eisenhower's 1952 campaign, Morrow was promised a position in the Eisenhower White House, but only after six months of continual pressure by longtime RNC Minorities Director Val Washington was he finally offered a job in the Commerce Department. It took two more years before Morrow was appointed to the White House post of Administrative Officer for Special Projects, and, even then, he was not formally sworn into office until 1958.[14] Overcoming obstacles in still-segregated Washington, D.C., did not make life outside the White House any easier. Morrow personally experienced the affronts of local party leaders on his many speaking tours. "It has never ceased to shock me," he wrote, "when the officials in the state or county dealt with me on the basis of a 'child' or 'boy' rather than as a full-fledged man with a responsible position in the office of the President of the United States." He urged that additional time, resources, and discussion be put toward incorporating African American voters more fully into the fabric of Republican Party life. Morrow continued to be willing to serve the administration. First, however, he insisted that "I, too, must have the support and respect and buildup from my own colleagues before I can appear on any scene as an apostle of a doctrine and a philosophy that must counteract the effective tactics of the Northern wing of the Democratic Party." Unless this happened, he predicted that there could not be a Republican victory in 1960.[15]

Nixon continued to maintain and develop his personal popularity as a civil rights advocate throughout 1958 and 1959. In March 1958, Val Washington congratulated the vice president and his wife for their attendance at a party hosted by a local black leader. To Val Washington's knowledge, this marked the first time any vice president had visited an African American's home. "You have helped our cause immeasurably," he told Nixon. "The members of the press, particularly the colored press who tend to lean toward the Democrats, were impressed and pleased by your thoughtfulness."[16] In April 1959, Roy Wilkins pressed Nixon to capitalize on Eisenhower's gains since 1952, arguing that given Ike's 17-point increase in black support in 1956, an additional 11 percent gain "would make a horse race of the election in many sections of the country." Wilkins urged action immediately to take advantage of this opportunity.[17] Nixon himself realized the symbolic importance of including advocates for traditional black concerns in party deliberations, and he urged Charles Percy, the chairman of the Republican Committee on Program and Progress, to include a social welfare expert on the committee. Democrats had used experts in this field to their advantage since 1933, he told Percy, encouraging many black Republicans to trade allegiances. Now, the Committee on Program and Progress gave the GOP "a golden opportunity to come up with positive suggestions that will refocus our welfare programs on the social problems of today, rather than twenty-five years ago."[18]

Despite his interest in appearing sympathetic toward African American causes, however, Nixon's behind-the-scenes actions often demonstrated more reluctance and pragmatic maneuvering than his black supporters were aware of. Morrow, for example, was shunted off by Nixon staffers in January 1959 when he told Nixon secretary Rose Mary Woods that it was time for him to have a "five-minute personal chat with the 'boss.'" In response, another staff member told aide Bob Finch that Nixon would not see him—"nor should he"—asking Finch to call Morrow for Nixon and take over the situation.[19] Why exactly Nixon "shouldn't" see Morrow remains a mystery, but clearly he did not want to listen to what the frustrated White House official had to say.

Earlier that same year, on the occasion of the NAACP's fiftieth anniversary, Nixon specifically instructed his aides to tone down a congratulatory letter to be sent to the organization's anniversary celebration. The original draft lauded the NAACP for charting a "most effective" middle course and gave the organization credit for "solid accomplishments." Nixon, however, directed his aides to write a far less enthusiastic letter. "Don't give them credit for the work," he said, "just say it has progressed." The finished letter was a pale reflection of the original.[20] No doubt Nixon intended to avoid looking too supportive of an organization many Southerners still considered subversive. He already had lived down years of association with the Monrovia, California branch of the NAACP, which awarded him an honorary membership when he was a southern California congressman in the late 1940s.[21]

Perhaps most notable among Nixon's behind-the-scenes subterfuges was his exhaustive effort to avoid meeting with African American leaders in early 1960, during deliberation of a second civil rights bill. On January 6, Charlie McWhorter reported to Nixon aide Don Hughes that he had received a call from Roy Wilkins, requesting an appointment with Nixon on January 14. Wilkins wanted to bring a delegation of 20 to 25 heads of organizations involved in civil rights, including A. Philip Randolph, Martin Luther King, Jr., and United Auto Workers head Walter Reuther. On January 12, Nixon told Hughes to contact the group and tell them that he would like to see them but was completely booked that week—"or whatever they have asked for." Attorney general and Nixon friend William Rogers had told the vice president that after January 27, Wilkins would not be able to co-ordinate his group members' schedules, so Hughes should tell Wilkins that Nixon was busy until then. "I think we can get out of it this way," Nixon explained. "If they buy settling for a date after January 27th I will be stuck with it." Hughes was told to inform them that Nixon had commitments in Florida that could not be broken and that he had talked with and shared the attorney general's favorable civil rights views.

By January 22, Wilkins had become frustrated with Republican congressional leaders' reluctance to support a discharge position that would get the civil rights bill out of the House Rules Committee. Blaming "Halleckism," or the conservatism of House minority leader Charles Halleck, Wilkins warned Nixon via telegram that "this performance [is] not calculated to generate love for the Republican Party and its candidates among Negro voters."[22] In response, Bob Finch told fellow Nixon aide Agnes Waldron to pen a response to be "signed by someone other than RN" and express the vice president's confidence that meaningful civil rights legislation would make it through Congress in 1960. Nixon would continue to fight for all measures "reasonably designed to secure the primary rights of all American citizens."[23]

Nixon's reluctance to meet with the civil rights leaders might have been predicated partly upon his desire to avoid affiliation with Reuther, the scourge of anti-union conservatives. Nixon and his staffers also desired, however, that the vice president keep his public distance from leaders like King, Randolph, and Wilkins. Nixon's hope of bringing new regions under Republican control, symbolized by his fifty-state campaign later that year, dictated maintenance of a middle-of-the-road position. Hindsight demonstrates how truly middle-of-the-road such figures as King, Randolph, and Wilkins were, but in 1960, many Southerners—as well as the head of the FBI, J. Edgar Hoover—looked upon these men as dangerous and possibly Communist-affiliated. Already conditioned against civil rights leaders by their own racist inclinations, individuals like Hoover and some of Nixon's southern supporters found subversive tendencies behind any attempts to better the position of African Americans in society. Whatever Nixon's true feelings, he believed close ties would prove a greater liability than an asset.

Pressure from the Left

Even as he avoided Wilkins and his cohort, Nixon could not ignore the pressures mounting upon him from Nelson Rockefeller's on-again, off-again interest in a challenge for the 1960 nomination. As chronicled in chapter 1, Rockefeller's actions throughout late 1959 and the first half of 1960 were sufficiently erratic to frustrate and befuddle supporters and opponents alike. Nonetheless, his presence generated significant pressure upon Nixon to address liberal issues like civil rights. In September 1959, Urban League Chairman and Rockefeller friend Lester Granger gave the governor a letter from Louis E. Martin, the executive editor of the prominent *Chicago Defender* newspaper. Martin, who was in the midst of a two-year assignment in Nigeria to help rejuvenate the Nigerian press, reminded Granger of his interest in supporting Rockefeller. He described the governor as a "fresh broom and . . . a good, hard campaigner for the cause he champions." Martin was registered as a Democrat and had even worked as assistant publicity director for the Democratic National Committee in 1944, but "the plug-uglies that seem to be on top in the Democratic camp don't inspire me."[24] Black newspapers paid attention when Rockefeller enrolled as a life member of the NAACP—an obvious difference in approach from Nixon's continual reminders that his own membership had been honorary, temporary, and 14 years past.[25] A recent Gallup poll might show that Rockefeller trailed Nixon by 43 points, but the *Baltimore Afro-American* editorialized that since the vice president had been "running" for the past eight years, "Governor Rockefeller, therefore, makes a very handsome showing, one that he need not be ashamed of."[26]

Rockefeller encouraged such friendly commentary by drawing overt links between the GOP's anti-slavery heritage and the present situation. Speaking before the Western States Republican Conference in Los Angeles on November 13, he contended that

> The Republican Party was founded on a fundamental purpose—to halt the extension of slavery. Our party's creation was based upon a concern for human beings. That opposition to slavery, that concern for people, is as valid now as when our party was founded.

Citing a long list of activist Republican stands, Rockefeller lauded the establishment of the Department of Health, Education and Welfare under the Eisenhower administration. To combat the Communist menace, he argued, Americans must achieve a sense of national purpose based upon shared values—the most important of which was "the brotherhood of man under the Fatherhood of God."[27]

As Rockefeller's fact-finding tours progressed throughout the fall of 1959, African American newspapers continued to follow his progress with interest and at least some support. On October 31, for example, the *Pittsburgh Courier* reported on the New York governor's speech before the fifteenth annual dinner of the Alfred E. Smith Memorial Foundation in New York

City. Rockefeller warned against the dangers of those in political life changing their convictions on matters like civil rights "as you change your audiences." Rockefeller drew on connections between civil rights at home and
support for the United States abroad, a theme Nixon had endorsed in the
past and African Americans often cited to encourage support for their struggles in the 1950s. "The United States cannot win respect and trust of black
men in Nigeria or Ghana," he said, "until we have honored the citizenship
of Negroes in Georgia or Alabama." Extending this common form of rhetoric
beyond the usual, narrow attention with legal rights, he went on to argue
that the United States could not "stir the hopes of slum dwellers in Calcutta
or Jakarta, if cities here are too lazy or fat to clean their own slums or if the
economic growth of America slows or falters." In so doing, he forged a clear
link between liberal social and economic policies and success in the Cold War
struggle. On November 7, the *Baltimore Afro-American* published an editorial cartoon depicting Rockefeller and John F. Kennedy holding placards that
proclaimed their recent statements on civil rights (Rockefeller) and religious
and racial intolerance (Kennedy). Captioned "Bad Political News for Bigots,"
the cartoon offered the two men as examples for their respective parties.[28]

Outside the newspaper world, some African Americans continued to
show strong interest in a Rockefeller candidacy. Danny Ryan, a "personal
friend" of Sugar Ray Robinson, wrote to Rockefeller asking whether he
might consider Ryan as a publicity man in his campaign. A Republican,
Ryan wrote that "our country needs a man like you for President and if you
will ignore my offer to bring you to the White House where you belong, I
will feel offended." With his boxer friend's help, Ryan assured Rockefeller
that he could garner him many votes among "Puerto Ricans and the colored people."[29] Public relations expert Walter Hiles also wrote to the governor to offer the services of his firm, Ebony Advertising Co. of San Francisco,
in the campaign.[30]

Not all black leaders, however, were impressed with Rockefeller's intentions or credentials. Baseball legend Jackie Robinson, for example, authored
a thrice-weekly column in the *New York Post* where, in addition to commentary on sporting news, he offered insightful reflections on the state of American political affairs. A Hubert Humphrey fan at first, Robinson indicated
his lack of enthusiasm with some of Rockefeller's actions. On November
25, for example, he castigated the governor for extraditing a black fugitive
named Willie Reid to Florida. In spite of Rockefeller's statement that the
Florida governor had promised "safe custody" for Reid, Robinson wondered
whether Rockefeller was aware that the constitutional guarantees of due
process and equal protection often "aren't worth the parchment they're
written on" when applied to African Americans in the South. Given his

"fine record" in New York since his escape, Reid had "more than compen-
sated for any past trouble in which he might have been involved"—trouble
about which Robinson was perhaps rightly skeptical, given the southern
legal system at the time. "I feel Gov. Rockefeller should have thought of
that," he concluded, "rather than hope to gain a few Southern votes."[31]

Rockefeller's withdrawal from the presidential race in late December 1959
brought a mixed reaction from the black press. The *Baltimore Afro-American*
printed an editorial cartoon depicting an elephant labeled "GOP Bosses"
singing "yes, sir, that's our baby" to an autographed photo of Nixon. The
caption read, "Poor Rocky! He Didn't Have a Chance." The paper's written
commentary, however, reflected a more ambiguous reaction to Rockefeller's
news. On the one hand, the governor's decision was a "bitter blow not only
to the more liberal elements in his own party, but to independent voters as
well." With Rockefeller's withdrawal, African Americans had lost a potent
lever upon Nixon's statements and activities. On the other hand, however,
with Nixon as the assured Republican candidate, "the Democrats are left no
room to travel on the conservative road." As a result, "political sense dictates"
that they seek out someone with a more liberal record on foreign policy, civil
rights, and economic issues. Citing Kennedy, Humphrey, California governor
Pat Brown, and Adlai Stevenson as possibilities, the *Afro-American* reflected
that the chances of "so-called 'moderates'" like Stuart Symington or Lyndon
Johnson seemed increasingly dim.[32] Such a situation did not bode well for
Republicans, but it demonstrated African Americans' intention of carefully
gauging candidates' support for civil rights issues. Without divulging his own
preferences, editor John Sengstacke of the *Chicago Daily Defender* reflected
that the Republicans would benefit from all the recent publicity surrounding
Nixon and Rockefeller, as well as Eisenhower's continued good standing and
the settlement of the 1959 steel strike. Nonetheless, "the conviction persists
among the unpaid experts that the Democrats' chances have improved considerably with the sudden withdrawal of Gov. Rockefeller."[33]

Jackie Robinson, on the other hand, viewed Rockefeller's withdrawal as
a potential boon to the GOP. Despite the predictions of Democratic leaders,
Robinson believed they might find Nixon would have surprising appeal for
many undecided voters, especially African Americans. Robinson was a registered independent, but Nixon had charmed the baseball pioneer as early
as 1952. The two men had been introduced in Chicago when the Republican National Convention coincided with a Dodgers road trip. The future
vice president had recalled specific details of an intricate play Robinson had
made in a UCLA football game 13 years prior, impressing Robinson with
his memory, and he went on to impress the athlete with his civil rights-
related statements in office. Following his retirement in 1956, for example,

Robinson traveled for the NAACP as chairman of its Fight for Freedom Fund, and he often quoted a statement Nixon had made while traveling in Ethiopia. "We shall never be satisfied with the progress we have been making in recent years," Nixon stated on this 1957 trip, "until the problem [of racial discrimination] is solved and equal opportunity becomes a reality for all Americans." Robinson was not a civil rights conservative. Starting in 1958 he even made several criticisms of the NAACP's hesitation in pursuing some anti-discrimination causes. But he was a fervent anti-Communist, a fan of capitalism, and impressed by the GOP's image of relative "moral austerity" in comparison to Democrats' southern ties and machine politicians. Biographer Arnold Rampersad has summarized Robinson's political identity as "Republican at heart, albeit a liberal Republican on the key matter of civil rights."[34]

Accordingly, Robinson encouraged his readers, and especially those concerned about civil rights, to give the vice president serious consideration. Nixon's record, while not so great as Humphrey's, was very attractive compared to those of the other candidates seeking the Democratic nomination. "I think it should be made clear," Robinson cautioned, "that many people whom I've talked with, whose first concern is civil rights, would not hesitate to support Vice President Nixon." Citing his growth in office and his foreign policy skill, Robinson lauded Nixon's 1953 comment, upon returning from extensive travels in Asia, that he felt every congressman should make a similar trip to "profit by the experience of seeing colored governments running their countries." Democrats should not be complacent about their chances against Nixon. "If it should come to a choice between a weak and indecisive Democratic nominee and Vice President Nixon, I, for one, would enthusiastically support Nixon."[35]

Despite his formal exit from the race, Rockefeller's involvement in civil rights remained active behind the scenes as he positioned himself as a "liberal conscience"—and hopeful draftee—of the Republican Party. Civil rights was the topic of one of the dozens of position papers penned by experts for the Rockefeller organization. Just two weeks after the governor's withdrawal, issues coordinator Horace Craig scheduled a meeting on civil rights "to discuss issues and recommended positions" with guests including the author of a position paper, Clarence C. Ferguson, Jr. of Rutgers Law School; Harris Wofford, then the assistant to Father Theodore Hesburgh on the Civil Rights Commission; John V. Lindsay, then a Manhattan congressman and member of the House Judiciary Committee; and two New York City attorneys. Although unable to attend, Lester Granger was also invited.[36] The resulting civil rights position paper, put into preliminary form by the beginning of April, urged development of a civil rights program based upon the three pillars of voting rights, education, and economic opportunity—namely, the opportunity provided by jobs. Cautioning that "our posture in the countries where non-whites predominate or where the racial tensions are a vital political factor will be deeply affected by the kind of leadership we demonstrate at home in the next few years." Among other goals, the proposal sought to strengthen enforcement powers in school desegregation suits and eliminate federal aid to discriminatory housing programs.[37]

Meanwhile, Nixon's formal campaign for the nomination began among mixed signals from supporters and the press. Columnist Rowland Evans, writing in the *New York Herald Tribune*, suggested that Nixon's candidacy might bode well for Republicans' chances of regaining African Americans' support. Democrats, he contended, had not yet succeeded in convincing northern blacks that their party stood for equality and dignity, while the vice president had been comparatively successful in imparting this feeling.[38] As chairman of the President's Committee on Government Contracts, the vice president garnered good press in March for his announcement that the committee would mount a twin drive to enforce equal opportunities for black craftsmen among both employers and unions.[39] Also in March, a poll of students and faculty at the historically black Tuskegee Institute in Alabama yielded wins for Nixon among both groups, and a majority of black high school students in Galveston, Texas, chose the vice president in an April poll.[40] Further cause for optimism came in late April, when a Gallup poll of African Americans' sentiments regarding the two parties showed that when asked which party was doing the most for blacks, 28 percent of respondents chose the GOP with only 25 percent selecting the Democrats.[41] With almost half of respondents feeling neither party's actions were adequate, the door was open for either the Democrats or the Republicans to make significant gains.

The most important black leader in the Republican Party, however, was less than enthused by the Nixon organization's early performance. In April, Val Washington returned from a month of outreach work in Colorado, Oregon, Washington, and California, and he reported his dismay at conditions in a telephone call sent on to Nixon staffer Bob Finch. People were thinking about election issues even at this early stage because of the active fight for the Democratic nomination, and the absence of any real effort by Nixon or his staff to mobilize behind concrete issues was creating feelings of apathy and disinterest. Although many of his contacts were among "his own people," Washington cautioned that he found the same attitude among whites. In California, he had heard several complaints to the effect that Nixon's palace guard, and most notably Finch, was keeping people away from the vice president.[42] Washington, an Indiana native and former general manager of the Chicago *Defender*, had been a prominent figure in

GOP politics since 1944, when he co-sponsored a booklet describing the forward-thinking policies of Republican governors in Illinois, New York, and Ohio. In 1948, he became national political director of the Midwest Council of Negro Republican Clubs. Later that same year, Washington took on the position of RNC director of "Negro activities," and he served as an assistant campaign manager for the GOP ticket of Thomas Dewey and Earl Warren. Operating under a variety of titles, Washington remained in charge of the Republicans' African American division throughout the 1950s and was called upon to participate in high-level political discussions with Eisenhower administration officials at election time. Little is known of Washington's motivation for involvement in the GOP, but he was a strident advocate for African Americans within the Eisenhower administration and a frequent critic of Democratic civil rights failures. In 1956, for example, he had labeled Adlai Stevenson "more Copperhead than egghead," citing the candidate's grandfather and namesake's Confederate sympathies during the Civil War.[43]

The troubles Washington and other key GOP officials encountered had ripple effects, creating the impression for some black party loyalists that they were insufficiently dedicated to voter outreach. Emmett Cunningham of the Michigan Democrats and Independent Voters for Eisenhower, for example, expressed his concern to Nixon that Washington, Fred Morrow, and others seemed to be suffering from complacency. Cunningham was a sales specialist with ten "unlimited" telephone lines in the Detroit area, and he hoped to establish a beachhead among voters softened by the Eisenhower administration's civil rights advances and confused by a recent Harry Truman statement opposing sit-in demonstrations. "Each of these glaring issues have [sic] been permitted to pass," he complained, "without being played up by an alert Republican Press."[44]

Further evidence of trouble brewing in Nixon outreach efforts came with Finch's reaction to a report from Nixon staffer Charlie McWhorter. Clarence Mitchell, the head of the Washington, D.C., NAACP, was not at all enamored of Democratic front-runner John Kennedy. Since joining Nixon's staff in 1957, McWhorter had dined occasionally with Mitchell to take his pulse on key issues. He reported in March that Mitchell was quite bitter about Kennedy's votes during consideration of the 1957 civil rights legislation to send the bill to virulently racist Mississippi Senator James Eastland's committee and to approve the jury trial amendment. McWhorter relayed that Mitchell told him, ". . . there are a lot of Negroes that can't be bought." Unfortunately, rather than taking a proactive approach to McWhorter's news, Finch simply scrawled a petulant "why don't they do something about it" across the memo.[45]

Finch's attitude on this and other occasions belied his background as an Inglewood, California, lawyer; Los Angeles County Republican Party official; and failed candidate for Congress in a predominantly Democratic district. He was not a southern segregationist, nor was he actively involved on either side of the civil rights debate. First and foremost, he was a Nixon loyalist. Other constituent groups and Nixon friends criticized the impermeability of Nixon's palace guard, so Finch's hesitation in admitting outside opinions may have been a systemic problem as much as it was a specific reaction to African American leaders. Even so, his callousness in dealing with the requests of African American Republican activists suggests a lack of dedication to their cause—and a lack of attention to the significance of African Americans as a constituent group. Other Nixon staffers, including San Diego newspaperman and general campaign press secretary Herb Klein, displayed similar inattention to the importance of African American outreach over the course of the campaign. Nixon's problems were therefore compounded by the actions of those closest to him. The vice president cannot be excused for his staff's failure to respond to African American constituents, but it is possible that in some cases he was not even aware of the additional problems they created for his candidacy. He also was undoubtedly the recipient of bad advice.

Nixon did reach out to Jackie Robinson, meeting with him and attorney general Bill Rogers in May. Robinson wrote to Nixon that he had enjoyed the meeting but advised the vice president that if he waited much longer to speak out authoritatively on civil rights, "it will be hard to convince people that your interest isn't motivated by politics." Nixon needed to come up with things he had done to further the cause of civil rights before 1955. Kennedy had sent copies of Nixon's record prior to 1950 to several columnists, including Robinson, and "believe me, it's most difficult to answer people who seem to have documentary evidence of what you did or said. When you withhold positive things, an image isn't easy to erase, but it can be done if you display a warmth or as much sincerity as you can regarding the Negroes status [sic]."[46]

Overall, however, the vice president and his advisers appeared more interested in garnering southern support, prompting editorial castigation by the *Baltimore Afro-American* for remaining silent during civil rights deliberations early in the year and reportedly advocating a weak civil rights plank in the 1960 Republican platform. Nixon had also failed to repudiate a "Confederate" speech made on his behalf by Arizona senator Barry Goldwater, who "proudly told a cheering Mississippi audience that it had far less to fear from Nixon than from any of the possible Democratic nominees."[47] Both sides noticed Nixon's reluctance to alienate the southern vote. *Birmingham*

[Alabama] *Post-Herald* editor John Temple Graves, for example, sent a probing letter to the vice president in mid-1959, observing that both Nixon and Eisenhower had begun to use the term "discrimination" in lieu of "integration." Nixon directed his staff to reply to the editor by outlining his stand "against immediate total integration and for moderation in this field." In response, Graves wrote several columns encouraging consideration of the vice president—and he kept the pressure on Nixon, contending in March 1960 that "The South is the wave of your future since you'll never win the Negro or labor votes."[48]

Prodded Toward Action

While Nixon and his staffers dawdled, Rockefeller began making his way back onto the political scene. Writing in the *Amsterdam News*, New York City Councilman Earl Brown referred to Nixon's moderate civil rights course as "burying civil rights as quickly as possible." By contrast, he wrote, Rockefeller stood out as the only possible presidential contender who had said anything "important and meaningful" on the subject of civil rights. Recently, Rockefeller had praised black college students for their southern sit-in strikes, and he came out "swinging hard for justice for the Negro" in a recent Chicago address. "No opportunist or demagogue," Brown wrote, "he has demonstrated moral courage, honesty and sincerity about handling the nation's number one problem while others have ducked it. He has brought the controversy a kind of native evangelism or liberalism which is critically needed." Unfortunately, Rockefeller's straightforward stand was one of the reasons why his party's leaders had scratched the New York governor from the list of possibilities. "Probably the greatest shot-in-the-arm this country could get at this time," Brown concluded, "would be for some Republicans to start a draft for Rockefeller and raise the roof at the G.O.P. nominating convention in Chicago in an attempt to nominate him. Even if he should lose it would do the country a lot of good." In the same issue, the *Amsterdam News* took an editorial shot at Nixon, arguing that he had been largely ineffective on the President's Committee on Government Contracts and could not therefore be trusted to further civil rights in the White House.[49]

Rockefeller's big leap back onto the national scene, however, came on June 8 with his ten-point statement criticizing Nixon for failing "to make clear where this party is heading and where it proposes to lead the nation." Rockefeller stated in the introduction to his ten points that "no matter is more critical than civil rights," and he devoted point eight to a plea that Americans "practice at home such a respect for law and equality as we wish to preach—and serve—in the world at large." While he acknowledged that

in comparative terms the Republican record on civil rights was a "very cred-
itable one," he warned that "all deliberate speed" must not be allowed to
turn into a rationale for sabotage. Rockefeller concluded his point by calling for a cooperative effort by leaders throughout the nation to enforce and
advance civil rights goals.[50]

The New York governor's ten-point statement prompted a resurgence of
interest in another Draft Rockefeller campaign among Americans from all
walks of life, African Americans among them. William J. Davenport of the
Bronx, for example, wrote to Rockefeller on June 10 to thank him for "coming out of the gopher hole, the country—and mankind under U.S. leadership needs you for President. I'm Joe Common, negro, merchant marine
Radio Officer, small landlord, and hoping that your merits are true value.
If I can help your campaign I'll do so." Echoing conditions Fred Morrow
had reported to Nixon back in 1958, Davenport informed Rockefeller that
the local Lincoln Club had "limited interest in me," but he was willing
to help if called upon.[51] The *Pittsburgh Courier* lauded Rockefeller for having "his say on the Republicans' wishy-washy attitude on civil rights" despite being "critically lashed" by fellow members of his party.[52] The *Chicago
Daily Defender* warned that while Nixon, with the nomination all but sewn
up, seemed complacent toward Rockefeller's criticisms, "Mr. Rockefeller's
charges of evasiveness and slickness will damage Mr. Nixon in November,
particularly in New York. He will not get the Negro vote by smothering
the civil rights issue."[53] One national publication to partially buck the pro-
Rockefeller trend was *Jet* magazine, which reported in mid-June that Nixon
was sufficiently popular to ensure that Rockefeller was on most African
Americans' list as a *vice* presidential candidate.[54] Even as a vice presidential possibility, though, the governor remained prominent among African
Americans, putting pressure on Nixon to come out more strongly in favor
of a strident rights stand in the 1960 Republican Platform.

Even Jackie Robinson, by this point the subject of rumors that he supported Nixon despite his own claims of being uncommitted, lauded Rockefeller's comments, although on somewhat different grounds. In the long
run, he wrote, the governor's challenge should prove a "healthy stimulus"
as the Republican Party hashed out its position on various issues. Robinson
agreed with Rockefeller that Nixon's views needed wider circulation, and
he told the vice president so when he met with him in May. In this spirit,
the baseball legend requested and received permission from Nixon to make
public a letter the vice president had written to Robinson regarding civil
rights. In it, Nixon agreed with Robinson that "no political party or special
interest group can take the American Negro vote 'for granted'"; mere "lip
service and demagoguery" in the area of civil rights would be less successful

than ever in 1960. Nixon himself believed in taking a strong civil rights position "not only for the clear-cut moral considerations involved, but for other reasons which reach beyond our nation's borders." First, the United States could not function as a true leader of the free world unless it showed "consistent, direct action in strengthening our moral posture in this field." Failing this, it would suffer in the eyes of emerging and nonaligned nations. Furthermore, Nixon pointed out that the Cold War struggle was economic as well as ideological. Practically speaking, "to deny ourselves the full talent and energies of 17 million Negro Americans in this struggle would be stupidity of the greatest magnitude." Robinson applauded Nixon's comments, admonishing his readers that

> . . . anyone who expects—as some readers have indicated—that Negro Americans should defer their quest for full and equal rights and opportunities until the world has solved the problems of disarmament, Berlin or Khrushchev, had better get wise to the idea that it is because of this very weakness that America's back is to the wall. When we seek needed friends in a world over two-thirds non-white with Jim Crow still squatting on our doorstep, we are handing our enemies a club with which to beat our brains out without having to fire a single atomic missile.[55]

Robinson's public airing of Nixon's civil rights statement aside, however, Rockefeller continued to enjoy the momentum in the struggle over definition of the Republicans' civil rights policy. Val Washington urged the Nixon campaign staff to hire more African Americans for fieldwork throughout the nation, reporting that his contacts knew the contents of Rockefeller's diatribe but were unfamiliar with Nixon's own positions. Meanwhile, Rockefeller continued to make high-profile speeches.[56] In an appearance before the National Sunday School and Baptist Training Union Conference in Buffalo, New York, the governor advocated, among other steps, an executive order forbidding housing discrimination; empowerment of the National Labor Relations Board to refuse to certify discriminatory unions; federal money to help cities and localities desegregate; legislation empowering the attorney general to bring court cases forcing school desegregation; a permanent ban on racial discrimination in all government contract work; and equal employment opportunity in all federal agencies. The *Baltimore Afro-American* lamented the fact that Rockefeller was not a candidate for the presidency, but opined that "if he keeps talking like this he is certain to influence the thinking of both Messrs. Nixon and Kennedy."[57]

Influence Nixon he did, although not without continued controversy. As the platform committee began deliberations in Chicago, Rockefeller used his ample resources to publish two treatises, one for Republican leaders and one for the platform committee, laying out his ideas on issues ranging from foreign policy to domestic affairs. Civil rights were an important factor in both and would become a near sticking point in Rockefeller's final and most controversial attempt to influence party direction, the already described "Compact of Fifth Avenue" released following a meeting between Nixon and Rockefeller at the latter's New York apartment on July 22.

While conservatives vigorously opposed several points in the two men's agreement, the most hotly contested provision was domestic point four regarding civil rights. Nixon and Rockefeller wrote that the Republican civil rights program must "assure aggressive action to remove remaining vestiges of segregation or discrimination in all areas of national life." The civil rights plank should "express support for the objectives of sit-in demonstrators" and commend the actions of businessmen who had voluntarily desegregated their lunch counters.[58] Southerners fought vehemently against the strong proposal, a process outlined in chapter 5. Nixon, however, finally mobilized his own considerable resources behind the more strident stand that Rockefeller's tireless urging had forced him to take. Upon his arrival in Chicago, Nixon mounted an all-out campaign to ensure passage of the strong rights provision. He summoned key members of the platform committee to his suite one by one and insisted that the current, moderate plank in the platform be rewritten to match the Compact proposal. One of his aides later reported that "we collected every political IOU we held in the country that night."[59] Meanwhile, Nixon faced continuing pressure from Rockefeller, whose statement during a July 24 NAACP rally that he was willing to start a floor fight on the issue was seconded by one of Nixon's key liberal supporters, Pennsylvania Senator Hugh Scott.[60] Again, Rockefeller's influence had given African Americans the leverage they needed to influence Nixon in a more liberal direction.

Nixon and Rockefeller succeeded in gaining a strong civil rights plank for the 1960 platform. The plank acknowledged that in "a nation dedicated to the proposition that all men are created equal—racial discrimination has no place." Discrimination could not be reconciled with the Constitution, and in a deeper sense it was immoral and unjust. "As to those matters within reach of political action and leadership," the platform stated, "we pledge ourselves unreservedly to its eradication."[61] Many commentators gave Nixon full credit for his work, concluding that his efforts on behalf of the plank were sincere and not merely politically motivated—a common charge against him.[62] Black editorial commentary, however, indicates that despite the strides Nixon made, African Americans continued to have cause for concern regarding Republicans' intentions.

The *Chicago Daily Defender* voiced optimism on July 25 that the GOP plank would be "unequivocally strong or stronger" than that of the Democrats. Citing the Republican Party's antislavery origins, the *Defender* conceded that Republicans had "the intellectual capacity to recreate the image of Abraham Lincoln and champion once more in a clear and unmuffled voice the legitimate cause of the Negro people." If party leaders were bent on "continuing their middle-of-the-road policy in order to woo dissatisfied Dixiecrats into their camp," however, "they will have committed political suicide on the very spot where they won their laurels fully a century ago." The same day, the *Defender* lauded Rockefeller's role in bringing liberal civil rights goals before the convention.

By July 28, however, the *Defender*'s optimism had disappeared, despite the success of Nixon and Rockefeller's stronger plank. Editor Sengstacke resented the reality that American citizens should still be forced to plead for their basic rights, midway through the twentieth century. He conceded that the plank "so grudgingly inserted in the GOP platform is better than the one the simple-minded moderates tried to ram down the throats of the delegates," but he criticized the party for offering too weak a token of sympathy in its reference to ongoing sit-in demonstrations.[63] On August 1, the newspaper concluded its comments on the Republican platform by pointing out that the 1960 plank constituted the strongest declaration of civil rights support ever made by the Republican Party. This was only to say, however, that in previous years, "having enunciated the principle of social justice in its broadest application, the GOP leadership went to sleep on its own premise and on the correlative burden of its responsibility." In contrast, the Democrats had drafted a plank giving uncompromising support to the sit-in demonstrators and committed to a final date for completion of school desegregation in 1963.[64]

The *Baltimore Afro-American* prepared a comparison of the principal differences between the two platforms, noting the school desegregation time line as one example. Republicans had condemned the idea of a deadline as producing a de facto moratorium on desegregation before that date. The *Afro-American* pointed out, though, that their plank was lacking in enforcement power, with the attorney general given the right to intervene in desegregation cases only if economic coercion or the threat of physical harm prevented defendants from filing suit themselves. The parties made similar calls for a permanent commission on nondiscrimination, but Republicans shied away from use of the controversial term "FEPC" (Fair Employment Practices Commission). In terms of voting rights, the Republicans' pledge for specific literacy regulations went further than Democrats' more vague commitments. Democrats promised action to end discrimination in all federally assisted housing programs, including loan programs for private homes, while Republicans mentioned only federally subsidized housing projects. Finally, both parties mentioned alterations to the filibuster rule, but each was fuzzy in different aspects concerning how it proposed to do so. Overall, the *Afro-American* awarded the prize for best leadership of his party to Kennedy, cautioning that Nixon needed to step out from the shadow of "Ike's 'Middle of the Road' band wagon."[65]

Losing the Symbolic Battle

Republicans, then, faced some serious burdens as Nixon and his running mate, United Nations Ambassador Henry Cabot Lodge, entered the general election campaign. Lodge himself was one potential bright spot for the party. Jackie Robinson argued that Nixon's choice of a "distinguished statesman and diplomat for the Vice Presidential nomination is in sharp and refreshing relief to the shoddy political deal which resulted in the designation of Lyndon Johnson for the Democratic second spot."[66] Robinson remained far more skeptical of Kennedy than most African American newspaper commentators, expressing frustration and concern over, for example, Kennedy's invitation to Arkansas governor Orval Faubus to sit on the dais with him during his acceptance speech.[67] Lyndon Johnson, however, was a popular target of concern, given his Texas roots and his role in attempting to water down the 1957 civil rights legislation. Lodge, by contrast, had a strong civil rights record. Scion of the Boston Brahmin Lodge and Cabot families, he had distinguished himself as a senator while still in his thirties. Following his 1952 reelection attempt and subsequent defeat to, of all people, John Fitzgerald Kennedy—a defeat due in part to his active role in the Eisenhower campaign—Lodge was appointed ambassador to the United Nations. During the 1950s, the United Nations was a prominent feature in American life. UN debates were often televised, and, as a result, over the course of his nearly eight years as ambassador, Lodge's stature as an articulate, handsome warrior against the Communist menace grew exponentially.

Lodge's later description of himself as having been "pitchforked into a national campaign for vice president" indicates that he was something less than wholeheartedly in favor of his own selection, but the ambassador's patrician upbringing instilled in him a strong sense of duty.[68] Clay Blair of the *Saturday Evening Post* wrote at the time that Lodge's prominence as UN ambassador made him the most widely known and discussed vice presidential candidate since Theodore Roosevelt in 1900. A post-election Gallup poll indicated that Lodge was more popular among Americans than Kennedy, Nixon, or vice president-elect Lyndon Johnson.[69] Republican leaders attempted to play up the contrast between Lodge and Johnson, pointing out in the August 24 edition of the Republican National Committee publication *Battle Line*, for example, that "the Democrats wrote a civil rights plank promising the moon and then nominated to run on it a man who has spent 20 years in Congress voting down or watering down civil rights measures."[70]

The GOP could take some comfort, also, from the statements of civil rights elders like A. Philip Randolph, who wrote in the *Pittsburgh Courier* that the only sound course of action for African Americans was nonpartisanship. Both parties were split into liberal and conservative factions, so neither could deliver on its civil rights pledges alone. Rather, by voting for the candidate of their choice and remaining free of the vest pockets of either party, African Americans could maintain a most significant strength—political unpredictability. "The policy of rewarding friends and punishing enemies which has been followed by the AFL for decades," Randolph argued, "I consider to be eminently sound for the Negro and labor today."[71]

For his part, however, Kennedy had taken the first of his symbolic steps to convince African American voters that despite his party's segregationist legacy and such personal misjudgments as his 1957 civil rights votes, he was a sincere advocate of civil rights. On August 4, the *Chicago Defender* reported that the Kennedy campaign had formed a new civil rights section to advise the Democratic nominee on civil rights matters and assist in preparing "position papers" on the subject. Kennedy's civil rights section would not be merely a convenient place to confine African American supporters. Rather, the section's staff would include "a representative group of people of all races and creeds from all sections of the country." Furthermore, African American employees were to be "integrated on a functional basis in all parts of the campaign." This represented a sharp departure from previous practices.[72] Kennedy also benefited from a symbolic advantage that was beyond either nominee's control—he was a member of a religious minority. As the *Baltimore Afro-American* reported, election of a Catholic would set an encouraging precedent. "Then there must be the first Jew to live in the White House, and then there must be the first colored President of the United States. All of these in due course, and in due time. And this is one good reason why this should begin now."[73]

Following the conventions, Congress went back into session, and Republicans used this opportunity to press Kennedy to deliver on civil rights promises made in the Democratic platform. When he failed to make good on platform pledges, Republican leaders peppered the media with press releases that demonstrated Democrats' continuing willingness to kowtow to southern opposition. Widespread black support for Democratic candidates in such a legislative environment was still far from a foregone conclusion.

On August 10, for example, New York Attorney General Louis Lefkowitz proclaimed that the Democrats had "talked big about a Fair Employment Practices Act. But with an opportunity to insure that at the very least there would be no discrimination in carrying out government contracts they brought out their biggest guns to kill the measure."[74] Two days later, Val Washington castigated Kennedy for leading Democrats in having "downgraded civil rights to the status of second-class legislation." The Leadership Conference on Civil Rights had asked both parties for an "August downpayment" on civil rights promises. Kennedy responded that he was ready now, as in the past, to vote for civil rights measures, but "on Tuesday, the very next day, Kennedy eagerly led his colleagues in voting against civil rights. I doubt if the Leadership Conference will trust Kennedy's promises again." According to a disgusted Washington, Kennedy had said the civil rights bill had been killed "so that it would not get in the way of more important legislation." By contrast, "Republicans believe civil rights legislation has first priority and their Senate performance proves it."[75]

Nixon's most prominent statement on civil rights issues came during an August 17 appearance in Greensboro, North Carolina. The vice president deserves full credit for conducting a detailed discussion of civil rights in a southern city, although North Carolina's political climate was in many ways closer to that of a border state. In press conference comments, Nixon argued that the Republican platform was superior to the Democratic platform in several respects, especially because:

> . . . it is responsible; it is an honest platform; it does not promise more than can be achieved; its legislative proposals are ones that we think are reasonable and that, if they were enacted, would help the cause of better understanding and progress in this field rather than to set it back.

Nixon's mention of rights proposals as having the capacity to 'set things back' had to have put some African American listeners on edge, given its similarity to past Eisenhower comments such as his statement before NAACP leaders a few years prior that "you people have to be patient." Nixon proclaimed that the GOP's civil rights position would be the same in all regions of the country—North, South, East, or West—an admirable goal, although as will be seen in chapter 5, some deviations from this model occurred as the campaign progressed. He went on to stress that while legislative action was important, "any law that we pass in this field will only be as effective as public support for that law is developed." This, he indicated, was one of the key roles of a president as national leader.

Finally, asked his views on the sit-in strikes that had originated in Greensboro in early 1960, Nixon responded that he supported their objective. He was tepid on their tactics, however, stating that "as far as the means for the purpose of achieving that objective is concerned, we there have to look at the legal problems involved." In the end, he argued that the best way to solve the problem was demonstrated by the actions of the attorney general, who had recently met on a voluntary basis with major chain store operators and helped them reach a voluntary decision to desegregate their lunch counters. Waiting for the law was not an adequate response in many areas of the country, and civil rights were a national problem. Rather, the United States needed to develop leadership at all levels of government and in the opinion-making media that could effect voluntary change.[76]

Nixon's Greensboro remarks met with quite positive reactions in some circles. The *Charlotte Observer* reported that the crowd in Greensboro's Coliseum was "very big and enthusiastic. . . . It was not the kind of crowd that diligent party workers whip together to fill empty seats." The *Washington Post* commended the vice president for beginning his bid for southern votes "in serious and commendable fashion. . . . Mr. Nixon gave no indication in Greensboro of any intention to trim on civil rights issues."[77] Margaret Hannah of Citizens for Nixon-Lodge in Pittsburgh wrote to request a recording of the vice president's remarks so black groups in the area could play it at their meetings. The Nixon-Lodge campaign was happy to oblige.[78] While not perhaps directly tied to the Greensboro appearance, the *New York Citizen-Call* reported that Harlem Democrats were hinting at a switch to Nixon. Ignored by Tammany Hall and reform Democrats, Harlem leaders were sufficiently impressed by Nixon's words and actions to consider throwing their support in his direction.[79]

Behind the scenes, however, trouble simmered within the GOP's organizational ranks. On August 30, Nixon aide Stan McCaffrey responded to a letter from Carl Shipley, the chairman of the Washington, D.C., Republican Party, concerning a suggestion from the Virginia White Speel Republican Women's Club that a civil rights division be created in the campaign—with Rockefeller as chairman. McCaffrey informed Shipley that it was his understanding that a special civil rights division would not be created within the Republican organization. Using Nixon's Greensboro rationale, one he would often employ to avoid placing blame on the South for its actions, McCaffrey wrote that "it is felt these matters are ones which are affected in so many issues of the day, as well as in all parts of the country." The Republican platform and its civil rights plank reflected the convictions of the party and of Nixon and Lodge. This, the Nixon aide implied, would have to be enough. Nixon was correct in emphasizing the national nature of the civil rights problem. In so doing, however, he abstracted the issue to such a degree that concrete attempts to solve specific problems were abandoned. The problem was so vast that little could be done. Given Kennedy's early

August description of the depth and breadth of his own civil rights division, black voters were placed with a clear and unpleasant contrast between Democratic outreach and Republican lack of commitment.

August also brought further indication that Nixon was less than thrilled about the prospect of meeting with black leaders. Nixon was scheduled to meet with Clarence Mitchell, Roy Wilkins, and a third leader, Roy Millenson, at the beginning of the congressional session, but Bill Rogers had called Wilkins to say that the vice president would not be able to see them as planned. Since then, the leaders had held a meeting, "although not very productive," with Kennedy but had heard nothing more from Rogers. Charlie McWhorter asked fellow Nixon aide Don Hughes whether Nixon wanted to see Wilkins, Mitchell, and Millenson. "In any event, Mitchell would like to get some word one way or the other." This time, Nixon did finally cooperate, returning Mitchell's call.[80] Campaign field-workers might well have wished he had done so sooner; by the time the call was placed, the *Amsterdam News* had run a headline proclaiming that "Nixon Shuns NAACP on 'Rights' Program. 'Too Busy' to Talk on Civil Rights."[81] The *Baltimore Afro-American* also reported, almost two weeks later, that Wilkins and the NAACP were having trouble getting past Nixon's keepers, a problem they had not experienced with Kennedy.[82]

Meanwhile, in another symbolic move, Kennedy managed to co-opt appeals to civil rights on the basis of Cold War ideology—and leave egg on the face of Jackie Robinson. Since 1959, Robinson had been one of a number of influential African Americans to support Kenyan labor leader Tom Mboya's plan to bring young Africans to the United States for college. More than eighty students came in 1959, the first year of the program, when Robinson, singer Harry Belafonte, and actor Sidney Poitier solicited private donations for the cause. In 1960, they asked the State Department for assistance. Their request was denied, but Kennedy, on behalf of the Kennedy Foundation, offered them $5,000. Eager to cast Nixon as a hero in contrast to Kennedy, Robinson moved to use his connections to the vice president to make the State Department reconsider. By mid-August, he thought he had achieved success, announcing in his column that a Nixon aide had called with news of a $100,000 contribution from the Department of State for transportation of African students. The vice president had expressed deep interest in the project, Robinson said. By his next column, however, Robinson had to admit he had been misled—State had given no support, but Kennedy in-law Sargent Shriver had offered over $400,000 from the Kennedy Foundation. This was enough to support the African-American Students Foundation for three years, and the organization had accepted.[83] Not only did this incident challenge Robinson's credibility; it offered Kennedy the opportunity to demonstrate his support for the kind of outreach programs that would stimulate international understanding and provide further incentive to grant civil rights to African Americans. After all, Americans did not want these Third-World residents coming to the United States only to discover racial segregation and discrimination.

As the general campaign got under way, Washington continued to express his frustration regarding the lack of Republican organization among minority groups. At the end of August, for example, he reported his unhappiness with conditions in San Diego and Los Angeles. No work had been done among African Americans or Latinos in San Diego County and the surrounding environs, and the situation had deteriorated over the past month among the same groups in Los Angeles. The Nixon-Lodge campaign could have taken this report as a heartfelt attempt to prod the GOP organization into action. Instead, the aide who transcribed Washington's phone call added his own insulting commentary. "It's my impression," he wrote, "that Val is perpetually inclined to believe that nothing is being done among his people, but I pass it along for what it's worth."[84] The Republican Party's most tireless African American advocate, an individual who had headed minority outreach efforts since the mid-1940s, was simply shunted aside. Nixon's campaign squandered its best resource in the black community, even as it responded to the recommendations of new, white constituents in the South.

Campaign leaders solicited the help of several other sympathetic African American figures, including some who served in pioneering positions in the Eisenhower administration. In September, Fred Morrow left the White House to become a campaign staff assistant, and Archibald Carey, who served both on the UN delegation and the Civil Rights Commission, served as a field coordinator in Chicago just before the election.[85] Several individuals—including S.B. Fuller of the Fuller Brush Company, Los Angeles businessman George Sevelle, and newspaper publisher William O. Walker—received letters on August 18 requesting their help, given their "special insight and knowledge" into conditions in their communities.[86] Sevelle took on a "command position" in Nixon-Lodge's outreach organization.[87]

Most notably, Jackie Robinson finally joined the Nixon team, having decided that Nixon was "better qualified" than Kennedy and "more aggressive on civil rights." As a result of his decision, the liberal *New York Post* dropped his column for the duration of the campaign season, firing him at the end of the year.[88] Robinson served as a black campaign spokesman for Nixon-Lodge—the *only* public spokesman, to Morrow and Washington's chagrin.[89] Morrow, despite being promised a prominent and vital spot in the campaign hierarchy in return for his two months' unpaid service, was given no funding, secretary, nor anyone to answer his mail. "Black leaders from all over the nation called me day and night for financial help and literature," he recalled, "and they could not believe me when I reported that neither was available." Washington was stuck in a similar predicament, given almost no money and forced to conduct a national campaign with a staff of about five people. Robinson, Morrow later wrote, "made a great personal sacrifice to help Nixon, the man of his choice. Yet he, too, had a heavy and broken heart over the ignorance with which the campaign was conducted."[90] This sidelining of knowledgeable and prominent African American leaders contrasts disturbingly with the experiences of longtime activists like Washington in the 1940s and early 1950s. Meanwhile, Nixon encountered pressure from southern party leaders to keep his civil rights statements to a minimum. Captivated by the prospect of breaking apart the solid South, the vice president sacrificed an outreach effort with strong possibilities for success.

September polling figures indicated that Nixon was sitting about even with Eisenhower's 1956 levels of support. A "Sum of the People" poll published on September 4 awarded Nixon 29 percent of the black vote nationwide, with Kennedy receiving 60 percent, and 11 percent of African Americans undecided. In the North, Nixon had 29 percent to Kennedy's 58 percent, and in the South, 30 percent to Kennedy's 62 percent.[91] As of the end of September, Nixon was actually ahead of Kennedy among black voters in Arkansas, Minnesota, Utah, and Washington.[92] Nixon continued the practice of tying civil rights at home to the Cold War abroad. Speaking before the Booker T. Washington Political Club in Portland, Oregon—a club that had recently changed its name from the Democratic Club to support Nixon—the vice president remarked that he had visited 55 countries as vice president, and 95 percent of them were nonwhite. "It is awfully hard to preach the dignity of man abroad," Nixon said, "and to have to explain the prejudices at home in the United States."[93]

Meanwhile, however, the Kennedy campaign was beginning to plaster African American newspapers—a form of media that, to Morrow's consternation, Nixon almost completely ignored—with advertisements.[94] One paper, the *Pittsburgh Courier*, featured a single Nixon ad and at least 16 advertisements for Kennedy, including 4-page photo-laden spreads, favorable commentary from Eleanor Roosevelt, obvious allusions to Kennedy as Franklin Roosevelt's political heir, and endorsements from celebrities like Cab Calloway, Mahalia Jackson, and Harry Belafonte. One paper included *two* four-page ads in a single edition, inundating readers with favorable information about the Massachusetts senator while Nixon remained on the sidelines.[95]

Vice presidential candidate Lodge marked one bright spot for the Nixon campaign. On September 14, Lodge named Jewel Stratford Rogers, a former assistant attorney general and an African American, to be his special consultant on civil rights for the campaign. The former United Nations ambassador seemed to understand the symbolic importance of appearances in the black community, visiting, for example, the offices of the *Chicago Defender* while on a trip to the Windy City.[96] At the end of the month, Los Angeles County Republican Central Committee Chairman Pat Hillings sent a report to Nixon regarding Lodge's recent Southern California visit. Hillings had learned that the ambassador would have been willing to make more appearances than the Washington, D.C., staff had indicated—including appearances before racial and minority groups. Hillings suggested that the staff at Nixon-Lodge headquarters were not fully tuned in to Lodge's wishes and how he could be most effectively used.[97]

On October 12, however, Lodge made a promise, while campaigning in Harlem, that an African American would occupy a cabinet-level position in the Nixon administration. Nixon's southern supporters quickly let him know of their dismay. Nixon attempted to reel in his vice presidential nominee, contending that he aimed to select the best men for his cabinet without regard for "race, creed or color." Lodge did modify his statement the next day in campaign visits to Virginia and North Carolina, saying he could not actually pledge anything as the number two man on the ticket. His statement was an expression of what he felt should be done, not a Republican commitment. Even after a 45-minute campaign meeting with Nixon, Lodge refused to backtrack further, while Nixon continued to equivocate with noncommittal statements.[98]

Reaction to the controversy was pointed and angry. In a representative example, the *Chicago Daily Defender* editorialized that Lodge's about-face "lends support to the Democratic charge that Republicans have succeeded in forging a 'Harlem propaganda line,' and a 'Dixie line.'" Contrary to earlier pledges, the Nixon campaign appeared to be making different claims in different parts of the country. Most disturbing for the *Defender*, however, was the sharp division of opinion between Lodge and Nixon. While Lodge made his pledge in Harlem, Nixon was in Los Angeles stating that he would not appoint an African American just because he was black but would "'attempt to appoint the best man possible without regard to race creed or color.'" "Mr. Nixon is not fooling anyone," the *Defender* contended, by resorting to this cliché. Who would be so naïve as to believe that of two men under consideration for a cabinet post, one Negro and one white both of equal ability, training and experience that the Negro would get the approving nod? Nixon's use of this worn-out cliché was his way of telling

African Americans that a Nixon cabinet would not reflect any advances for Americans of color. "So what Henry Cabot Lodge says North or South on this question is strictly for the birds. Mr. Nixon is not yet in the White House; and may never get there."[99]

From October 12 onward, any momentum Nixon's campaign among African Americans might once have had began to fall apart. On October 22, the *Baltimore Afro-American* reported that while the Democratic National Committee was flooding the press with releases aimed at black voters, Nixon-Lodge had released almost nothing appealing. Nor was there any decent Nixon campaign literature aimed at black voters. Jackie Robinson was reportedly becoming increasingly frustrated by the lack of turnout at his speaking engagements and threatening to quit.[100] A mid-October poll of Cleveland and Cuyahoga County black voters demonstrated that in at least one urban area, support for Nixon was plummeting quickly, with Nixon receiving only 17.8 percent of the vote to Kennedy's 72.2 percent.[101]

Then Martin Luther King, Jr. was thrown in jail. On October 19, King joined students staging a sit-in at Rich's department store in Atlanta. All the protesters were arrested, and King refused bail to remain with the students in jail. The students were released on October 24, but King's release was denied on grounds that his arrest violated the terms of a suspended sentence that the civil rights leader had received in September for driving in Georgia with an Alabama license. King was transferred to another rural Georgia jail to serve a four-month sentence. While Nixon remained silent, John F. Kennedy made a much-publicized call to Coretta Scott King, and the Kennedy campaign brought successful pressure on local law enforcement to release King on bail. Nixon claimed in his memoirs that he felt it would be improper for him or any other lawyer to interfere personally in the proceedings, citing the American Bar Association's *Canons of Professional Ethics*.[102] We can never truly know Nixon's intentions, but the incident looked terrible to black voters and rather attractive to many white Southerners. Although fears of widespread anti-Catholic voting in the South never materialized, the specter of this possibility likely influenced both men's decisions. By speaking out, Kennedy could at least improve his chances with black voters, while Nixon's silence might appeal to whites inclined to abandon the Democratic Party rather than vote for a Catholic.

Scholars disagree regarding the significance of Kennedy's call at the time, but in such a close race, this event as much as any other might well have sealed Nixon's defeat.[103] During a service of thanksgiving at Ebenezer Baptist Church in Atlanta, King's father, the Rev. Martin Luther King, Sr., publicly stated a pledge he had made to Kennedy staffer—and former Rockefeller aide—Harris Wofford earlier that day. "I had expected to vote against

Senator Kennedy because of his religion," the elder King stated, indicating that among at least one constituent group, Kennedy's phone call improved his chances as a Catholic as well as an apparent civil rights advocate.

> But now he can be my President, Catholic or whatever he is. It took courage to call my daughter-in-law at a time like this. He has the moral courage to stand up for what he knows is right. I've got all my votes and I've got a suitcase, and I'm going to take them up there and dump them in his lap.

King's associate in the Southern Christian Leadership Conference, Ralph Abernathy, followed the senior King's statement with a call to "take off your Nixon buttons." King himself continued to maintain a position of neutrality, but his supporters' course was set. Taking advantage of this fortuitous turn of events, the Kennedy campaign printed a pamphlet composed entirely of statements made by black preachers and the King family titled "'No Comment' Nixon Versus a Candidate with a Heart, Senator Kennedy."[104]

Nixon's black advisers, few though they were, did not sit idle while the events of the King incident unfolded. Unfortunately for the vice president's electoral chances, however, he and his handlers would not be swayed. Morrow begged Nixon's managers to have the vice president make a statement about King's jailing. When they demurred, he urged Herb Klein, Nixon's press secretary, to take action and even penned a telegram for Nixon to send to the mayor of Atlanta. Klein pocketed Morrow's draft, saying that he would "think about it." Finally, Morrow left the campaign train altogether, disgusted by the Nixon team's performance.[105] Robinson begged the Nixon campaign to make a direct show of support for the embattled civil rights leader. Staffer Bill Safire recalled Robinson's vehement arguments at a midwest campaign stop: "[Nixon] has to call Martin right now, today. I have the number of the jail." Safire took Robinson to see Finch, who granted access to the vice president. After ten minutes, however, Robinson returned to Safire, dejected. "He thinks calling Martin would be 'grandstanding,'" Safire recalled Robinson saying and then adding: "Nixon doesn't deserve to win." Only former Dodger executive Branch Rickey, who had brought Robinson into major league baseball and served as a father figure to the player, was able to convince him to stay with the campaign.[106]

In the wake of King's release, most African American newspapers came out in favor of Kennedy. Those that did not make a specific endorsement, like the *Pittsburgh Courier*, ran news analysis articles indicating where they expected, and perhaps preferred, African Americans to cast their votes. Even the *Courier*'s article titled "The Case for the Republicans" concluded that "the Republicans have a good case . . . but they have chosen to IGNORE the

Negro voter. The Democrats . . . brilliantly advised and willing to listen . . . have gone after this vote with intelligence and imagination. They'll get the Negro vote . . . because they worked for it!"[107]

Disastrous Results

Election Day, of course, brought news of Nixon's narrow defeat. Republican National Committee research analysis indicated that Nixon's numbers among black voters represented a substantial falloff from Eisenhower's levels of support in 1956. The Republican Party had essentially retreated eight years, back to levels last seen in 1952. In sample areas like the South, African Americans who had made a major transition to Ike in 1956 returned to the Democratic fold, and in northern cities, with the exception of two New York City precincts, black support for Nixon dipped slightly below 1952 levels. In Missouri and Illinois, Kennedy's plurality among African Americans exceeded the plurality by which he carried the states. The same, researchers indicated, might be said of South Carolina.[108] Morrow later concluded that Kennedy's intervention in the King case won him the election, a sentiment echoed by historian Clifford Kuhn. Kuhn even argued that black voters constituted more than the margin of victory in at least six states.[109]

African Americans like Morrow and Jackie Robinson who had thrown their influence behind Nixon lamented the shortcomings of his campaign strategy. Condemnation of the campaign staff's strategic errors was rife. Nixon supporters were reluctant to believe the worst of their chosen candidate, although internal evidence demonstrates that in many cases the campaign intentionally discounted black support in favor of southern outreach. In the March/April 1961 edition of *The Young Republican News* (New York), Robinson blamed Nixon's defeat on advisers who said Nixon would lose South Carolina and Georgia by going into Harlem. Robinson contended that supporters who would abandon Nixon over a Harlem visit were already gone. He termed Nixon's no-comment stand during the King incident a mistake and bemoaned the fact that Kennedy had appointed no African Americans to his cabinet. "I'm sure that Mr. Nixon would have appointed at least one Negro," he contended. In a remark that echoed the sentiments of campaign workers from all walks of life around the country, Robinson criticized the Republican Party for appearing, rightly or wrongly, to be a "two week party." To win the black vote, he concluded, Republicans must work year-round. Robinson had no regrets about his position in the campaign. "I did so because I believed," he wrote to Nixon. "I thought we ran a poor campaign, but nevertheless I feel I supported the right man. No amount of criticism will change that feeling."[110] Morrow also remained loyal toward

Nixon, although his longtime connection to the Republican organization made the loss more personally devastating for him. "The election was a traumatic experience for me," he wrote to the former vice president. "In the areas of my concern and responsibility, I could see the election being lost, but could not reach your ear to let you know. My efforts and appeals were completely stymied, and to this day, I cannot figure out why."[111]

Other campaign field-workers indicated that in addition to missing important opportunities like the chance to intervene in the King incident, Nixon's handlers did not recognize the many smaller chances the vice president had to create feelings of goodwill among African Americans. Elaine Jenkins, a volunteer for Val Washington in 1960, told Nixon that he had been overly protected by supporters who did not convey to him the clues, cues, and aids that might have given him a chance to select his own course of action. During his Denver visit, for example, Nixon's motorcade had passed within two blocks of the largest predominantly African American school in town, at the end of the school day. "School children climbed over fences and ran across yards to get to the procession. Their disappointment was resounded in every crevice of the community. A simple example, but one that was to be repeated in hundreds of instances."[112]

Fallen Spans and New Bridges

The election of 1960 marked the end of an era for the Republican Party. Val Washington resigned his post, and Morrow left government service. Despite his early skepticism about Rockefeller, the New York governor's forthright sincerity impressed Robinson as the two men campaigned in Harlem and Brooklyn. Following the election, Robinson pledged his support to Rockefeller, assisting him in outreach to the African American community.[113] The supporters of Barry Goldwater who would take control of the party machinery over the next few years were almost wholly focused upon the Sunbelt states of the South and Southwest, effectively surrendering urban minority voters to the Democratic Party. Goldwater's 1961 comment that the GOP "ought to go hunting where the ducks are" signaled an end to African American voter outreach that lasted four decades.

By the end of the twentieth century, voting patterns had shifted so dramatically that in predominantly African American precincts, 80 or even 90 percent of the vote often went to Democratic candidates. Meanwhile, the Republican Party took the formerly yellow-dog Democratic South by storm, scoring impressive victories among white voters. Nixon's refusal to make a wholehearted effort to reach out to African American voters quite possibly lost him the election in 1960. Nixon did win more black votes than any Republican candidate has since, but the choices he made in his first presidential campaign dictated the party's future course. By surrendering the symbolic high ground to Kennedy and failing to adequately support African American outreach efforts, he squandered what might have been the party's last opportunity to reach out to African American voters in the context of the anti-Communist consensus of the 1950s. The black community responded accordingly, abandoning support for Nixon once it became clear that black voters could not convince him to wholeheartedly support civil rights efforts.

Ironically, some scholars have argued that Kennedy's symbolic campaign efforts proved to be just that—mere symbolism unaccompanied by much action, especially before 1963.[114] By 1964, the progress of the civil rights movement and heightened white backlash had effectively dissolved the anti-Communist consensus. Eight years later, however, the southern connections Nixon had begun to cultivate in his first race for the presidency won him the election. Today, of course, the South is almost solidly Republican. Realistically, then, it could be speculated that Nixon's short-term loss translated into an enormous long-term gain for the GOP. Morally speaking, refusal to make a strong endorsement of civil rights for all Americans was no victory. In political terms, however, Nixon had set in motion a transformation that would make the GOP the majority party.

3 "Nixonfeller" and the Remnant

National Review and the Election of 1960

"The ascendancy in the 1960 conventions of a new generation and new tactics suggests that they mark the end of the postwar period, without yet revealing what the nature of the coming period is to be. In ideas, both Kennedy and Nixon linger in the past, while their behavior seems to strain toward the future."—*National Review* editorial, August 13, 1960[1]

As late as 1945, no organized, effective conservative movement existed in the United States. After thirteen years under Dr. New Deal and Dr. Win-the-War, conservatism was a fragmented and largely impotent asterisk on the checklist of American intellectualism. Most Americans viewed conservatives as "anti-industrial Southern agrarians and the anti-New Deal tycoons who led the Liberty League," artifacts of a bygone era when America could actually be a fortress and Americans were self-sufficient farmers.[2] Surely the time for conservative ideology was past in an era of international cooperation, economic planning, and dramatic growth.

Then came the Cold War—and the New Deal consensus began to crack. Even before then, the first trickles of dissent had begun to spring from behind the dam. George H. Nash's *The Conservative Intellectual Movement in America Since 1945* remains the signal work in understanding how conservatism went from outmoded backwater to perhaps the dominant ideology of twenty-first-century America. Nash traced three strains of conservative thought growing out of the New Deal, the terrors of totalitarianism, and the nascent Cold War struggle. First, there was a group of intellectuals

Nash describes as "classical liberals" or "libertarians"—people who were concerned primarily with creeping statism. These individuals often referred to themselves as "individualists," casting themselves into relief against those who favored "collectivism."[3] Second, he describes a group labeled "new conservatives" or "traditionalists." These people, who tended to refer to themselves as "traditionalists," urged America to return to traditional religious and ethical absolutes. Finally, Nash mentions a strain of individuals motivated primarily by "militant, evangelistic anti-Communism." This mode of thinking was shaped by the ex-leftists who were its leaders—people such as Whittaker Chambers and James Burnham who had seen, to varying degrees, Communism's horrors.

These strains of thought proceeded for several years along mostly separate courses, although a young conservative might read and benefit from such divergent sources as Albert Jay Nock, who described a "Remnant" within society that might survive the ravages of statism; Richard Weaver, author of the self-explanatory 1948 treatise *Ideas Have Consequences*; and *Witness*, Chambers' seminal account of the Alger Hiss case and Chambers' life as a Soviet agent.[4] New journals adhered to various of these mindsets, from the anti-statist *Human Events*, which went through a series of incarnations during the late 1940s and 1950s, to Russell Kirk's *Modern Age*, a scholarly journal that examined the world from a largely traditionalist perspective beginning in 1957.[5] Meanwhile, the Cold War climate of the 1950s fed fires of frustration in young people like William Rusher, a "comprehensive but shallow" Republican Party activist from New York state who was sufficiently disillusioned by the Eisenhower administration's abandonment of Joseph McCarthy in 1954 to seek shelter in the conservative movement.[6]

Coexistence of these three strains was possible in part, as Rusher later described, because the three functioned on different "levels." Traditionalism offered a philosophical defense of ideals, while classical liberalism's economic nature served to form a "grand strategy." Finally, anti-Communism served as a tactical grounding for conservatives eager to take action.[7] Conservatives needed a catalyst, though, that would weave these strains into one cohesive fabric. The catalytic reaction began in the mid-1950s when an Austrian émigré by the name of Willi Schlamm began discussions with the brilliant young firebrand William F. Buckley, Jr.[8] From these meetings sprang a weekly, then biweekly magazine by the name of *National Review*. While the two were co-founders, Schlamm understood from the start that his 28-year-old counterpart's youth and enthusiasm would prove to be a catalyst for the conservative movement and insisted that he become the sole editor in charge. Schlamm, who found working for anyone a difficult task, eventually left the magazine.[9] For the next 49 years, however, Buckley—who began his writing career by graduating from Yale and then promptly indicting it for godlessness and collectivism in *God and Man at Yale* (1951)—would be the dean of the single most important development in the post–World War II conservative movement.[10]

Nash argued that if *National Review*, or something like it, had not entered into American life, "there would probably have been no cohesive intellectual force on the Right in the 1960s and 1970s."[11] Buckley's sharp-witted little journal was that important. A few members of the growing conservative intellectual community disagreed with the magazine's approach. Traditionalist Peter Viereck distressed fellow conservatives with his refusal to make liberalism a target and his kind words for Adlai Stevenson. Whittaker Chambers, an anti-Communist Quaker, used the magazine as a weapon through which he declared war on libertarian Ayn Rand—with resultant fireworks. And former socialist—and continuing atheist—Max Eastman left the publication in 1958, irritated by Buckley's insistent advocacy of religion's role in the conservative movement. None of these, however, created any popular alternative to *National Review*'s ideals.[12]

National Review was, therefore, the only publication challenging the liberal consensus in an organized, mass-distributed format. Unabashedly intellectual and everlastingly cutting, it provided information and opinion, and it also gave conservatives a forum for discussion and a means of belonging. *National Review* brought the conservative masses—to borrow a "leftist" term—together. A businessman in Topeka and a housewife in Anaheim could both read L. Brent Bozell's political commentary or James Burnham's thoughts on foreign policy and feel that they were part of a larger movement. This, in the end, was *National Review*'s most important contribution. In so doing, it fueled the prodigious growth that Rusher characterized as the signal characteristic of the conservative movement in the late 1950s.[13]

This contribution, in turn, was founded upon the concrete intellectual framework developed by an important member of the *NR* staff. In his 1962 book *In Defense of Freedom*, editorial staff member Frank S. Meyer developed a new framework for talking about conservatism. Calling this framework "fusionism," he argued that conservatives must absorb the best of *both* branches of the conservative mainstream—the libertarian impulse toward freedom and the more traditionalist ideal of virtue. Meyer believed that humans needed both liberty and an organic moral order.[14] Again, this definition of conservatism encountered criticism and challenge. In the end, however, fusionism triumphed—and one William F. Buckley, Jr. personified "fusion" more than anyone else in the movement.[15]

NR's significance in the conservative world, then, is second to none. The publication did for conservatism what William Lloyd Garrison did for abolitionism, or colonial broadside editors for independence—even if individuals might quibble with the relative merits of each undertaking. As such, understanding how Buckley and his *NR* gang viewed the 1960 election is essential to our analysis of how this event affected the direction of the Republican Party heading into the last forty years of the twentieth century—and beyond. It is also essential in understanding how contingent conservatives' support for Republicanism truly was in 1960. The writers and editors of *NR* forged varying levels of contact with and commitment to the GOP. Third parties and nonpartisan pressure groups were seen by some in the conservative movement as viable options. The behind-the-scenes deliberations of the *NR* staff when faced with the question, for example, of a Nixon endorsement, elucidate the tensions present within conservative ranks. While conservatives would eventually win control over the future of the Republican Party, their adoption of a Republican identity was not a foregone conclusion.

A Morass of Modern Republicanism

Buckley's history followed a different trajectory from many of his cohorts at *NR*, who came to conservatism as adults disillusioned with the New Deal and socialism or were moderate Republicans radicalized by the Eisenhower administration's opposition to Joseph McCarthy. Buckley's father, a Texas oilman with business connections in Mexico, was a friend of Albert Jay Nock's and a passionate conservative. While *NR*'s chief foreign policy specialist, James Burnham, flirted with collectivism and publisher William Rusher stifled feelings of opposition to the eastern establishment following a childhood move from Chicago to New York, Buckley enjoyed dinner-table conversations with Nock and the rest of his large family. Moving on to prominence as the head of the *Yale Daily News* following a stint in the army, Buckley proved a constant challenge to school administrators even before he matriculated and wrote his famous indictment of the college. In 1954 he joined his Yale colleague and new in-law, L. Brent Bozell, in authoring *McCarthy and His Enemies*, a defense of the Wisconsin senator's investigative activities.[16]

Others, including Rusher, shared the indignation that Buckley and Bozell felt when faced with such episodes as Nixon's speech on behalf of Eisenhower in 1954, when the vice president compared McCarthy's tactics to shooting wildly at rats. Understanding that Communism was what he was *against*, Rusher found himself wondering in the wake of Nixon's comments

what he was *for*. He found solace and direction in sources like Chambers'
Witness, Friedrich Hayek's *The Road to Serfdom* (1944) and Russell Kirk's *The
Conservative Mind* (1953). Further influenced by Burnham's *Web of Subversion* (1954) and Kirk's *Academic Freedom* (1955), Rusher was convinced by
mid-1954 that his lot lay with conservatism.

While Kirk is generally categorized as a traditionalist conservative, the
tenets of conservatism as outlined in *The Conservative Mind* came to sig-
nify the program of *NR* circa 1960. Kirk cited six "canons" of conservative
thought, beginning with a belief that "a divine intent rules society as well
as conscience, forging an eternal chain of right and duty which links great
and obscure, living and dead." As a result, "political problems, at bottom,
are religious and moral problems." Second, conservatives expressed "affec-
tion for the proliferating variety and mystery of traditional life," in contrast
to the stultifying uniformity of most radical systems. Third, conservatives
believed that civilized society required orders and classes—"the only true
equality is moral equality." Fourth, conservatives believed that "property
and freedom are inseparably connected, and that economic levelling is not
economic progress." Fifth, conservatives placed their faith in prescription,
favoring the controls of tradition and "sound prejudice" over the "anarchic
impulse" of human emotion. Finally, conservatives recognized that change
and reform were not synonymous—"innovation is a devouring conflagra-
tion more often than it is a torch of progress." Society would and must alter
over time, for "slow change is the means of its conservation." Providence,
rather than man, was the proper inspiration for such change.[17]

Conservatism as practiced by Buckley and his colleagues was grounded
in religious as well as in social, political, and economic belief. Buckley was
a lifelong Catholic, and many others on the *NR* staff, including Rusher and
Meyer, converted to Catholicism as adults. Catholic laypeople, including
Buckley, were influential in working out many of the principles of post–
World War II conservatism. The church's hierarchical nature, traditions, and
faith in natural law were highly conducive to conservative thought. Only
in the 1960s, in the wake of disagreements and divisions within American
Catholicism following Vatican II and with Protestant evangelicals mobilizing against the unrest of the age, did Catholicism lose momentum as a
defining force for American conservatism.[18]

Buckley's religious beliefs, however, and those of many members of his
staff did not preclude them from making what commentator E.J. Dionne
has termed the conservative movement's first political breakthrough—in
this case, an intellectual breakthrough that formed the basis for conservatism's eventual success in the political realm. Even as they internalized
Kirk's traditionalist tenets, Buckley and the bulk of the *NR* senior staff

succeeded in brokering a theoretical compromise between conservatives who revered tradition and religion and those who valued the free market economy above all else.[19] Kirk's fourth "canon" was essentially elevated to a status of equal importance with the other five. This breakthrough was articulated in Frank Meyer's "fusionism," introduced above. Meyer argued that virtue was humankind's ultimate goal. Virtue was only meaningful, however, if individuals sought and arrived at it voluntarily. As Donald Devine, a conservative political scientist in the Reagan Administration, put it, fusionism consisted of "utilizing libertarian means in a conservative society for traditionalist ends."[20]

The late 1950s were a period of both growth and frustration for the editorial staff of *NR*. On the one hand, their magazine—while consistently hovering near the brink of financial meltdown—was fostering a thriving dialogue within conservative circles. On the other, the political world outside *NR*'s office walls provided cause for consternation. Biographer John Judis has called Buckley's 1959 book *Up From Liberalism* the fullest expression of the young editor's political philosophy, and it provides a helpful glimpse into conservatives' reaction to the Eisenhower years. As Buckley put it,

> America, most historians teach us, has sought to avoid the extremes, to be flexible without resembling Silly Putty; to be principled without being arch. I think our country is not clearly enough avoiding the former extreme. I think she is in danger of losing her identity—not on account of the orthodoxy that we are being told in some quarters threatens to suffocate us; but for failure to nourish any orthodoxy at all.[21]

Eisenhower's Modern Republicanism, with its "passion for modulation," was incapable of withstanding the onslaught of the liberal offensive.[22] The "Eisenhower Program" was essentially an attitude, "undirected by principle, unchained to any coherent idea as to the nature of man and society, uncommitted to any sustained estimate of the nature or potential of the enemy."[23] Its danger was not so much in its program as in its lack thereof and subsequent susceptibility to liberal inroads. Buckley discussed several of liberalism's dangers, including its one-sided perception of free speech—let the chief prosecutor of Stalin's purges speak, but strap that muzzle on Joseph McCarthy—and its predilection toward philosophical relativism. The key problem for Buckley, however, was his conviction that "the salient economic assumptions of liberalism are socialist."

Up From Liberalism cautioned against extremism, a stand *NR* would take on multiple occasions. The conservative might not care for federal social security, Buckley noted, out of concern that it "sew[ed] seeds that could lead to economic destruction; but then it is also true that being born with Original Sin is a poor way to start out in life." Social Security did not translate into the collapse of the economy; it was merely a step in the wrong direction. Equating one with the other weakened conservatism's cause.[24] That said, Buckley cautioned that a long string of small extravagances could lead to a "stagnating if not a crippling overhead." The best course of action for the government in society was to enhance the freedom of the individual to acquire property and dispose of that property in the manner he preferred. This would maximize the ability of individuals and localities to tailor solutions to their own situations.[25]

Buckley's frustrations, and his programmatic preferences, were paralleled in the pages of *NR*. Even before the 1958 election, *NR* expressed dismay over the direction of Republican Party politics and the probable outcome of the New York gubernatorial race, in which liberal Republican Nelson Rockefeller was making a splash. In late September 1958, an editorial on the departure of Modern Republican guru Arthur Larson from the White House described his liberal doctrine "*as a matter of principle—against* principle." A doctrine without principles, *NR* concluded, was bound to fail. [26] In early October, contributor Frank Chodorov opined that regardless of who was elected, "the next Governor of New York will be a socialist."[27]

Later in October, in an article on the 1958 elections titled "Here Goes Nothing," George Morgenstern commented on the applicability of Charles Lamb's famous phrase to modern Republicans: "I am determined that my children shall be brought up in their father's religion, if they can find out what it is." Modern Republicanism, he concluded, was little more than a cult of personality—a venue in which the eminently likeable and ebullient Rockefeller was incomparably well equipped. Meanwhile, he mentioned, the *New York Times* had concluded that Vice President Richard Nixon's hapless campaign on behalf of doomed Republicans throughout the nation revealed him as "something old, something new, something borrowed from [Murray] Chotiner [his longtime campaign manager], somewhat blue." Going on to reveal the bemused dispassion with which most *NR* writers viewed the vice president, he pointed out that "A more interesting subject of speculation, still to be resolved, is whether it is true that he carries concealed razor blades in his bubble gum."[28] An editorial on November 8 painted a slightly more positive view of Nixon, pointing out that the vice president appeared to be developing a political personality independent of the administration. While continuing to reserve judgment, the writer held out hope, "and there are grounds," he wrote, "for hoping."[29]

Given the gloomy outlook described above, the disastrous outcome of the 1958 elections had to have come as little surprise to the *NR* staff. Even so, political columnist Bozell's post-election wrap-up, titled "The 1958 Elections: Coroner's Report," demonstrated the deep frustration and dismay with which conservatives regarded the Republican Party. The GOP as the traditional vehicle of conservative political action was dead, he wrote. Referring to Rockefeller as a "caricature of Eisenhower," he labeled his victory as personal and predicted that in the ideological morass of Republicanism circa late-1950s, Rockefeller would doubtless become the party's next presidential nominee. Rockefeller's victory was a crippling blow to Nixon, the one whom conservatives, however skeptical, had hoped might take up their cause. While party regulars might remain pledged to Nixon, they were so weakened by six years under Eisenhower, Bozell predicted, that they would not play a decisive role in candidate selection. Nixon could either wed himself to liberals or mobilize the conservative arm of the party— or, in a semi-wittingly prescient comment Bozell quipped, "There is, of course, a third course, and Mr. Nixon may attempt it: that is, he may try to do both at the same time." However, even as he added up the party's losses—the defeat of Senator Bill Knowland, "national ideological spokesman," in the California gubernatorial race; statewide Democratic sweeps; the election of Vermont's first Democratic congressman since 1856— Bozell held out a certain apocalyptic hope. Conservatives lost, but so did liberals. Bozell saw no ideological moral in the electoral results. While the GOP at the national level might be dead, local organizations continued to offer hope for revitalization from the grassroots. These grassroots groups could send the Republican Party rising once again like the proverbial phoenix (coincidentally, the name of Barry Goldwater's hometown), or they could organize to form an entirely new party as the Republicans of the 1850s sprang from the Whigs.[30] The former is precisely what did happen in many parts of the country, particularly in the South and West, over the course of the 1960s.[31] Meanwhile, however, party leaders and national intellectuals needed to sort out what had happened and plan for the next presidential election.

NR staffers did not become much more optimistic in the weeks after the 1958 election. On December 20, the editorial page predicted that 1960 would be a repeat of the Taft/Eisenhower fight between party stalwarts and liberals, with Rockefeller snatching the nomination from Nixon. Under Eisenhower, the editorial stated, the party had disintegrated into "an ineffective apparatus of spasmodic protest against Democratic excesses." With Rockefeller at the helm, the writer suggested, even these spasms would cease. He even went so far as to suggest that Eisenhower might need to step down and give Nixon an opportunity to "convince the people that the Republican Party is the party of individual freedom and national survival, and is relevant to their future."[32] In late January of 1959, Bozell waxed melodramatic once again, proclaiming that "this is probably the best way for a party to die: Lincoln would have preferred his ship to break up on the rock of principle—the way it was put together."[33]

A Shadow Program for Conservatives

Meanwhile, however, life went on, and the pages of *NR* throughout 1959 provide helpful insight into the issues and perspectives conservative intellectuals held to be important leading into the 1960 election. In the world of economics, *NR* writers entered into the debate over controlling inflation and maintaining economic growth that was so paramount to the American political economy in the 1950s and 1960s.[34] On January 17, for example, *NR* criticized former Eisenhower administration economic adviser Gabriel Hauge for suggesting at an annual American Economic Association meeting that Americans might cause inflation by overpaying themselves for what they produced. Goods pay for goods, *NR* argued; there can't be "overpayment" in the system as a whole. The cure for inflation was to stop adding to the nation's money supply.[35] Rising costs were a theme the magazine returned to on multiple occasions, including a comment in June 1959 that next to the Soviet Union, inflation was America's greatest contemporary enemy.[36] In July, *NR* further noted that the interim report of the Nixon-headed Cabinet Committee on Economic Growth would not please liberal economists. Among other things, the report evidently concluded that wages sometimes affect prices.[37] A pithy little poem submitted by one William H. Sharp provided further insight into *NR*'s views on "The Complete Cycle of Government Social Planning":

> Great obsession,
> Intercession,
> Slight recession,
> Bad depression,
> Retrogression,
> No confession.[38]

In foreign policy, *NR* took a predominantly hard-line stance, although a look back on the magazine's commentary provides an illuminating window into the benefits of hindsight. On January 17, for example, *NR* professed its doubts that Fidel Castro was a Communist.[39] The magazine did take a surprising stand against travel restrictions for suspected subversives,[40] but it cautioned against efforts to legislate, mediate, or otherwise cajole the Soviets into cooperation on the international scene. On April 25, for example, an editorial lamented Nixon's initiation of a drive to give the International Court of Justice the authority to adjudicate disputes arising between two nations over interpretation of treaties. "Any revolutionary worth his salt," *NR* sardonically concluded, "will eat Rule by Law for breakfast."[41] While Nixon was said to have handled himself like a decent, courageous man on his August trip to the Soviet Union, the magazine argued that the mere fact of his trip "served to anoint and legitimize" the Bolshevik regimes.[42] When it came time for Khrushchev to make his own visit to the United States in fall 1959, *NR* trumpeted its opposition but also cautioned against taking the Soviet leader anything less than seriously:

> Khrushchev is a man of total devotion to an ideal. He is a man of courage. A man of resolution. A man of extraordinary forensic and dialectical skill. A man. The contrast [with leaders of the West] is clear.[43]

The Khrushchev visit proved to be one of the rare times that *NR* offered praise for Governor Rockefeller. The New York liberal also happened to be an implacable foe of Soviet Communism, and *NR* commended him for the "realism" of his stand against trading with the USSR.[44] Bozell further congratulated Rockefeller for his anti-Soviet line in the November 7 issue.[45]

On the issue of civil rights, *NR* demonstrated some of the reasons why Southerners were shortly to become so wedded to the conservative wing of the Republican Party. In March, for example, one issue offered ample evidence of *NR* appearing to cater to Southerners' most extreme fears about racial integration. In a comment regarding Martin Luther King, Jr.'s comment to audiences in India that the United States would be fully integrated in "all phases of social life" by 2000, the *NR* editor asked, "Does he consider the family unit a 'phase of social life?'"[46] Miscegenation was a fear shared by whites around the country, but such a comment added fuel to the fire of civil rights opponents' basest concerns. Buckley has acknowledged that the "cultural coordinates of our household were Southern." Both his parents were born in the South, and when Buckley and Schlamm initially recruited writers for *NR* they made a concerted effort to attract southern agrarians.[47] This connection gave the pages of *NR* a certain pro-South sympathy. Later in the same March 14 issue, for example, Richard Weaver wrote that "the attack on the Southern school system is but one front of a general attack upon the principle of an independent, self-directing social order, with a set of values proper to itself." Liberals' fight against segregation, he threatened, was but one phase in a larger attempt to destroy the American way of life: "The same charges of inequity leveled against the Southern regime will be leveled against capitalism, private property, the family and even individuality."[48] By abstracting desegregation efforts from the immediate problems of vast social inequality and unjust legal practices, Weaver was able to turn attention away from Southerners' own failings and paint the region instead as the bulwark against liberal efforts to subvert traditional society.

On the political scene, *NR* views were borne out through the magazine's commentary on the developing tone of the 1960 election. In July 1959, for example, *NR* editors could barely conceal their delight at the results of the Young Republican convention recently held in Denver. Despite lavish financing by Nelson Rockefeller, the Young Republicans elected as president a young Kansas banker named Ned Cushing who "scarcely bothered to conceal his pro-Nixon sentiments." To add insult to injury for Rocky, the convention also adopted a conservative platform opposing federal aid to education, opposing the "judicial usurpation of legislative prerogatives," favoring anti-trust legislation to break up big labor, favoring the reduction of taxation and the national debt, and opposing U.S. recognition or U.N. admission of the "pirate governments" of Red China and East Germany. The magazine recorded "A smiling eye-witness to Nelson Rockefeller's humiliation: Vice President Richard Nixon, whom the delegates welcomed with a thunderous ovation."[49]

Reading Richard Nixon

The vice president continued to be an ambiguous figure for *NR*'s cadre of conservatives. At times, as above, the magazine looked kindly upon the man from Yorba Linda, even using him as a tool to increase magazine readership. On July 6, 1959, for example, Nixon staffer Charles McWhorter received a financial-plea form letter from Buckley that cited, as one rationale for support, "it is read by the Vice President, and members of his staff."[50] The implication was that Nixon agreed with the magazine enough to read it and could be further influenced in a conservative direction by its pages. This rumor of vice presidential readership circulated widely. Even before McWhorter received his letter, he had fielded a call from Robert Spivack of the *New York Post* about an alleged Buckley comment that Nixon read every issue of *NR* and was "in agreement with substantially all of its contents." McWhorter reported back that Nixon did not read the magazine cover to cover but was briefed on the contents of this and all such publications by his staff. It would be hard to generalize, he said, about any agreement with the magazine's contents.[51]

Rumors aside, Buckley himself indicated his appreciation of Nixon on more than one occasion. The young editor first met Nixon in 1957 and wrote the vice president a thank-you letter relating that "before seeing you I told Whittaker Chambers it was not likely that I would fail to be impressed by someone who had impressed him; and the unlikely did not happen." In reference to closing remarks by Nixon regarding the "need to hang together," Buckley pointed out that "I do not think your position (or any other) is the last word on the subject; a little tension between the tablet-keepers and the governors is good for both of them." He concluded, however, by adding "I hope you know we mean well, and well by you."[52] In November 1959, Buckley expressed his frustration in his column, "The Ivory Tower," over the "putative superiority of Nixon over Rockefeller, and the dumbfounding failure of the Harvard professors to see it." He went on to speculate that the reason for the academy's Rockefeller love-fest was

> Symbolism. Nixon symbolizes the Right in this country, and does so quite apart from whether he is its adequate symbol; Rockefeller symbolizes the (non-radical) Left; and the academic community is in spiritual league with the Left.

Despite this frustration, however, Buckley concluded that most people, despite their ability to be manipulated, were essentially conservative. "The conservative will get more support from the people than from the academicians."[53]

Buckley's voice of qualified praise was not, however, the only voice resident within the pages of *NR* as 1959 headed toward 1960. At the beginning of December, the magazine announced an upcoming forum on the question of whether Richard Nixon deserved conservative support. Speaking in his favor was longtime Nixon friend and journalist Ralph de Toledano, while Frank Meyer was scheduled to speak in opposition. *NR* prefaced this event with a statement indicating the deep reservoir of uncertainty in which conservatives were mired.

> The preponderant answer to that [above] question by American conservatives is Yes, so frightened are we by the specter of Nelson Rockefeller, et. al. But there are complications, deep complications, that range from Mr. Nixon's recent statements on such weighty matters as the invitation of Khrushchev to this country, to preemption by the federal government of states' rights, and the suspension of nuclear tests. *National Review* has not taken a corporate position on the Nixon question—and may never do so, for we may decide to relay responsible conservative arguments, and let the reader make his own choice. But we are certainly not going to act as though the problem did not exist.[54]

Gubernatorial candidate Nelson Rockefeller and running mate Malcolm Wilson enjoy hot dogs and the Manhattan skyline while on the campaign trail in 1958. Courtesy of Rockefeller Archive Center

Claude Barnett (right), director of the Associated Negro Press, and White House Staffer E. Frederic Morrow (left) join President Dwight Eisenhower in admiring a copper tray destined for presentation in Africa in 1958. Courtesy of the Dwight D. Eisenhower Presidential Library

Baseball legend Jackie Robinson (left) and comedian Joe E. Brown (right) chat with Eisenhower at the White House in 1958. Robinson often showed his support for liberal Republican policies and would become a fervent Nixon backer in 1960. Courtesy of the Dwight D. Eisenhower Presidential Library

Arizona Senator Barry Goldwater signs copies of his paradigmatic book *Conscience of a Conservative* at a rally in Boston in 1960. Courtesy Arizona Historical Foundation

Goldwater stands before a bank of eager supporters at the Republican National Convention in July 1960. Courtesy Arizona Historical Foundation

Party leaders, left to right: California senator Thomas Kuchel, Rockefeller, former New York governor Thomas Dewey, Michigan governor George Romney, Goldwater, and Labor secretary James Mitchell. Courtesy Arizona Historical Foundation

L. Brent Bozell (left) and William F. Buckley, Jr. promote their jointly authored book, *McCarthy and His Enemies*, in 1954. Within a year, Buckley began publication of *National Review*. While Buckley, especially, became a mentor to Young Americans for Freedom, the two men's youth illustrates the vibrancy of the conservative movement circa 1960. *Los Angeles Times* Photographic Archive, ca. 1918 (Collection 1429). Department of Special Collections, Charles E. Young Research Library, UCLA.

Despite lukewarm conservative support for the vice president, Goldwater was a dedicated campaigner for the 1960 Republican ticket. In this photo, he addresses a crowd at a rally in Las Vegas, Nevada, on October 12, 1960. Courtesy Arizona Historical Foundation

Richard and Pat Nixon chat with South Carolina GOP chairman Greg W. Shorey in 1960. Courtesy South Carolina Political Collections, Thomas Cooper Library, University of South Carolina

The aftermath of Nixon's hugely popular rally at the statehouse in Columbia, S.C., left reams of paper and the distinct impression that Dixie was "all for Nixon."

NR's editors would continue this debate privately throughout the campaign.

In the next issue, Meyer's column offered a glimpse into his arguments at the Forum—and his position on the side of those conservatives who did not view Nixon with Buckley's friendly regard. Meyer wholly rejected pragmatists' argument that Nixon as president would be better than a Democrat even if he was not as conservative as preferred. "What use is it," he asked,

> to spend energy to achieve political power if the positive result is going to be nothing better than a mild decrease in our rate of growth towards collectivism at home and our surrender to collectivism abroad; if, negatively, energies that might be devoted to building a serious conservative opposition are diverted and drained off from that task?

Nixon, he argued, was no more an ideologue than Eisenhower, and "like Eisenhower—though for different reasons—he drifts with the tide." The reason for Nixon's drifting tendencies, Meyer concluded, was the result of his "aiming for the Presidency and subordinating all principles to that aim." Conservatives should not waste their time on Nixon; rather, they should work for conservative congressional candidates and local causes, then prepare for 1964.[55] While most conservatives did, however half-heartedly, support Nixon in the end, a substantial minority of *NR*'s readers would agree with Meyer over the course of the electoral season. In August, for example, a reader from Snyder, New York, proposed a write-in ticket of Goldwater and Virginia Senator Harry Byrd, and in September a reader from Falmouth, Virginia, proposed staging sit-in protests in voting booths come Election Day.[56]

At least one of *NR*'s most prominent pens took action beyond the bounds of the magazine. For several years, lawyer and one-time Notre Dame dean Clarence Manion had sought to mobilize conservative opinion through such means as his weekly radio broadcast *Manion Forum*. In 1959, Manion turned his attention to the 1960 election, organizing a group of prominent conservatives from around the country to push for a draft of Barry Goldwater as the Republican presidential candidate. While Goldwater himself repeatedly expressed his skepticism about the movement and his reluctance to be drafted, Manion and his cohort pushed on.[57]

As the summer of 1959 progressed, and Rockefeller loomed ever larger on the scene, Goldwater expressed to *Arizona Republic and Gazette* publisher Eugene Pulliam his belief that "in the event something occurs that prevents [Nixon's] getting [the nomination] and Rockefeller is suggested, then we must be ready to fight."[58] This "ready to fight" status evidently included cooperation with Manion's group, which aided them in preparing for publication a little book of principles to be called *Conscience of a Conservative*. It has been well established that the ghostwriter of the book was L. Brent Bozell. The minutes of a January 23, 1960 meeting of Goldwater for President activists indicate the enthusiasm with which Bozell supported a Goldwater candidacy. While he doubted Goldwater's chances of winning the nomination, he believed as few as fifty Goldwater delegates at the convention would send a clear signal of conservatives' significance, laying the groundwork for a more successful campaign in 1964. As such, he urged the assembled committee to raise sufficient money for an organized, national appeal, sending three or four people on a speaking tour that would promote Goldwater and his ideals as expressed in *Conscience*.[59]

Chronicling the Campaign

The end of 1959 brought with it Rockefeller's declaration that he would not seek the presidency in 1960, and despite *NR* conservatives' opposition to the New York governor, they viewed his exit from the race as a blow to the debate over the future of the GOP. Without Rocky, the magazine editorialized, Nixon would not be able to define himself and his positions until after the July convention. A push from the right from someone like New Hampshire Senator Styles Bridges or General Albert Wedemeyer—for most of *NR*'s editors, Goldwater was not yet on the presidential radar screen—would compel Nixon to measure his own views against a truly conservative position. With competition from the center courtesy of a man like U.N. Ambassador Henry Cabot Lodge or John J. McCloy, Nixon would have to define himself in relation to Modern Republicanism. "But with Rockefeller bowing out of the race," *NR* concluded, "Republicans are left with no means of registering their impact on Mr. Nixon before he gets the shoo-in notification that he is their Mr. It."[60]

Even after his exit from a race he never officially declared, Rockefeller remained in the news, and, therefore, in the pages of *NR*. In February, the magazine commented that Rockefeller's failure to even mention the vice president at a $100-a-plate GOP fund-raising dinner, as well as his continuing willingness to comment on national and international concerns, "suggest to some that he would be the willing subject of a miracle."[61] In March, *NR* reported on the machinations of Arthur Goldsmith, "Manhattan Machiavelli," as he sent out personal anti-Nixon letters to top East Coast society figures and telephoned for financial support for the "not-altogether-dormant Rockefeller Presidential campaign."[62]

March also brought the New Hampshire primary, however; and while Bozell pointed out that uncontested primaries are just a test of organizational prowess, on this front Nixon succeeded admirably. Nixon was *liked*, he pointed out, by the people who made up the Republican Party organization, from precinct workers through top leaders, and he predicted that New Hampshire would be just one example of pro-Nixon sentiment across the country. With regard to ideological affiliation, Nixon proved to be plausible with both liberals and conservatives, having it both ways, despite Bozell's earlier prediction that he could not.[63] Even so, the vice president continued to face early criticism, with *NR* reporting in early April that GOP chairman Thruston Morton and former chairman Leonard Hall told Nixon that he would lose the election if it were held immediately. Despite the New Hampshire results, conservative Republicans remained merely lukewarm, having been most recently annoyed by Nixon's sympathy for federally funded medical aid to the elderly. In the same issue, however, the editors pointed out that the one man in the United States who thought Nixon would not receive the nomination was Harold Stassen—who was by now infamous for his inability to make predictions and for his unreasoning hatred for all things Nixon.[64]

Meanwhile, a certain Arizona Senator was blazing his way onto the electoral scene. *NR* reported on Goldwater's appearance before the South Carolina State Republican Party Convention and his unanimous selection as that delegation's choice for the presidency. Goldwater's success in South Carolina prompted the state parties in Minnesota, North Dakota, and Mississippi to invite him to their conventions. Conservatives around the country also began promoting Goldwater as a vice presidential option. *NR* reported that a *Human Events* poll of GOP county chairmen showed strong support for Goldwater as vice president, and he also won the vice presidential endorsement of all 450 college delegates to the Midwestern Young Republican meeting held in Des Moines on April 9.[65] In the midst of all this excitement, *Conscience of a Conservative* hit bookstore shelves.

NR loved *Conscience*. Meyer published a rapturous review of Goldwater's groundbreaking book in the April 23 issue, and in a May 7 editorial, the magazine gloated over Goldwater's ability to turn two credos of the left on their heads. First, an unabashed conservative position was *not* always going to be dismissed as "Neandertal." Second, a book published by a vanity press did indeed have a chance of getting press coverage and selling thousands of copies—Goldwater's book had definitively proven this potential.[66] Goldwater's book was a declaration of his conservative philosophy, along lines that quite closely paralleled *NR*'s editorial positions. The conservative, Goldwater argued, could "claim a familiarity with the accumulated wisdom and experience of history, and he is not too proud to learn from the great minds of the past." Furthermore, conservatives believed that

. . . the economic and spiritual aspects of man's nature are inextricably inter-
twined. He cannot be economically free, or even economically efficient, if he
is enslaved politically; conversely, man's freedom is illusory if he is dependent
for his economic needs on the State.[67]

Here were the fundamentals of Kirk's six canons. Goldwater—or rather, Bozell as ghostwriter—went on to outline how conservative principles applied
to such topics as states' rights; civil rights; farm, labor, and taxation issues;
the welfare state; education; and the Soviet menace. Nixon's star paled with
every issue in the light of all this Goldwater hoopla, with William L. White
dismissing the vice president's advocacy of "progressive conservatism" as
a "hermaphroditic goal."[68] The Goldwater steamroller continued through
successive weeks as Young Republican groups and college organizations
pronounced their support for the Arizonan as either presidential or vice
presidential nominee.

As the convention neared, however, Bozell put a damper on all the
Goldwater excitement with a reasoned look at conservative options that
roughly matched his initial beliefs back in January. It still seemed likely,
he concluded, that Nixon would win the Republican nomination on the
first ballot. An affirmation of conservative principles, however, in the form
of Goldwater delegates from South Carolina, Arizona, and any other state
that might care to join them in retaining their votes for the Arizona senator, would be a meaningful political act. Conservatives' most urgent task
in 1960, Bozell argued, was to make sure their ideological position was preserved as a recognizable political alternative. The Republican Party needed
to realize that Goldwater "is a different kettle of fish from Nixon." By casting their first vote for Goldwater, even if Nixon was later selected by acclamation, Goldwater delegates would have served notice to the party that
conservatives were still in business. Such a move would continue Goldwater's goal, though refusing to discourage his supporters, of urging Nixon
away from a leftward course. It would also establish Goldwater as a potential candidate in 1964, as well as promoting him for the vice presidency,
although Bozell himself felt the senator could do more good by retaining
his present position.[69]

Preliminary convention proceedings gave *NR* conservatives hope that the
conservative voice would be reflected in the party platform. While speaking
before the Republican Platform Committee the previous week, Goldwater
"sparkled," receiving a standing ovation. By contrast, *NR* noted, Rockefeller's comments received little applause—and much of what he did receive
came from Adlai Stevenson backers in the galleries who were looking for a
new candidate. In a comment that indicated the frustration conservatives

felt toward the mainstream media, the editorial noted that Rockefeller received front-page coverage in the *New York Times*, while Goldwater was relegated to two column inches on page 19. Bozell commented on July 30 (an issue published before the convention, despite its date) that, provided the GOP did not ruin it by imitating the Democratic platform, an actual two-party system seemed to be coming into existence.[70]

By the August 13 issue, however, the Republican National Convention was over, and with it, to judge from its pages, went the hopes of *NR* for 1960. Angry over Rockefeller and Nixon's last-minute agreement on platform issues—the "Compact of Fifth Avenue"—the magazine concluded

> The operative deal was between Rockefeller and Nixon, though it may not have been certain at first glance which was Antony, and which Octavius. Nixon, or Rockefeller, or Nixon-Rockefeller did not ask Senator Goldwater's advice and consent in selecting a Massachusetts liberal [Henry Cabot Lodge] for second place.

The contrast between the two parties' political platforms could be measured only in shades of gray, although *NR* did concede that they differed a little and by a consistent pattern. Overall, the *NR* editorial staff concluded that the ascendance of a new generation to the presidential nominations of both parties marked the end of the postwar period, without yet revealing the direction in which the future would lead. Both Nixon and Kennedy appealed to the future but did so on foundations of old ideas.[71]

That said, *NR*'s post-convention tone was considerably more chipper than might initially be expected of the intellectual bulwark of a failed movement. This optimism was the result of the bright future this initial, failed effort portended for the conservative wing of the Republican Party. The convention was crawling with young people, the magazine reported, and the most serious among them were fans of Goldwater.

> They drove one Nixon aide into muttering in exasperation: 'Those damn Goldwater people are everywhere.' What's more, they are going to be around for a long time to come, which is something the Republican leadership should take note of.

As Bozell pointed out, by the end of the convention, Goldwater wore three hats, each making him a national luminary and potentially a national power. First, he was a member of the Rockefeller-Nixon-Goldwater triumvirate that dominated the convention. Second, he was the sentimental favorite of the party rank and file. In an open convention, Bozell argued,

Goldwater would surely have won the vice presidential nomination, and he might even have been chosen for the presidency. Finally, he was now the undisputed leader of the conservative movement, the first inheritor of the great Ohio Senator Robert Taft's mantle since his death in 1953. This accomplishment was all the more remarkable because "Goldwater organized nothing. He simply girded himself with a rounded position on public affairs, and walked onto the stage." Bozell's article was not an unqualified paean to the Arizona senator. He felt that Goldwater should have continued to fight the "Compact of Fifth Avenue" following his initial denouncement of it as "the Munich of the Republican Party," and he disliked Goldwater's convention speech addressing his followers as "naughty children." "The movement may have to make alliances with uncongenial political mechanisms, as Goldwater thinks it must," Bozell argued, "but it can never afford to support uncongenial candidates while muting its voice."[72] Overall, however, the future Bozell painted was bright. Conservatives might have lost the battle, but with a strong and courageous leader, perhaps they could win the war.

As *NR* staffers sloughed off the loss in Chicago and focused on the future, the magazine became important for another service it offered to its readers. The Topeka businessman and the Anaheim housewife introduced above could share a sense of belonging through the articles and commentary printed in *NR*, but they could also participate in the developing conservative movement more directly, with *NR* as facilitator: they could write letters to the editor. The "letters" pages of the magazine began buzzing as soon as the convention ended and continued on through Election Day. The sentiments *NR* readers expressed provide further insight into the tactics of the developing conservative movement.

The predominant emotion expressed by readers post-Chicago was disgust. Lionel Lokos of Flushing, New York, provides a good example: denouncing Nixon's "drooling love affair with the Left," he reflected that Nixon's motivation for cooperating with Rockefeller was his certainty that conservatives had nowhere else to go come November. "Well I, for one, have news for Mr. Nixon," Lokos stated. "On election day, I'm not going to the polls at all." In the same issue, Bernard F. Alder of Bryn Mawr, Pennsylvania, expressed similar sentiments, urging *NR* readers to vote just for GOP congressional and senate candidates and abstain from voting for either presidential nominee.[73] Others supported variations on Lokos' and Alder's plans, prompting Nixon supporters to write in as well and urge fidelity to the Republican Party. Tim Terry of San Marino, California, for example, proclaimed it "suicidal" for conservatives to deliberately aid Kennedy by refusing to vote for Nixon.[74]

Heading into the general election, *NR* continued to comment on campaign proceedings but with something of a resigned air. On August 27, Meyer deplored the specter of a president—regardless of the ruling party—

> whose effective opinions are automatically derived by a slide-rule out of the material the poll-takers automatically present, a President whose personal style is externally created by the impersonal prescriptions of the television system.

Nixon and Kennedy were not identical, but in Meyer's eyes they were symptomatic of a larger problem: "decades of the reduction of the political to the achievement of power by the pure calculus of material interests." Referring to Nixon as "Nixonfeller," Meyer melodramatically concluded that the present situation was a "revolt against the constitution of being itself. It is the American form of the twentieth-century revolution of nihilistic denial of man's nature." Conservatives were charged, he exhorted, with vindicating man in his full dimension, "taking his direction not from the movement of material forces but from eternal principle."[75]

Others on the *NR* staff accentuated the positive outcomes of the nomination fight. In September, Buckley lauded the formation of the new conservative youth movement Young Americans for Freedom—of which he played a key role in founding. The young people who met at his family's Sharon, Connecticut, manse to form an organization adopted a "tough-as-nails statement of political and economic convictions which Richard Nixon couldn't read aloud without fainting." With Goldwater as their hero, YAF would fight for the triumph of conservatism on positive terms. "It is quixotic to say that they or their elders have seized the reins of history," Buckley said. "But the difference in psychological attitude is tremendous."[76]

As the election neared, *NR* chronicled Nixon's and Kennedy's maneuverings with amused detachment. An October 8 editorial compared the candidates' first debate to the "splendid but innocuous maneuverings of a pair of Siamese fighting fish separated by a pane of glass."[77] The magazine declined to endorse or refute the entreaties of various groups within the conservative wing, some of whom urged support for Nixon and others of whom suggested boycotting the election. *NR*'s job, an editorial stated, was to remind conservatives that equally well informed people could differ on matters of political tactics, and it was "profoundly wrong for one faction to anathematize the other over such differences." The magazine itself did not intend to urge a particular course of action.[78]

To Endorse, Or Not to Endorse

Since before the convention, the declaration of non-intent had masked a heated debate among *NR* senior editors about the efficacy of endorsing or opposing Nixon, Goldwater, or any other candidate for the presidency. Back in May, Meyer laid out in detail his fascinating forecast for the future of conservatism. He predicted that the growth of conservative influence and intellectual bankruptcy of liberalism, combined with the weakened political opposition to liberalism in government resultant from Eisenhower's own liberal policies and Nixon's progressive movement toward the left, would result in one of two outcomes. On the one hand, historical circumstances might allow liberalism to stumble on long enough for conservative intellectual leadership to develop into political reality. On the other, liberalism might fail so spectacularly and so soon as to produce a political crisis that would result in the American people looking for new leadership uncompromised by previous association with the political establishment. Here he referred to the Third and Fourth French Republics as examples. Whatever the case, Meyer argued, it seemed to him that the responsibility of conservative leadership—meaning, first of all, *NR* was to maintain and develop an independent position vis-à-vis the dominant forces present in American politics. This meant that under no circumstances should *NR* compromise its legitimacy by endorsing Nixon.

A few months ago, he said, he would have recommended a completely independent and critical attitude, but now he felt that a positive option had become available. "The emergence of Barry Goldwater as a principled conservative," Meyer argued, "gives us a public political symbol through which our position is expressed in the political arena." Much as *The New Republic* had recently committed itself to Chester Bowles, *NR* could take the position that Goldwater was the only candidate conservatives could support and that between the conventions and the election the magazine would criticize both candidates on the basis of the standard they established before the conventions.[79]

Beyond Bozell's pre-convention column endorsing a vote for Goldwater on the first ballot as a stand for conservative principles, the *NR* leadership did not pursue Meyer's ideas further. The battle over the possibility of a Nixon endorsement, however, reemerged with vigor in September. Rusher offered a thoughtful analysis of the *NR*'s possibilities in mid-September. Frustrated by citizens' inability to express through the electoral process their unhappiness with both candidates, he did not plan to vote for either in November. "How can it possibly be contended," he asked, "that a serious conservative is effectively registering his opinion if he casts his vote for that one of the

two who is slightly preferable, although neither is in his eyes really acceptable?" It was on other grounds, however, that he determined that it would
be a "grave mistake" for *NR* to either endorse Nixon or advocate absten-
tion from the vote. Some might say they owed it to their readers to take a
stand, but Rusher argued that they would do readers the greatest service by
revealing that even among the editorial staff, opinions differed on whether
Nixon should be supported. The reasons *NR* could cite for supporting Nixon
were so vague that they would apply equally well to "every Republican
candidate who runs against a Democrat between now and the dissolution
of the Republic." If *NR* was to decide that the GOP really was the last, best
hope for America, then it should be forthright "and not pretend that Nixon
is a particularly toothsome Republican, or Kennedy a uniquely malignant
Democrat." Politicians were usually most solicitous of those whose support
they hoped to get, not those they already had in their pockets, so withhold-
ing endorsement from Nixon might actually serve to bolster conservatives'
bargaining power if the vice president were elected. Finally, *NR* should not
kid itself that the candidates or the mainstream media would report a qualified endorsement as such. "Within forty-eight hours, it would be known
that '*National Review* has endorsed Nixon'—period."[80]

Fellow editor Priscilla Buckley, on the other hand, though not especially
enamored of Nixon, nonetheless felt an endorsement was in order. In the
end, she wrote to her brother that the struggle against Communism was
the issue of greatest importance in 1960: "Whereas Richard Nixon is hardly
the champion we would choose, the empirical evidence is that he and his
adviser are less apt to play the appeasement game than Kennedy and his
advisers." Priscilla Buckley also saw a difference between 1956, when *NR*
demurred from endorsing Eisenhower, and 1960, because the current election was bound to be a much closer race. If the magazine decided to endorse the vice president, she recommended that such an endorsement also
discuss the stands *NR* wished the candidates had taken. "This would give us
something to point to when, as we all know, Nixon does something ghastly
24 hours after his election and our readers say, 'Ha! Ha! Why did you support this dreadful man!'" She astutely pointed out, however, that if the
magazine declined to endorse Nixon and Kennedy was elected, *he* would
do something dreadful and readers would ask why *NR* didn't endorse Nixon
when it had the chance.[81]

As the deadline for the October 22 issue approached, James Burnham
made a final plea for—and Rusher against—endorsement of Nixon. Burnham revealed to Buckley that he had "so little personal enthusiasm for
Nixon that I may not be able to endure voting for him." Nonetheless, he
was convinced that conservatives' public opinion must be pro-Nixon. The

question was not one merely of Kennedy versus Nixon but of all the leftist forces aligned with Kennedy. These were the things that *NR* was against, and the only way to oppose them in 1960 was through an endorsement of Nixon.[82] Rusher, on the other hand, betrayed a frustration with the two-party system in general, arguing that both were nothing more than highly efficient vote-gathering machines. As such, working within the party system was pointless for individuals concerned with fundamental principles. The best course was to work outside the party system, through avenues of pure opinion like *NR*, until one of the parties—or, even better, a third party—responded to the massive change in public opinion that conservatives' extra-party work would engender. A vote for Nixon, on the other hand, merely strengthened the current, failed management of the GOP.[83]

Finally, however, Buckley settled the argument with the statement of noncommitment excerpted above. Explaining his decision to Burnham, he confided that he hated the thought of insulating *NR* from the political process: "I do not feel that ours is a monastic function of bead-saying in isolation from the rest of the world." Under the circumstances, though, he was forced to agree with Rusher on two points. First, he felt a good case could be made that conservatives would increase their leverage by remaining aloof from Nixon. Second, Buckley did not feel it was possible to declare for Nixon with reservations. "I don't think the system permits this," he said, pointing out that a good friend who a year ago was "elaborating his dislike for Nixon" was now, having been caught up in the machinery of politics, defending the vice president at almost every turn. Buckley hoped his editorial, "plus a very diligent disparagement of Kennedy, will end up satisfying you psychologically, even if you find us lacking in intellectual rigor."[84]

Having expected little, disappointment over Nixon's defeat was not exactly palpable among the *NR* staff. Nixon, a November 19 editorial concluded, chose to fight as a practical politician and a technician. This kind of politics is sometimes justified but only by one fact—success. Nixon did not achieve success, so his defeat was total, despite the small percentage margin.[85] Bozell pointed out that the narrowness of Kennedy's victory left Nixon in the picture, whereas a larger triumph would have spelled the end of his national political career. He disagreed with Frank Meyer that Nixon did not win any state that a conservative could not have won as well, citing Illinois (!), Ohio, California, Wisconsin, and Washington as examples. He felt that Goldwater could have scared off much of the anti-Kennedy vote "at the country's present level of political consciousness."

Meyer, on the other hand, argued that absolutely nothing of political significance for conservatives was at stake in the contest between Kennedy and Nixon. Conservatives needed to realize, he argued, that they had no stake in the GOP as such. The struggle to control the party was important, but it could not be the entire strategy. Conservatives must retain their ideological independence and strive to further their cause outside the bounds of Republican Party politics. Meyer seemed to share Bozell's concern about immediate acceptance of conservative ideology by a majority of Americans, but he argued that it was better to lose in 1964 and win in 1968 than to face another election like those from 1940 through 1960.[86] At a couple months' distance, Bozell began to speculate along lines more similar to his colleague. Nixon's loss removed the Modern Republicans from power. Now conservatives were "provisionally emancipated." If they kept their eyes on the target of national power, organized with all possible speed, preserved their freedom of action a la Meyer, concentrated their resources "in areas of natural advantage"—youth, the Midwest, and the Sunbelt—and created "a substantive vision of the political, economic and social orders" that would characterize a better society, success could be theirs. Nixon's survival was a source of irritation, but conservatives' situation was substantially improved if they husbanded their resources carefully and built a stable foundation for change.[87]

An Independent Voice for the Future

The conservative intellectuals of *National Review*, then, ended 1960 with a confirmed belief that the Republican Party needed a new direction—and a sense of hope that this move was underway. The year 1960 marked no triumph, but it marked a significant and far-ranging beginning. Young people were motivated to fight for a truly conservative candidate like Barry Goldwater. Goldwater's conservative credentials had been burnished and his image enhanced by the machinations at the Republican National Convention; conservatives now had a unifying figure behind which to assemble in the future. The "Nixonfeller" agenda had been coolly regarded, if not completely dismissed, by the American electorate, and in the absence of strong evidence to the contrary, conservatives could make a stronger claim that "me-tooism" was not going to gain victory for the GOP.

As the voice of the conservative movement, *NR* had provided a meeting ground for conservative ideas and a forum for their expression. Furthermore, it had forged a middle ground on which conservatives could work for change in the GOP—as Bozell had done and would continue to do through the Goldwater-for-President movement—without becoming beholden to unfavorable Republican decisions. Buckley's editorial statement of noncommitment preserved conservatives' independence. It also preserved their power as a pressure group to motivate rightward change within the Republican Party in the wake of Nixon's loss. As conservatism gathered steam heading into the 1960s, it would continue to build on the groundwork Buckley and Schlamm established in 1955.

Buttoned-down Rebels

GOP Youth and the Revolt against Liberalism

"... it is indeed the Liberal who is old—who has aged in the exercise of power—and it is the conservative who is young, angry, declassé. The evidence of conservative rebellion—substantive as well as symbolic—is everywhere at hand."—M. Stanton Evans, *Revolt on the Campus, 1961*

Any visitor to an American high school during the inevitable "Sixties Day" of Homecoming Spirit Week will quickly glimpse the outward cultural legacy of the 1960s—adolescents strolling the halls adorned in tie-dyed shirts and round glasses, peace signs, and peasant garb. These are the cultural cues of youthful rebellion, resistance to established authority and desire for a new mode of being. By the early 2000s, however, these teenagers came home to evening news broadcasts covering the daily activities of President George W. Bush and an increasingly conservative Supreme Court, debates over tax cuts and protracted legal battles over the display of the Ten Commandments in courtrooms. What has happened to the rebellious youth of the 1960s?

The short answer, of course, is that not all the youth of the 1960s were "flower children" or peace activists. Most were young people just like the youth of every generation, struggling to get through school, find work, start families, make it through war if drafted and, in most cases, avoid it if at all possible. Even more important in terms of the historical development of American political parties, the left wing was not the only source of youthful rebellion. As conservatives took increasing control over the political process at all levels of government, youth were no exception. Beginning in the 1950s, young conservative activists forged their own struggle for a new mode of American life, one based on what they viewed as traditional moral and economic principles. Their fight was just as threatening to the established order as their left-wing counterparts'—and, one could argue, more effective.

Both poles of American political life have seen the enduring impact of the 1960s generation. Young Americans of all political persuasions viewed the United States during this era as a land of opportunity with great possibilities for positive change. While their methods and their goals differed dramatically, both sides combined to move "political discourse from an arena dominated and largely controlled by elites to one that sought to take its cue from the popular imagination."[1] The Democratic Party continues to struggle with the legacies of Vietnam and the protest movement, as exemplified by the frustrations Senator John Kerry encountered during his 2004 quest for the presidency.

The Republican Party, on the other hand, is a far more conservative organization than it was in 1960. This conservatism is the legacy of a number of factors, including the development of a coherent conservative philosophy by activists such as William F. Buckley, Jr. and his cohorts at the *National Review* and the emergence of the South and Southwest as politically important regions. One of the most significant factors is the legacy of the conservative youth movement that grew out of frustration with the liberal establishment of the 1950s and flowered during the 1960 presidential campaign. Liberal and left-wing students often initially attempted to work through the political system, enjoying some success in areas such as civil rights and women's rights; however, over the course of the 1960s, some left-wing radicals turned toward violence or personal politics in their disillusionment with unbending institutions. By contrast, conservatives remained focused upon "the system." Working at the grass roots, they worked with conservative elders to forge an alternative political culture that captured the Republican Party, if not by Nixon's election in 1968 then certainly with the election of Ronald Reagan in 1980. In so doing, they profoundly reshaped the landscape of American politics.[2]

Youth of various ideological stripes participated in the race for the Republican nomination in 1960. Ultimately, however, conservative youth reigned triumphant, waging a far more successful battle for their principles—and with far greater fortune in mobilizing the support of their ideological heroes. In part, conservatives' success was the result of individual personalities. Barry Goldwater was a more congenial icon than Rockefeller, who consistently thwarted his supporters' attempts through his failure to commit to a single course of action. While Goldwater never explicitly ran for office in 1960, remaining loyal to Nixon and the Republican program, he did not hesitate to speak out when affronted. Goldwater responded warmly to youths' support, even as he played the role of elder statesman in cautioning them to be patient and wait for a more opportune moment.

Above all, however, conservatives benefited from the financial and institutional support of their movement elders. As social movement theorists have observed, the greater the level of social actors' access to diverse kinds of resources, the more likely they will be able to develop into an effective collective action group.[3] We also cannot underestimate the importance of specific political actors and institutional configurations at discrete points in time.[4] Nixon's stance as a middle-of-the-road Republican coming into the 1960 election meant that much institutional support that might otherwise have flowed toward Rockefeller remained in Republican Party coffers. Even as progressive Republicans like the National Students for Rockefeller argued that Nixon was insufficiently liberal, the bulk of Eisenhower supporters believed that Nixon had the nomination sewn up; a dollar for Rockefeller was a dollar wasted. By contrast, conservative leaders like Buckley recognized the value of encouraging a conservative youth movement. As a result, Youth for Goldwater and its post-convention antecedent, Young Americans for Freedom, enjoyed the financial and leadership contributions of their conservative elders. Goldwater youth also benefited from the availability and widespread distribution of conservative books and publications. While liberals such as Rockefeller commissioned expert studies, Goldwater wrote *Conscience of a Conservative*, a slim, easily read paperback that outlined basic conservative principles. Other movement elders also established networks to distribute conservative literature to young people.

As in other realms, the triumphs of 1960 were incremental rather than total. In the words of conservative columnist John Chamberlain, "many of the affected students are still not old enough to vote. . . . But four years from now, eight years from now, 12 years from now, the pressure on the old parties from the youngest workers and convention delegates may tell a different story."[5] Youthful conservatives did not attain all of their goals, but they succeeded in rendering their brand of Republicanism the most viable option for the future. Meanwhile, young liberals effectively lost any lingering momentum they might once have enjoyed. A variety of student and young-adult groups took part in political activities leading up to and during the electoral season, and their contributions will be noted where relevant. The story of youth involvement during the 1960 campaign, however, can best be told through the activities of three groups: National Students for Rockefeller, Youth for Goldwater, and College Youth for Nixon.

National Students for Rockefeller

As a liberal Republican and governor of a large eastern state, Nelson Rockefeller was representative of the dominant arm of the GOP circa 1960. Every Republican candidate since 1940 had come from this wing of the party, including Dwight Eisenhower, although the general's Kansas upbringing and unknown ideological stance made it possible for him to charm many more conservative supporters in 1952. When Rockefeller took New York by storm in the disastrous year of 1958, many Republicans of a more liberal stripe believed he could be their next Eisenhower. Young liberals were no exception. A core of active supporters, led by Harvard student Bruce K. Chapman, coalesced around the new governor and began to promote his presidential candidacy in early 1959. Chapman, a freshman at the time, led a trio of three other freshmen and a lone junior, Mark K. Adams, before the Harvard Student Council in April of that year. Announcing their intent of forming the first student Rockefeller group in the country, "so far as any of its members know," Students for Rockefeller also became the first candidate-focused organization on the Harvard campus leading up to the 1960 election. Chapman reported that he expected a bandwagon movement for Rockefeller to gather speed "by Christmas at the latest."[6]

In May of that year, Harvard Students for Rockefeller joined the newly formed Students for Humphrey in taking a poll of Harvard students in campus dining halls that showed Rockefeller triumphant over all but one potential Democratic nominee: "egghead" favorite Adlai Stevenson. By contrast, Nixon garnered a minority of the vote against all five Democratic possibilities.[7] Even more significant for Rockefeller's youthful backers, only 28 percent of students polled considered themselves Republicans, while 33 percent claimed Democratic affiliation, and 39 percent professed to be independent.[8] Students for Rockefeller eagerly ran with this evidence of the New York governor's independent appeal, pointing out that commentators ranging from archconservative David Lawrence to consensus liberal Arthur Schlesinger, Jr. had praised Rockefeller's "constructive philosophy of government." The governor took a courageous and realistic attitude toward current problems, the Rockefeller backers proudly proclaimed, citing his experience in many levels of government—as well as his average score of 57 percent support versus Nixon's dismal 37 percent in their poll.[9]

From the beginning, however, support from above for Rockefeller's youthful supporters was lacking. Chapman later recounted that he first visited the New York Republican State Committee in March 1959 to state his support for Rockefeller and his hopes of starting a student organization. The public relations agent to whom Chapman was directed repeatedly stated "with stiff formality" that the committee's actions were predicated upon the wishes of the governor, and the governor had announced no intention of running for president. The frustrated Chapman contended this "cold indifference to tendered support was, I think, symptomatic of too great caution." Even a bit of interest in his group's plans would have been encouraging, but the meeting and a subsequent, unanswered letter mailed on April 10 provided no such solace. Despite this disappointment, Harvard Students for Rockefeller had gone forward with its organization and activities. At the Young Republican National Convention in June, George Sallade asked Chapman to become national chairman of Students for Rockefeller. Following the confidential approval of the New York Young Republicans' president, he accepted—a bit of "quiet, effective support" that he pointedly contrasted with the state committee's lack of interest.[10]

In addition, Chapman's enthusiasm for Rockefeller's independent appeal might have been premature, given the governor's need to win a Republican nomination before he could reach out to Americans of all political affiliations. From the start, Young Republicans more closely tied to the Republican Party indicated only lukewarm support toward Rockefeller. A Harvard Young Republican Club poll conducted the evening before the cafeteria canvass indicated that 67 percent of Young Republicans preferred Nixon to the governor or any other Republican candidate.[11] The 1959 Young Republican National Federation convention provided further evidence of members' preference for the vice president and probable nominee, with a coalition of southern and western delegates defeating pro-Rockefeller New Yorkers' attempts to impose a 'Rockefeller Republican' national chairman upon the federation.[12]

As the Rockefeller for President Citizens' Information Center stepped up activity in fall 1959, a number of letters from interested students filtered through headquarters and were passed along to the enthusiastic Chapman. Chapman also used Alexander Halpern and the RFPCIC resources to evangelize for Rockefeller on his limited student budget. October 13, for example, Chapman wrote to Halpern and asked him to send information to students at the universities of Chicago, New Hampshire, Washington, Indiana, Adrian College, and his own campus.[13] Rockefeller was far more comfortable in informal settings, and, as a result, his interactions with students were generally more successful than his more formal meetings with adults. Following his November 1959 West Coast trip, for example, a Rockefeller aide reported that while Rockefeller's foreign policy speech at the Cow Palace was vague and hard to follow, his appearance at a Young Republican cocktail reception was "as different as day from night." The governor had shown warmth, enthusiasm, and an ability to speak well off-the-cuff.[14]

Rockefeller's own time, however, was limited, and his supporting staff continued to appear frustratingly indifferent toward their youthful contingent of advocates. In October 1959, University of Washington Young Republican treasurer Camden Hall wrote to Halpern requesting help with obtaining material and speakers as he attempted to organize colleges in Oregon, Washington, Idaho, Montana, Wyoming, and Alaska. "Both the Democrats and the Nixon people have been able to bring speakers out to the University," he reported, "while the Rockefeller group goes unheard. I have been asked when will Rockefeller people be out, and my only answer has been that I am not sure. Any solution to this will be greatly appreciated."[15] Chapman did finally have an opportunity to meet with Rockefeller aide Rod Perkins in September, a meeting that "gave us much needed faith in the 'legitimacy' of our group." He also enjoyed some support from the chairman of the California Rockefeller for President organization and from Republican financier Arthur Goldsmith. National Students for Rockefeller was formally announced on November 2, and a mass mailing of 400 printed letters to Young Republican presidents throughout the country garnered several favorable responses. Twenty-six Students for Rockefeller chapters had been organized by the end of November, despite organizational hiccups such as Chapman's discovery in October that a supposed Columbia activist had, instead of organizing 10 campus groups, organized none.[16] An enthusiastic Chapman told the *Harvard Crimson* in early November that he planned to spread "Rocky and Victory" literature, organize "Rallies for Rockefeller," take straw polls, sponsor speeches, advertise the "Rockefeller Record," and carry out a national letter-writing campaign to newspaper editors and Young Republican presidents. He reported gifts from two early Eisenhower supporters from Montana and New York and said the organization intended to increase its drive for contributions.[17]

Unfortunately, the charisma Rockefeller demonstrated in California was often clouded by his lack of forcefulness as a speaker, a problem many contemporaries and historians have attributed to his dyslexia. A three-college "Rally for Rocky" organized by National Students for Rockefeller fell prey to one of these off days. Chapman reported that while his after-dinner handshaking sessions were magnificent—the governor was a born schmoozer—Rockefeller's appearance did not actually influence many votes. Furthermore, no one on the governor's staff was available for any sort of logistical discussion with student leaders. Chapman contrasted this poor performance with the Nixon operation, "in which an advance man is sent to a city about to be visited by the Vice-President, and who confer with student as well as adult leaders."[18]

By December, Chapman's frustrations were boiling over. Thirty college chapters were active, with another ten in the process of organizing—a dramatic increase from the five colleges organized at the beginning of the fall term. Significantly, however, all but two of the twenty states listed in RFPCIC files as having college contacts were located in the Northeast, Midwest, or far West. Only Texas and Virginia, often viewed as southern border states, broke this trend. National Students for Rockefeller's support, then, came overwhelmingly from those regions of the country inclined toward progressive Republicanism in the past.[19] Students for Rockefeller had printed 3,000 "Rocky and Victory in '60" pamphlets for distribution to Young Republican leaders and states where Rockefeller had visited, and student receptions and rallies had been held along the routes of the governor's travels in New Hampshire, San Francisco, Eugene, Seattle, and Providence. The organization had urged a number of letter-writing, speaking, and polling duties upon its members and had even planned an extensive national campaign to place ads in fifty campus newspapers, publish a variety of campaign material, and travel to New York to petition Rockefeller to run. Unfortunately, Chapman reported, all of the national activities had been cancelled due to lack of funds. He had spent almost $200 of his own money, and while Arthur Goldsmith had given him $90 and promised more funding by the end of January, without these funds it was doubtful that the organization could be regenerated before late March. "In short," wrote the demoralized youth, "I am frustrated by having workable ideas and no means, no financial means, to put them into effect. I do not feel I can go further into debt, no matter how important I consider a Rockefeller candidacy."[20]

In light of evidence that the Rockefeller clan personally bailed out RFPCIC following the governor's withdrawal from the race, National Students for Rockefeller's elders probably had little cash with which to fund their erstwhile supporters' efforts. The lack of funding and organization endemic in National Students for Rockefeller was mirrored throughout the Rockefeller organization, although this would have been small solace to Chapman and his fellow workers. The students' efforts simply were not matched by sufficient enthusiasm from individuals or organizations with the financial resources to support a pro-Rockefeller effort. Rockefeller sounded acceptable to many, as the May 1959 Harvard poll indicates; however, he failed to inspire the fiery devotion or, even more importantly, build the organizational apparatus that a long shot candidate must have to enter the electoral mainstream. Following the governor's withdrawal, a group of Ivy League students attempted to bring the Rockefeller-for-President organization back to life with a write-in campaign in New Hampshire's March 8 primary. The students' movement did not get beyond the planning stage, no doubt due in part to the meager $14 treasury bequeathed by Students for Rockefeller to its successor.[21]

Youth for Goldwater

Elsewhere, however, a very different organization behind a very different candidate was garnering just the kind of enthusiastic support Rockefeller lacked. Conservative students in the 1950s often found themselves isolated from the GOP mainstream and its Young Republican organization. In the throes of Eisenhower's Modern Republicanism and an intellectual climate characterized by anti-McCarthyism, collegiate conservatives often felt isolated and powerless. A pro-McCarthy organization called Students for America flourished for a few years in the early 1950s and even harbored a national security division that maintained a direct liaison with anti-subversive government agencies. Otherwise, conservative students had for decades lacked any sort of organization through which they could mobilize for the furtherance of their ideological program.[22]

In his 1961 work *Revolt on the Campus*, journalist M. Stanton Evans described his own coming of age. Evans, who graduated from Yale University in 1955 and was something of a mentor to conservative college students nationwide in the early 1960s, served as assistant editor of *The Freeman*, managing editor of *Human Events*, and was on the editorial staff of *National Review* before joining the *Indianapolis News* in 1959. He became editor of the newspaper at the ripe old age of 26, retaining also a post as contributing editor to *NR*. As an undergraduate the young Evans found solace and conservative companionship in a number of publications, most notably those distributed through the Intercollegiate Society of Individualists (ISI). Started in 1953 by conservative author and editor Frank Chodorov, ISI was a clearinghouse for publication and distribution of conservative literature on college campuses. For a nominal fee, ISI mailed interested students copies of books such as Friedrich Hayek's *Road to Serfdom* or Richard Weaver's *Ideas Have Consequences*. While the organization was not itself activist, its educational mission motivated conservative students to form organizations on campuses around the country.[23]

By the late 1950s, conservative students had grown sufficiently strong in numbers and in organization to begin taking hold of mainstream Republican youth organizations. In 1957, for example, the Young Republican National Federation adopted a hard-line platform opposed to federal aid to education, all military assistance to Communist nations, United Nations membership for Communist China, and union shops. In 1959, conservatives at the biennial convention "openly repudiated" Eisenhower Republicanism, booed Chief Justice Earl Warren, and mobilized against liberal Rockefeller forces to elect conservative Ned Cushing of Kansas as chairman. All this was done without the support of New York or the East for the first time since the Young Republicans' inception two decades earlier.[24] Young conservatives benefited further from passage of the National Defense Education Act in 1958 and subsequent attempts to repeal the act's loyalty oath provision. Student activists Douglas Caddy of Georgetown and David Franke of George Washington University organized the Student Committee for the Loyalty Oath, which spread to encompass a large network of collegiate supporters nationwide and established communication and organizational links that would prove greatly beneficial in future efforts.[25]

Describing conservative students' motivation, Evans expressed frustration with what he viewed as the hallmarks of establishment liberalism: permissiveness—a lack of moral values—and statism. The 1950s had been characterized by liberal scholarship bewailing American conformity and calling for new, inevitably liberal, methods of reviving the populace by further equalizing wealth or expressing tolerance for Communists. Liberal elites failed to recognize, however, that American conformism *was* liberal— liberalism was itself the root problem. Until the country returned to a moral society and a free economy, Evans contended, the doldrums would continue. The results of liberalism were visible all around:

> Abroad, [the conservative youth] can observe the menacing advance of the Soviet Union, which the Liberals seem incapable of confronting with resolution. At home, he can observe the rise of the domestic state, with its crushing taxes and its latent capabilities for oppression. He can see that the bills for vast programs of government spending are going to be paid by someone—and it is clear that the someone is himself.

This was the reality that youthful conservatives perceived—"and the signs of conservatism [liberals were so unhappily noticing] . . . were the beginning of insurrection." If young conservatives did not act, they would be crushed under the weight of spending at home and the Communist menace from abroad. Furthermore, Evans admitted that "by some law of political oscillation, young people tend to rebel against the going order—or at least the more aggressive and resourceful young people do." These students were conscious that through their activities, "conservatism" had become "a vanguard movement"—conservatism was revolutionary. "They revel in the paradox," he observed. Conservatives were the new rebels, and they were out to change the fabric of American society.[26]

With a satisfying sense of commitment to overthrowing the old order, young conservatives found in Barry Goldwater their shining star of hope for the new decade. The origins of pro-Goldwater sentiment remain vague but were likely linked to his outspokenness on issues like labor reform and the Cold War struggle. Goldwater projected an image of brave independence, with his Arizona pioneer roots and his status as a top jet pilot in the Air Force Reserve. While Nixon plied crowds with generic platitudes, Goldwater argued that

> If [Nixon] would come out with a strong statement of 'conservative' principles relating to these problems [i.e. care for the aged and aid to education], you couldn't beat him with a club. People are desperately looking for a man who will give them 'conservative' leadership, tell the farmers to get back under the law of supply and demand, get the chiselers off the welfare rolls, tell people that their welfare depends on themselves, not on the Federal Government.[27]

Statements like these were golden for young conservatives frustrated by the liberal failings Evans cited in *Revolt on the Campus*. Goldwater's *Conscience of a Conservative*, published in early 1960, became a best seller in campus bookstores, and in April 1960 the first public demonstration of Goldwater's youth support came at a meeting of the Midwest Federation of College Young Republican Clubs. Evans characterized the meeting itself as something of a "stand-off," with a liberal candidate for chairman squeezing through by a mere five votes. More significantly, however, conservative delegates pushed through a resolution of support for Goldwater and endorsed him for the Republican vice presidential nomination.[28]

One of the delegates to the convention was a Northwestern University business student named Robert Croll, who was impressed by the conservative delegates' enthusiastic response to Goldwater. Croll decided that an organized effort to mobilize young people in support of the Arizona senator might send the nation a wake-up call. While Croll believed that Nixon had the presidential nomination locked up, he began calling a number of young conservatives, including Caddy; Franke; Robert Harley of the D.C. Young Republicans; Richard Noble of the California Young Republicans; and John Weicher, a University of Chicago student and former staff member at *Human Events*. A month after the Midwestern Federation convention, Caddy, Franke, Harley, Noble, and Weicher became the executive committee of Youth for Goldwater for Vice-President, with Croll as chairman.[29] The organization's two purposes, Croll declared on May 12, were to secure the vice presidential nomination for Goldwater and to work within the Young Republican National Federation for the political and economic philosophies espoused in *Conscience*.[30]

Unlike National Students for Rockefeller, Youth for Goldwater received extensive support from its elders in the conservative movement. *National Review* ran advertisements soliciting support for the organization, and elder statesmen such as former New Jersey Governor Charles Edison provided encouragement and financial assistance.[31] Rockefeller advocates had no comparable journal to lend intellectual and organizational support, nor did they enjoy the financial backing of elders who sought a significant change in the direction of Republican Party politics. Given Youth for Goldwater's focus on the vice presidency, Young Republican leaders were freed to pour lavish praise upon their conservative hero while remaining safely pledged to Nixon as the expected presidential nominee. On May 3, for example, the Wisconsin Young Republicans passed a special resolution lauding Goldwater, among other conservative declarations, thereby causing the liberal *Madison Capital Times* to ponder, "one wonders why they missed the Salem witch trials."[32] By June, Croll enthusiastically proclaimed to the *Chicago Daily News* that "we have been getting four replies for each mailing piece we've sent out," and by the middle of July, Youth for Goldwater boasted representation at 65 schools in 32 states.[33] A July Young Republican National Federation poll revealed that 37 percent of young Republicans favored Goldwater's selection for the vice presidency, while only 11 percent selected Henry Cabot Lodge. In a May and June poll of Republicans at California colleges and universities, Goldwater ranked 21 percentage points higher than his closest competition, Rockefeller.[34]

Youth for Goldwater established itself as a vocal critic of liberal Republicanism, denouncing Rockefeller, for example, when in his June ten-point statement he asserted that successful waging of the Cold War depended on increased government spending. To argue that the United States could not triumph without increased funding, Croll argued, was to give "aid and comfort to the very forces of weakness and confusion which have contributed so much to our series of retreats at the hands of the world Communist empire."[35] Elsewhere, Croll demonstrated that the Youth for Goldwater leadership was conversant with the history and development of post–World War II conservatism, pointing out in an interview that conservatism had been made respectable through the intellectual efforts of people like Russell Kirk.[36] The young conservatives supporting Goldwater had done their homework. They understood where they came from—and as events would prove, they had a clear idea of where they were going. This sense of ideological coherence and collective understanding was something that National Students for Rockefeller lacked. Chapman and his cohorts could tout Rockefeller's appealing characteristics, but they had no comprehensive critique of the alternatives.

Meanwhile, Goldwater himself was a far more cooperative potential candidate. While Rockefeller repeatedly refused to consider anything other than the presidency, the Arizona senator stated as early as December 16 that while he preferred to remain in Congress, he would take the vice presidential slot, and "anybody who would say they wouldn't is just a plain liar."[37] Despite his lack of a college education and his reputation for bluntness, Goldwater was a thoughtful man. He read in the field of conservative political philosophy and shared his desire to educate young people in conservative principles with close friend and column ghostwriter Stephen Shadegg.[38] Accordingly, he was more willing to placate and tutor his young supporters, roles that became evident during the events of the Chicago convention.

When the delegates arrived in Chicago at the end of July, so did students from around the country. Youth for Goldwater was not the only pro-Goldwater organization present, as older conservatives from Americans for Goldwater, Goldwater for President, and the Goldwater Coordinating Committee set up headquarters of their own in various buildings. As Evans put it, "Goldwater activity in Chicago was sporadic, disorganized, and thoroughly spontaneous." Many of the Arizona senator's student supporters were too young to vote, and they were all too young to wield much influence in party circles—but they could show their numbers and make noise for their candidate, and they did both with aplomb.[39]

Meanwhile, on July 23 Rockefeller announced the results of the "Compact of Fifth Avenue." As conservatives fumed and Goldwater decried this "Munich of the Republican Party," Nixon's nomination suddenly became more uncertain than at any point since 1956. Nixon's apparent sellout to liberal forces led some delegations to reconsider their support for the vice president and ponder the opportunity his apostasy offered for a "symbolic demonstration of conservative spirit"—a nomination of Goldwater for the presidency.[40] Goldwater realized that even after the "Compact," Nixon retained control over enough delegations to win the presidential nomination easily. His South Carolina supporters, however, defied his request not to have his name placed in contention.[41] Retreating to consider the situation, Goldwater decided, as author Rick Perlstein records, to have his name placed in nomination, have the standard seconding speeches given, and then give a speech withdrawing himself from the nomination process. As Perlstein put it, "he would give everyone a piece of his mind—on national TV."[42]

Before Goldwater's withdrawal speech, however, came Arizona Governor Paul Fannin's nomination address and a demonstration by Goldwater's conservative supporters that nearly raised the roof of the Union Stock Yards. As Evans, who covered the convention as a reporter, described it,

> A great wave of sound exploded into the vaulted reaches of the stockyards. The demonstrators charged through the rear entrances. Delegates leaped to their feet. State signs bobbed in the aisles: Louisiana, Georgia, South Dakota, Wyoming, Texas, Indiana, Colorado, even Massachusetts. The Indians [brought from Arizona] marched, delegates poured into the aisles, more demonstrators struggled into the amphitheater. . . . Surrounded by a melee of shouting humanity I could see nothing. I found my way back to the pressbox, clambered up onto a table, and looked out over the swirling demonstration.[43]

Enthusiastic as the demonstration had been, Youth for Goldwater were frustrated by what they termed obstruction by convention officials. In a letter to the editor printed in many national newspapers, James Kolbe of Arizona estimated that less than half of the 250 people with Goldwater demonstrator passes were allowed on the convention floor, while Nixon demonstrators were allowed to enter regardless of whether they had passes. The Goldwater demonstrators were marched directly down the side aisles and out, obstructed by standing delegates and out of sight of television cameras. The convention orchestra, which had played at "pain-point intensity" for eighteen minutes during the Nixon demonstration, played quietly and only briefly for Goldwater. "This letter," the frustrated youth concluded, "is to let your readers know that, had it not been for the actions of the convention authorities, what appeared on the nation's television screens would have been an even more stunning expression of loyalty to Goldwater and his principled conservatism."[44]

Goldwater's "piece of his mind" was an emphatic defense of the Republican Party and a strongly worded admonition to those who might be so frustrated by the machinations of the convention that they would be inclined to strike out on their own. In spite of differences, he argued, "the Republican Platform deserves the support of every American over the blueprint for socialism presented by the Democrats." He had been campaigning across the country for six years for Nixon, he said, and he saw no reason to change his mind that evening. "We must remember," he admonished, "that Republicans have not been losing elections because of more Democrat voters. Now, get this. We have been losing elections because conservatives too often fail to vote." Telling conservatives to "grow up," he summed up with a call to arms: "If we want to take this Party back, and I think we can someday, let's get to work."[45]

The Arizona senator's speech was geared toward the convention as a whole, but, given the youth of many of his most fervent supporters, his references to "growing up" have special significance. Goldwater might have been a renegade within his party, but in the end he was a party man. He believed in process and organization, and while he deeply believed that the GOP must adopt a more conservative agenda, he felt this transformation should be accomplished within the party and not via outside insurgency. Speaking before the Phoenix Press Club Forum the previous winter, Goldwater had expressed his views on third party movements in no uncertain terms: "If we can have a third party, we can have a fourth, and a fifth, and a sixth. We'd wind up like France. What we need, is two good parties."[46] Through his forceful words to the convention, the Arizona senator impressed upon many of his young admirers the importance of taking over the Republican Party, of working within the political process to effect conservative change. Over the next several years, his supporters would do just this—although they would also forge external networks to ensure that they supported conservative candidates of either party. Liberal Republican youth, by contrast, failed to build such external networks. Convinced, like Rockefeller and many other party liberals, that consensus politics continued to be the wave of the future, liberals did not feel the sense of urgency shared by conservatives who viewed their mission as one of salvation for the country.

First among these networks was an organization conceived in the aftermath of the Chicago convention. Determined to preserve the fervor of the Goldwater campaign, public relations specialist Marvin Liebman and former Governor Edison organized a luncheon meeting at the Pick-Congress Hotel, where they urged Youth for Goldwater's activists to keep fighting for conservative principles and goals. With Liebman's help, Caddy put together an interim committee charged with planning a conference in the fall that would create a more permanent organization of conservative youth. This conference became the Sharon Conference, held September 10–11 at the family home of conservative hero William F. Buckley, Jr. Historian Gregory Schneider has referred to Buckley as "the young conservative more responsible than any other for bringing together and making possible the movement toward political action." Over 90 young activists met and agreed to forge an inclusive, nonpartisan organization charged with furthering the conservative cause. United behind a statement of principles that came to be known as the Sharon Statement—forged by Evans—the youths proclaimed themselves Young Americans for Freedom.[47]

The various backgrounds of conference attendees reveal patterns somewhat at odds with common perceptions of young conservatives as financially well off or as products of the burgeoning Sunbelt. Instead, almost two-thirds of participants were from the East, with the Midwest representing about two-thirds of the remainder. Part of this disparity might be due to the conference location. More interesting, though, was the fact that a majority came from lower-middle- and working-class families. Sixty-four percent of attendees' fathers had never gone to college. Catholicism was the predominant faith, although several Jews and many Protestants were also among the founders. Catholics were important contributors to the development of the post–World War II conservative movement, and for many YAFers, Catholicism and conservatism worked together in much the same manner as they did for Buckley and other *NR* staffers profiled earlier.[48] Many participants came to YAF from interest in issues such as McCarthyism or the Hungarian Uprising, or from a shared family background. Their political views did not represent a sharp break from those of their parents.[49]

These findings are in keeping with a survey of conservative students undertaken by Evans for his 1961 book. Of 122 replies from around the country, Evans found that 51 percent had family incomes of $5,000 or less annually, and a substantial number held scholarships or took jobs to help with school expenses. Of 121 replies to the question, "Do you believe your parents have influenced your political beliefs?" 78 respondents replied "yes," with only 43 saying "no." The majority of the students described their parents as Republicans and conservatives—although most also said they considered themselves more conservative than their parents. Most students connected their conservatism to parental training and attitudes toward morality, self-reliance, and patriotism.[50]

These students' rebellion against liberalism, then, was not forged upon opposition to parental values or the self-interest of the moneyed elite. Rather, the activists of organizations like Youth for Goldwater and YAF were reacting *against* the people they viewed as the elites. The government programs that liberals proposed were fundamentally at odds with conservative beliefs in independent charity and bootstrap morality, and beyond this they had the potential to inflict real harm on already-stretched budgets. As predominantly religious people, many of them Catholics, any hint of coexistence with Communists struck deep-seated fear. Because these young people were not in revolt against their elders, they benefited from their support in a way that leftist radicals of the 1960s never could. Because they viewed liberal proposals as personal attacks on their well-being, with potentially disastrous effects for the future of American society at home and abroad, they maintained deep personal commitment to their fight.

College Youth for Nixon

Meanwhile, however, an election remained to be determined. YAF decided not to endorse a candidate in the November election out of fear that such a move would establish them as an "appendage" of the Republican

Party before their work had even truly begun.[51] Most signatories to the Sharon Statement, however, headed back to their homes and campuses to work on Nixon's behalf. One of them, founding secretary Carol Dawson of Dunbarton College in Washington, D.C., even served as executive secretary of College Youth for Nixon. Others served in state-level positions, including James Abstine, state co-chair for Indiana; George Gaines, state chair for Louisiana; and Howard Phillips, state chair for Massachusetts.[52]

Despite pressure from the left and the right, the vice president had proven to be a popular candidate among many college students in polls and mock elections throughout the spring. The students of Northwestern University chose Nixon over Adlai Stevenson in a bipartisan mock convention on April 23, and additional victories were won at Republican mock conventions at the University of Wisconsin, University of Syracuse, Earlham College (Richmond, Indiana), and Lindenwood College (St. Charles, Missouri), among other campuses. Spring campus polls at Yale, the University of Iowa, the University of Washington, and the University of Virginia all selected Nixon over Republican and Democratic opponents. Goldwater was not listed as a presidential possibility in any of these polls.[53]

College Youth for Nixon first organized during the primary season, promoting the vice president in mock conventions and publicizing his views. The May edition of the College Youth for Nixon newsletter provided readers with an analysis of Nixon's views that illustrated in bewildering detail the vice president's attempts to bridge the ideological divide. "Conservatism at its best is progressive," Nixon was quoted as explaining. "The Republican party in its greatest years has been progressive, while at the same time following conservative economic policies." If he thought "'let-the-government-do-it' type" government programs would work, he would "be the most enthusiastic radical in those fields you could possibly imagine." He did not, however, and as a result he favored the "truly progressive programs of the economic conservatives."[54] Why exactly government programs did not work was omitted, as was any explanation of how conservatism and progressivism could be synonymous. Nixon's attempts to cast himself as a moderate hybrid, drawing upon the best of both liberalism and conservatism, did not convince either side of the spectrum. Goldwater took issue with avowals of "progressive conservatism" on the first page of *Conscience of a Conservative*, arguing that they implied "ordinary" conservatism was opposed to progress. "America made its greatest progress," he argued, "when Conservative principles were honored and preserved."[55] Ideological fuzziness aside, however, College Youth for Nixon garnered sufficient support to boast 240 clubs by July.[56]

Nixon supporters who were also Youth for Goldwater enthusiasts voiced frustration with some of the vice president's more moderate stands. James

Abstine, who was also chairman of the Indiana Collegiate Republicans, wrote in a memo to Mid-West Volunteers for Nixon that he worried it might be hard to mobilize students amid widespread dissatisfaction with Nixon's stands on federal aid to education, the Connally Amendment, socialized medicine, and the loyalty oath.[57] Abstine believed Nixon's positions would cause recruiting problems among both Republican and independent students. He cited an April 30 meeting of the Butler University Republican Club, a group that endorsed Goldwater for vice president and despite continued support for Nixon stressed "complete disapproval of attempts to nullify the Connally reservation and attempts to adopt federal aid to education and plans for socialized medicine."[58] A year later, Abstine was honored with an award at a mammoth YAF rally in New York's Manhattan Center.[59]

To at least some extent, Republican Party leaders seemed to understand the importance of reaching out to young people. In 1957, pollster Claude Robinson pointed out that the GOP vote among 21- to 29-year-old voters had risen dramatically in recent years, from 38 percent in 1948 to 57 percent in 1956. One of the party's primary tasks needed to be solidifying and holding this youth vote.[60] In 1959, Pennsylvania Senator Hugh Scott told the California Republican Assembly that the GOP needed to become a younger party "both in years and in outlook." Party elders had to invite young people to participate and increase their interest in party activities. A training school for future party officials and candidates would be immensely helpful. "Enthusiasm is the very breath of a successful organization," Scott exhorted, "and we must welcome with open arms the zeal which young men and women can generate. Moreover, we must not shut our ears to their suggestions or close our eyes to the picture they draw of the views of their contemporaries."[61]

Ambitious plans aside, however, College Youth for Nixon's primary activities were dominated by the more prosaic roles of telephone calls, campus polls, demonstrations—students were exhorted not to miss the opportunities the football season provided—and canvassing. John DeBruyn, a University of Oregon junior and a member of the Young Republican Federation of Oregon's Executive Committee, was typical of the organization's non-YAF leaders. DeBruyn had been involved in student government on the Eugene, Oregon, campus and was a member of the Druids, the junior men's fraternity. One of 23 students throughout the nation appointed to the steering committee of College Youth for Nixon-Lodge following the convention, DeBruyn and his colleagues were charged with offering advice to the organization's members on ways of supporting the Nixon-Lodge ticket.[62] University of Oregon students' activities on behalf of Nixon took the form of canvassing operations at local supermarkets, passing out Nixon buttons, bumper strips, and campaign literature.[63] Like many affiliate groups, College Youth

for Nixon-Lodge was targeted toward young people of all political persuasions who could be convinced to vote for the vice president.

To a great extent, these activities included Nixon volunteers of all ages
and represented the kind of large-scale footwork necessary to gather votes.
Students were viewed as particularly gifted at "carry[ing] out the light-
hearted aspects of the campaign which are so necessary to give it zest and
in which the older party faithful consider themselves too mature to participate." Former University of California at Berkeley student body president Bill Stricklin also recommended that the campaign take advantage of
a hitherto untapped source of funds: students—"early in the Fall Semester
while [they] still feel solvent from their Summer employment."[64]

Students, then, provided unique skills—but they were to be used by the
campaign, rather than actively advising in the more "mature" activities
of the Nixon-Lodge effort. Such a program differed from YAF's mission of
helping direct the future of conservative politics. While Nixon aide Stan
McCaffrey passed along Stricklin's comments to the Nixon Volunteers staff,
he also relayed an anxious memo from Carol Dawson, who was concerned
about a lack of activity among college students in California. Dawson urged
campaign director Bob Finch to personally contact Nixon leaders in the state
and insist that they give some help to college leaders. As student leader Elaine
Solomon had reminded Dawson, there were over 22,000 students at Los Angeles City College alone, and the universities of California at Berkeley and
Los Angeles each had huge enrollments. "We estimate that one third of the
students enrolled in colleges all over the country are eligible to vote for the
first time this year. We know also that Richard Nixon is popular among these
young people. We *must* register them and get them to vote."[65]

When the election results were tallied, youth voting patterns matched
those of African Americans, white ethnics, and other groups who had
inched toward the Republican Party during the Eisenhower years but fled
to Kennedy in 1960. Voters aged 21 to 29 cast 5.7 million votes for Kennedy
but only 5 million for Nixon. The party Hugh Scott accused of appearing
too elderly proved to be so once again, with Nixon majorities only among
people aged 50 or above. Nixon's total among 21- to 29-year-old voters came
in over 10 percentage points below that of Eisenhower in 1956—when the
former general was 66 years old.[66]

Unlike other constituencies, Nixon's youthful supporters do not appear
to have spent much time on recriminations and catalogues of their frustrations with campaign staff. After all, the conservatives among them, at least,
had longer-term goals in mind. College Youth for Nixon's slick organizational manual and photo-laden newsletters provided a far more cohesive
organization for students than that experienced by, for example, African

American constituents. More to the point, however, Nixon youth leaders like Carol Dawson were part of an exciting new foray into youth politics. Fall 1960 marked a loss for Nixon but an important new beginning for YAF. The Gallup poll reported that despite Nixon's poor youth showing, he did manage to win majorities among young voters in the far West and South— two areas that, despite YAF's initial representation, would prove especially important in the GOP's rightward shift over the next two decades.[67]

The Future of Republican Youth

Nixon's 1960 defeat "opened the doors of opportunity" for young conservatives eager to turn the Republican Party in a more conservative direction. Like Goldwater and other older conservatives, YAF argued that the election represented a rejection of Eisenhower's Modern Republicanism.[68] With the help of their elders, the new organization undertook a massive fund-raising campaign aided by letters sent out under the signature of ultraconservative Wisconsin businessman Herbert Kohler and former New Jersey governor Charles Edison and by the donation of a mailing list from the National Association of Manufacturers.[69] YAF also enjoyed a "cozy relationship" with *National Review*, with Frank Meyer and William Rusher establishing especially close ties to the young ideologues.[70]

By contrast, the leaders of National Students for Rockefeller faded into the background during and after the Nixon campaign. Aware of the Rockefeller campaign's flaws, Bruce Chapman attempted to keep the spirit of liberal Republicanism by announcing the development of a magazine titled *Advance* in late 1960 that was charged with remedying the lack of a "'national voice and national intellectual leadership' in the modern Republican movement." Initially, liberal Republicans like New York Senator Jacob Javits and New Jersey Senator Clifford Case were reported to be interested in the new publication, and Chapman announced his plans to distribute the magazine to representatives of nearly all college Republican clubs and a variety of elected officials.[71] By 1964, however, *Advance* had ceased publication. Chapman, who moved the magazine to Washington, D.C., following his graduation, blamed its demise on the failure of rich liberal Republicans to provide financial support. Despite widespread distribution of a letter calling for "progressive Republicans" to "'institutionalize their movement' or face political suicide," donations were not forthcoming. Publications can consolidate and develop burgeoning movements, as *National Review* demonstrates. A publication produced by experts and leaders, however, could not spontaneously generate a movement. As a result of their insufficient attention to mass organization, GOP liberals lacked the institutions and support networks a successful movement required. *Human Events* was reported as gloating in an editorial that *Advance* and its staff had been "little more than annoying thorns in the sides of conservative and moderate Republicans."[72]

Overall, Rockefeller's appeals to national purpose and a strong national defense, among other proposals, wound up sounding disconcertingly similar to Kennedy's campaign rhetoric and inaugural address. Laudatory references from Arthur Schlesinger, Jr. had become a cross to bear rather than a feather to flaunt as the famed professor joined the Kennedy administration. While Rockefeller's liberal student supporters had tried to mobilize behind their candidate, the Rockefeller parent organization displayed the tactical ineptitude, indiscipline, and lack of foresight Nicol C. Rae described as typical of liberal Republican efforts during the declines of the 1960s and 1970s.[73] The example of *Advance* suggests that other GOP liberals were hardly better organized.

At Harvard, Howard Phillips, an active participant in both College Youth for Nixon and YAF, superseded Chapman and Mark Adams. Phillips, a native of Brighton, Massachusetts, became the first sophomore to be elected president of the Harvard Student Council in early 1960. Far from a fluke, Phillips "commanded the support of virtually all the members of last year's Council" and drew accolades for his dynamic leadership and creative thinking abilities.[74] That Phillips' popularity was not based upon his political predilections became apparent in 1961, when he was reelected to the presidency and *Time* magazine promptly cited the council's decision as an indication of a "sharp turn to the right" on college campuses. The Harvard Student Council sent a letter to *Time* arguing that the young conservative had been chosen on the basis of his "personal qualities and abilities," not because of his political philosophy.[75] Later in the spring, a squabble emerged between liberal and conservative factions of the Harvard Young Republican Club, as club president Tom Alberg was charged with omitting Phillips, a leading candidate for chairman of the Massachusetts State Young Republicans, from a slate of delegates to the state convention. Phillips, though in the minority among Harvard Young Republicans, accused Alberg's "ABC" coalition—the "C," interestingly, standing for one Bruce Chapman—of waging the "most ruthless, vicious campaign I have ever seen." By May, Alberg and Phillips had emerged as two leading contenders for the national college Young Republican chairmanship. Meanwhile, Phillips had been the subject of a resolution of "strong disapproval" by members of the student council, who objected to the president's use of his name and council office on the letterhead of the Committee for an Effective Peace Corps, "a group with extreme political leanings."[76]

In the end, Phillips' tenure as student council president was, in the words of the *Harvard Crimson*, "abruptly terminated by an academic probation notice" at the conclusion of the spring 1961 term. Phillips also lost his bid for the national college Young Republican chairmanship, although he managed to thwart Alberg's attempt by throwing his support behind a conservative Midwesterner. The events of Phillips' controversial spring and summer, though, demonstrated the depth of support young conservatives like the former council president enjoyed from their older patrons. Rather than dismiss Phillips' collegiate struggles as parochial, William F. Buckley, Jr. called attention to them in the pages of *National Review*, defending the student against charges that he had misused the prestige of his office in such episodes as the letterhead incident. "To begin with," Buckley pointed out, "no one in his right mind would believe the Harvard student body is conservative." If Harvard students were truly concerned about misrepresentation, they should examine some of the generalities coming out of fund-raising operations like the Harvard Development Council. Moreover, the idea of Harvard sending a letter to *Time* denying its conservatism was reminiscent of the Chamber of Commerce of Italy, Texas, wiring the League of Nations in 1935 to state that it should be absolutely clear that it was not Italy, Texas, that was invading Ethiopia.[77] Buckley's argument bore a great deal of truth, but there was also something rather disingenuous about bringing Phillips' trials into the pages of *NR*. The act of disavowing any indications of widespread Harvard conservatism, after all, also enabled the *NR* editor to publicly broadcast the conservative inclinations of at least one very prominent member of the Harvard community. From this seed, perhaps more conservatives might find solace—and the movement might grow.

Moving to the Right

Nineteen-sixty, then, marked a turning point for Republican youth as it did in so many other arenas. Conservative activists entered 1961 with a vibrant new organization and a raft of plans for the future. Liberals, on the other hand, were left bereft of a leader or a direction to take them through the next decade. While some liberal youth would organize once again for Rockefeller in 1964, his erratic performance proved as frustrating four years later as it did in 1960. Other liberals found themselves either in the shadows of the media-savvy governor or failed to respond to their supporters' overtures sufficiently quickly to hold off the Goldwater tide. Henry Cabot Lodge, for example, became the target of a draft attempt in early 1964 but was out of the country at the time, serving as ambassador to Vietnam. He won the New Hampshire primary as a write-in candidate but refused to leave his diplomatic post and run for the nomination, although he later regretted his failure to try and forestall what he viewed as an extremist takeover of his party. By the summer of 1964, Lodge was home, having resigned as ambassador due to his wife's ill health. Frustrated by the laissez-faire economic policies of the Republican Platform Committee's majority, he appeared before the committee with Milton Eisenhower and George Romney to plea for a "Republican-sponsored Marshall Plan for our cities and schools." Lodge received standing ovations from thirty members, but the other seventy responded with complete silence to the man who had chaired the same committee sixteen years prior. Lodge was later heard to exclaim, "What in God's name has happened to the Republican Party! I hardly know any of these people!"[78]

Conservatives, on the other hand, enjoyed the excitement of youthful rebellion while maintaining financial, organizational, and ideological ties to their elders that made their political future brighter than that of other 1960s rebels. As Robert Claus, president of Wisconsin's Conservative Club, put it in the early 1960s, "You walk around with your Goldwater button, and you feel the thrill of treason."[79] Young conservatives' 'treason' was not against their elders but against the liberal establishment. As a result, they were able to serve as shock troops for a multigenerational movement, fundamentally changing the nature of American politics over the next two decades.

"Dixie Is No Longer in the Bag"

South Carolina Republicans in 1960

> "Oh Dixie is no longer in the bag
>
> Oh Dixie is no longer in the bag
>
> It's a hundred odds to ten
>
> That the South will rise again
>
> For Dixie is no longer in the bag."
>
> —"Here Comes Nixon," 1960[1]

In 1961, Barry Goldwater took the stage in the solid South stronghold of Atlanta, Georgia, and made a prototypically bold statement. "We're not going to get the Negro vote as a bloc in 1964 and 1968," he told his Republican colleagues, "so we ought to go hunting where the ducks are."[2] Scholars Jack Bass and Walter DeVries trace the development of the "southern strategy" generally associated with Richard Nixon's 1968 election back to this statement, arguing that it marked the beginning of a conscious outreach to the white southern electorate on the part of the Republican Party.

Goldwater's unabashed declaration of racial priorities certainly fed the white backlash movement that would contribute to his victory in five southern states in 1964. Focusing only upon race, however, obscures longer and more significant trends in postwar southern politics. As early as the 1950s, the Republican Party began to undertake efforts to gain support in the states of the solid South, and by 1960, a native party organization was beginning to develop. Race mattered to these nascent Republicans, but the complete story of GOP development in the South is far more complex.[3]

As early as the 1920s, economic conditions and concerns about what pundits have since termed "social issues" challenged the integrity of the Democratic solid South. In the wake of plummeting cotton prices and Republican candidate Warren Harding's declaration that he was "highly sympathetic to Southern problems," the GOP carried Tennessee in 1920 and gained 40 percent of the vote in Arkansas, Georgia, Kentucky, and North Carolina.[4] Protestant dissatisfaction with the Democrats' selection of Catholic New York Governor Al Smith in 1928 also brought Southern- ers into the GOP fold, although as political strategist and author Kevin Phillips has pointed out, large-scale defections were limited primarily to the outer South and were attributable in part to economic concerns.[5] The 1944 election marked the last year that Democrats received over 70 percent of the regional vote for president. Even before World War II, conservative southern Democrats had begun to form a voting bloc with conservative Republicans in Congress, with several signing a bipartisan "Conservative Manifesto" in 1937.[6] Postwar, the relatively liberal civil rights planks in the Democratic platform of 1948 spawned the well-known backlash of the Dixiecrat movement.

With the sudden and massive growth of the urban South during and after World War II, city-dwelling Southerners gradually began to identify their economic interests as resting with the Republican Party.[7] Depending on the civil rights climate and which candidate was deemed more accept- able to segregationists, black belt counties were also developing a tendency to vote Republican.[8] By 1952, the immensely popular Dwight Eisenhower was able to carry four southern states, and even after the Eisenhower ad- ministration's racial policies—and especially *Brown v. Board of Education*— had soured some voters on the Republican, Adlai Stevenson actually lost ground, with seven states going for Ike.[9] Some scholars argue that the great- est gains for Eisenhower between 1952 and 1956 came from African Ameri- can wards where the administration's enforcement policies on racial issues won favor.[10] Given the persistent disenfranchisement experienced by many black Southerners, however, Eisenhower had to have retained significant white support. A 1960 study of Republicanism in the urban South indicates that, with a few exceptions, white support held steady and in some cases even increased.[11] Despite the continuing myopia of contemporary intel- lectuals like historian Clinton Rossiter, who stated in 1960 that "the South, which becomes more of a minority every year in terms of both interests and numbers, wants to remain Democratic," a transformation of southern politics was underway.[12]

The history of South Carolina is almost a caricature of all that has com- posed southern political style. As the home of John C. Calhoun and the first state to secede from the Union, its states' rights credentials are unimpeachable, and its first city, Charleston, has long been the paragon of southern gentility and culture. Add in the populist tendencies of "Pitchfork" Ben Tillman and the racial hysteria of "Cotton Ed" Smith, among others, and all the major ingredients of the South's political history are in place. By the 1950s, it was also, as Godfrey Hodgson has explained, "perhaps the most conservative state in the South."[13]

Despite the state's long history of Democratic loyalty, then, its politicians and voters were at the forefront of the wave of southern frustration with the New Deal Democratic Party. Local candidates could appeal to their racially, economically, and culturally conservative constituents under the banner of the state Democratic Party, but such a strategy was of course impossible on the national level. As early as 1952, Eisenhower was only 10,000 votes short of an overall win in the state, with all but about 10,000 of the 168,018 South Carolinians who voted for the ex-general doing so under the banner of "South Carolinians for Eisenhower" rather than on the Republican ticket. In 1956, the state bore witness to some of the frustration mentioned above over Ike's civil rights policies, and the 54.6 percent of voters dissatisfied with Democratic candidate Adlai Stevenson split their votes fairly evenly between the Republican ticket and independent electors pledged to segregationist Virginia senator Harry Byrd.[14] By 1960, contemporary commentators like Samuel DuBois Cook could declare that the state constituted "perhaps the best example of the growth of Southern Republicanism in presidential elections." While Nixon lost South Carolina, he did so by fewer than 10,000 votes, with all his supporters voting a Republican ticket—and as recently as 1948, the Republican candidate had secured less than 4 percent of the South Carolina vote.[15] South Carolina urbanites would prove the most enthusiastic Nixon supporters in the entire old Confederacy, with a whopping 63.2 percent of city residents voting Republican.[16]

Cook's initial opinion of South Carolina Republicanism proved durable. Scholars including Earl and Merle Black have described South Carolina as the most notable developing stronghold of Republicanism in the Deep South between 1952 and 1964.[17] What remains to be studied, however, is how this process took place. The South Carolina Republican Party circa 1960 serves as a window into both the process of southern realignment and the manner in which a political group with certain defined interests works to gain recognition and influence in a presidential selection process. The South Carolinians were not successful in their initial goal of gaining the 1960 GOP nomination for Barry Goldwater, but they did demonstrate their growing strength and significance—and Richard Nixon and the Republican Party clearly received their message.

Race was a factor in 1960, but issues ranging from labor to the conduct of the Cold War mobilized South Carolinians as well. The rise of Republicanism in South Carolina was not a one-dimensional process. Rather, South Carolina Republicanism reflects the development of a brand of conservatism unique to the South but tightly connected to the conservatism growing in the country as a whole during this period. Racial conservatism played a larger role in the South than in other regions, acting as a catalyst for movement into the Republican Party; however, economic concerns, in particular, also played a significant role. In 1960 especially, migrants and business leaders were dominant in the party's state leadership, illuminating the various strains present in South Carolina's conservative culture. The growth of southern Republicanism has in turn affected the development of national Republican Party rhetoric on issues ranging from civil rights to the role of organized labor. The 1960 election offers a means of exploring this story without some of the more obscuring effects of the racial backlash in 1964.

Going for Goldwater

While white Republicanism in twentieth-century South Carolina began slightly earlier, as described above, the story of 1960 begins in 1959, with a different speech by Barry Goldwater. The Arizona iconoclast had been elected to the Senate for the first time in 1952, breaking into the political structure of his solidly Democratic state. The GOP, realizing his potential as a mobilizer of the party's conservative base, had selected him to chair the Republican Senatorial Campaign Committee as early as 1955. Goldwater distinguished himself quickly in the Senate as a labor foe and military advocate, highly desirable traits in a region dripping with military bases and anti-union sentiment. Accordingly, the young senator caught the eye of a young Republican transplant to the Palmetto State.

Gregory D. Shorey, Jr. was born in Arlington, Massachusetts. He was a graduate of Boston University, where he attended law school and earned the first graduate degree awarded in the field of public relations and marketing communications—an auspicious beginning for a future party functionary. He first became active in the Republican Party as a teenager, working on behalf of his father's candidacy for town meeting member. After a stint in the Navy during World War II, he devoted much of his time while in law school to working on behalf of Republican candidates. These early connections would reemerge later in life, as many of the young activists he worked with in the 1940s became active in the Goldwater for President movement. Following graduation, however, Shorey headed south to take advantage of an opportunity to purchase the assets of and retool a firm that had produced surgical dressings during World War II. By 1952 he had become a prominent figure in South Carolina GOP politics, serving as state chairman of Eisenhower for President in 1952 and 1956; Republican elector in 1952 and 1956; state executive chairman from 1954 to 1956; and state chairman from 1956 to 1962.[18]

As a southern transplant, Shorey demonstrates one of the trends that contributed to the development of the two-party South. While significant support for the GOP came from native Southerners who came to identify economically—or, in backlash years, racially—with the Republican Party, another important source of early leadership came from Northerners flocking toward newly vibrant southern industry during and after World War II.[19] Young soldiers also brought home wives from around the country, further diversifying the southern population.[20] The growth of the Sunbelt was underway. As a businessman, Shorey further exemplifies the kind of individual active in the early development of the South Carolina GOP. Other early Republicans, such as textile magnate Roger Milliken and grocery store heir J. Drake Edens, were also business leaders concerned about labor costs and promotion of a favorable regulatory environment for investors in their industrializing region. These individuals hailed predominantly from inland manufacturing centers like Greenville, Orangeburg, and Spartanburg rather than the "old South" low country region surrounding Charleston. All but two of thirteen delegates to the 1960 convention hailed from upstate, and all seven Republican Party state officers in 1960 were from the interior midlands or piedmont.[21]

Republican Party activity in South Carolina during the 1950s was an uphill process against a variety of entrenched interests. Most notably, Republicans like Shorey struggled against the Democratic hegemony of their state, sending out press releases that newspapers were unlikely to run and appearing before civic organizations at which Shorey recalled that he was "always a speaker oddity." In addition, the party faced internal struggles as new, young leaders attempted to take the reins from longtime officials who were primarily concerned with patronage appointments. Shorey and his compatriots worked to persuade local candidates to run for local offices in an attempt to forestall charges of "carpetbagging" and promoted the theme that the South needed a two-party system that would be more responsive—and responsible—to South Carolinians' needs. Even New Deal programs had failed to bring the South out of widespread poverty, they proclaimed, and in the process the New Deal system challenged the autonomy that southern states held so dear.[22]

By 1959, Shorey was focused on the next presidential election year, and while victory mattered to him, he did not feel that ideological compromise was the way to achieve it. In March 1959, for example, Citizens for Rockefeller Committee Chairman George Wahr Ballade wrote to Shorey, touting liberal New York governor Nelson Rockefeller as Republicans' best choice. Shorey's response was polite but straightforward—and opposed:

> I personally cannot endorse your sentiments with reference to the need for a more liberal approach nor a candidate that subscribes to these factors or ideals. To the contrary, it is my strong conviction that a strong, unrelenting conservative is the only answer to the future of our Party. We must distinguish ourselves from our Democrat socialists [sic] opposition and unless we do so, we will never consolidate the conservative interest of our Country against the onrush of socialism that is rapidly overtaking us.[23]

While he refrained in this letter from specific reference to his preferred alternative, Goldwater captivated the young manufacturer. In fall 1959 Shorey "borrowed" the Arizona senator from the South Carolina Banker's Convention, which was being held in Greenville. With the assistance of Republican National Committeewoman Pat Barnes, textile executive Roger Milliken, and a statewide radio broadcast organized by local civic leader Jesse Helms, he introduced Goldwater to a Republican Party fund-raising dinner as his choice for the 1960 nomination.[24]

The Arizona senator must have made a good impression on South Carolina Republicans during his first visit, as he was invited to return and speak at the Republican State Convention in March 1960. Meanwhile, Goldwater's paradigmatic *Conscience of a Conservative* had been published to glowing reviews in South Carolina newspapers. With the publication of *Conscience*, Goldwater's name and stature as the party's leading conservative became known far beyond the circles of attentive politicos like Shorey. William D. Workman, Jr., a prominent political reporter and columnist for the Charleston *News and Courier*, referred to the book and its author as "one of the most encouraging books—and one of the most forthright citizens—to appear on the national scene in many a year."[25]

While pre-convention press releases indicated merely that Shorey had secured Goldwater as the keynote speaker, *News and Courier* editor T.R. Waring confided to Workman on March 21 that he had been confidentially advised of the party's plans to nominate Goldwater for president. Even some prominent state Republicans were unaware of this move, Waring noted, explaining that state GOP financier Milliken had told him the move was "designed to call attention of GOP bigwigs and Nixon personally to conservative sentiment in these parts."[26] Here, then, the state party's intention of putting pressure on the national organization is clear. South Carolinians, unhappy with the idea of a Modern Republican approach to party politics, were signaling their discontent—and, perhaps, looking to start a movement.

Sure enough, after listening to their conservative hero speak on March 26 in Columbia, the delegates to the Republican State Convention nominated Goldwater for president by acclamation. The Arizona senator's speech demonstrates the many reasons why South Carolinians found him so appealing. Goldwater denounced the Democratic Party for leading the country down "the road to socialism," arguing that—as a result of "radical" government—individual initiative was destroyed, and "the lazy become parasites of the workers."[27] Read through a contemporary lens, Goldwater's language appears coded in the same manner that Ronald Reagan spoke of "welfare queens" in the 1980s. Significantly, however, America had not yet experienced the Great Society years that mobilized so many members of the white working and middle classes into believing that their tax dollars were going to fund programs geared toward ungrateful African Americans in the smoldering inner cities. Rather, Goldwater's prominence—and South Carolina's interest—was in opposing what both viewed as abuses of labor power. In 1957 and 1958, Goldwater had ridden to prominence on the Senate Rackets Committee, investigating corruption in organized labor. He had stood alone in April 1959 in opposition to the Kennedy–Ervin labor bill. While Eisenhower had long been involved in the issue of labor reform, public legend and Goldwater's own account described his one-man stand as a wake-up call to the president, who vetoed the limited piece of legislation. The administration called upon members of the House to sponsor a stronger, substitute bill, and in September 1959 both houses passed the Landrum–Griffin Act, a much stronger piece of legislation that cracked down on labor corruption, coercive picketing practices, and abuses of trust and power.[28] South Carolina Republicans, who "view[ed] with alarm the increasing control exercised by big labor barons and their criminal cohorts," were strong advocates of right-to-work laws and opposed industry-wide collective bargaining—and Goldwater was their most prominent ally in the Senate.[29]

Moving on to other issues, the Arizona senator urged Republicans to adopt a platform that was not merely a "dime store New Deal" and concluded that Eisenhower's attempts to organize a summit meeting with Khrushchev could do "nothing but negotiate" away "freedom." Finally, Goldwater demonstrated his appeal to racial conservatives. While the senator said he agreed with the intentions of civil rights advocates, he denounced "ideology"-based Supreme Court rulings and attacked liberals who would, in the words of the Columbia *State*, "wreck the constitution in order to enforce civil rights."[30] Here, of course, his professed fidelity to the Constitution neatly complemented many white Southerners' desires to maintain their segregated societal system.

Inspired by Goldwater's fervor, the South Carolina Republicans adopted a conservative platform that the Charleston *News and Courier* described as reading "like the party platform of the old national Democratic party before it was corrupted by the Dealers with their socialist doctrines."[31] The convention secretary was instructed to communicate South Carolina's decision to support Goldwater to leaders of state parties who had yet to meet and suggest they take a similar course. W.W. "Duck" Wannamaker, who was elected as national committeeman at the convention, was revealing in his comments following Goldwater's address. "You are not only a great American, sir," Wannamaker said, "but you could pass for a great Southerner any time, any place, and, best of all, to us you sound like a South Carolinian of whom we can all be proud."[32] Indeed, political writer Michael Lottman argued in 1970 that without this convention "love-in," South Carolina Republicanism might never have gotten off the ground. As it was, Goldwater himself later alluded to the significance of this early support in persuading him to seek the presidency in 1964.[33]

Proselytizing to the Masses

Shorey did not limit his Goldwater activism to the state level. In addition to his South Carolina Republican Party responsibilities, he took on the role of national co-chairman of the Goldwater for President Committee. Shorey's quest for his chosen leader took on dual qualities of optimistic idealism and realistic practicality. A June 24 fund-raising letter signed by Shorey and co-chair Aubrey Barker of Arizona expressed their confidence that Goldwater would provide "brilliant, courageous and principled leadership," but they also recognized that "as political realists . . . the chances of his nomination appear to be slim." Nonetheless, they argued that if even 50 delegates cast votes for Goldwater, "the cause of principled Republicanism would be immensely enhanced." Shorey and Barker were devoted, but they were not dogmatic—or party-suicidal. After informing recipients that a copy of *Conscience* was headed their way and asking them to write back and indicate their views regarding the nomination, they closed their letter by stating that they desired harmony and party unity and would support Nixon if he were nominated.[34]

A Workman column published before the national convention provides further evidence of Shorey's approach. Shorey was aware, Workman wrote, of the difficulty of securing the first-place spot for his man, but he felt the vice presidency was within reach—and would be immensely helpful for the GOP. With Goldwater on the ticket, Shorey argued, Republicans would carry every state in the South. Shorey's desire was to weld the southern states into a "formidable voting bloc within the Republican National Convention . . . thereby influencing the course of the party." Workman quoted Shorey as proclaiming that "The shadow of [the late U.S. Senator] Bob Taft will rise up and prevail."[35]

Shorey's allusion to the Ohio senator christened "Mr. Republican" by his supporters was an interesting choice. On one level, the idea of Taft as a role model made good sense. Taft, often cited as the last of the isolationist, economically conservative "Old Guard" Republicans who characterized the party pre–World War II, cooperated with conservative southern Democrats on a variety of legislative fronts as early as the late 1930s and especially during the war. He favored a strict interpretation of the Constitution and limited government. All of these factors made him a favorable figure for southern conservatives. On the other hand, Taft favored abolition of the poll tax, supported federal bills against lynching, and possessed a "singular lack of interest in abstract thought," laughing when interviewers asked if he had read books by conservative philosophers.[36] As such, he was hardly on the same page as Southerners worried about federal civil rights legislation or the burgeoning, ideologically rigorous conservative movement that was beginning to take hold among some right-wing Republicans.

The tendency of South Carolina Goldwaterites to view Taft as their role model might reflect the economy-focused conservatism of state party leaders like Shorey. It might also reflect conservatives' growing tendency to perceive of "strict constitutionalism," whatever the historical reality, as the antithesis of the "judicial activism" that had produced such rulings as *Brown v. Board of Education.* In any event, Taft was their man, and Modern Republicans like Nelson Rockefeller were their foes. The distinction came to a head just before the national convention, when Nixon made a trip to the New York governor's Fifth Avenue apartment to iron out differences between their opinions and develop mutually satisfactory recommendations for the party platform. As Rockefeller had been dropping in and out of the race, and generally irritating the party rank and file since 1959, Nixon's attempt to conciliate him was meant to smooth over intraparty tensions. Unfortunately, in the vice president's attempt to smooth over some differences, others came angrily clashing into the open. The "Compact of Fifth Avenue" made its way onto the AP wire on the morning of July 23. Rather than release his Arizona and South Carolina votes to Nixon, as had been planned, Goldwater used an already scheduled press conference to castigate Nixon for his "sell-out on nearly every point that once separated the Vice President and the Governor." Referring to the fourteen-point agreement reached by Nixon and Rockefeller as "immoral politics," Goldwater argued that if Republicans alienated their conservative supporters, the liberals who were attempting to "take over" the party would inherit "a mess of pottage."[37]

In a meeting at the Conrad Hilton Hotel, Nixon aide Charles McWhorter struggled to convince Goldwater supporters that the agreement was not meant to sidetrack their efforts. The senator and his supporters, however, continued to believe that Rockefeller was up to no good, and Nixon had been placed in a compromising situation.[38] Shorey, sensing a shift toward Goldwater, predicted that the senator would receive as many as 120 first-ballot presidential votes from states including Nevada, Virginia, Nebraska, Mississippi, North Carolina, and Louisiana.[39] "Thanks to the attempt by Governor Rockefeller to impose his will in a dictatorial fashion upon this convention," Shorey told reporters, "and to Vice-President Nixon's apparent acquiescence in the governor's demands, the sentiment of the convention has suddenly become restive, dissatisfied and flexible."[40]

While several points in the "Compact" were controversial, it was point nine, which called for "aggressive action" to eliminate segregation and discrimination and a statement of support for the objectives of sit-in demonstrators, that infuriated southern delegates.[41] South Carolinians had been hard at work to secure an acceptable civil rights platform plank, and as late as July 21, Wannamaker had written to Workman that the delegation had hopes of an acceptable platform.[42] Even in the midst of the furor aroused by the announcement of the "Compact," Wannamaker retained some optimism. "The Platform situation may not be as bad as it appears," he wrote to Workman. "As is human nature people don't like to be told what to do and resentment helps us." Roger Milliken and Pat Barnes were doing great work on the Platform Committee, he wrote, and "Greg is doing an impressive job of coordinating the diverse Goldwater groups."[43] In addition to their behind-the-scenes work, South Carolinians played a role in the theater of the debate, with Barnes gaining the floor to defend Texan John Tower's minority report on civil rights. As historian Rick Perlstein records, Barnes proceeded to read a "stirring defense of the go-slow approach to Negro rights." Liberals protested that "Nixon could never agree with that"— at which point Barnes revealed that the book from which she read was Nixon's *The Challenges We Face*.[44]

Meanwhile, however, Nixon stood firm on his civil rights position, dropping all other engagements on the Monday before the convention to work for the strong plank's passage.[45] In the end, the vice president was able to negotiate a compromise with all sides whereby an original, non-Rockefeller foreign policy plank was approved, but an only slightly modified Nixon/Rockefeller position on civil rights passed with a majority. Cognizant of his lack of support, Goldwater told his Arizona delegation that he did not wish his name to be placed in nomination. The South Carolinians, however, had different ideas. Milliken argued that his state had sent its delegates to vote for Goldwater, and that was what they intended to do. Shorey continued to believe that Goldwater could garner significant, if distinctly minority, support on the first ballot. "You can't put him in a region. He's so grassroots," he said, using language that anticipated the future character of pro-Goldwater activism.[46] Retreating to consider the situation, Goldwater decided, as described in chapter 4, to have his name placed in nomination, have the standard seconding speeches given, and then deliver a speech of withdrawal, attempting to redirect the enthusiasm of his erstwhile supporters in the process.

Having received their senatorial lecture, the South Carolinians would acquiesce. Before Goldwater took his turn at the podium, however, Shorey was able to make a seconding speech for his nomination. Shorey's speech illustrates a few of the reasons he and the South Carolina GOP found Goldwater so compelling. First, Shorey opened his speech with the declaration: "This man is all man." Coming from a region with a tradition that privileged strident masculinity, Goldwater's he-man persona was important. Second, Shorey heralded Goldwater's credentials as a "proven political giant killer. He took on the best the Democrats had to offer in his home state of Arizona," Shorey said, "and cracked wide open a traditionally solid Democratic state, that has since elected many distinguished Republicans." For Shorey and others struggling to establish a two-party system in South Carolina, Goldwater's example was profoundly encouraging. Finally, Shorey argued,

> No other man in our time has so vigorously defended our Constitution, individual liberties, sovereignty of states and free enterprise system. He is for the little man and against domination by anything big—government, business or labor.[47]

Here were the familiar political positions for which the South Carolina Republican Party—and, in truth, many South Carolina Democrats—stood. Certainly "sovereignty of states" was an appeal for states' rights, but Shorey's emphasis on business and labor demonstrates South Carolina Republicans' concern with smoothing the path for development in their region.

Moving On to Nixon

The senator, however, had made his proclamation, and South Carolina Republicans complied with his request, shifting their energies toward electing Richard Nixon. The ease with which the state GOP made this transition testifies to both Goldwater's persuasive power and the party's multifaceted political allegiance. Goldwater's continuing appeal was evident, as local Republican clubs organized "Goldwater Speaks" luncheons and advertised that since Goldwater supported Nixon, South Carolinians should also.[48] The Arizona senator doggedly campaigned for the Nixon-Lodge ticket, and, in a nod to his popularity with southern audiences, the campaign sent him on a number of speaking tours through the region. Barnstorming through South Carolina cities including Columbia, Dillon, and Orangeburg, Goldwater declared: "Before the convention, you work to get your philosophy to prevail. Afterwards you work together. After all, Nixon and I agree far more than we disagree."[49] Columnist Holmes Alexander, on the road with Goldwater, observed that "Coattails are a-flyin' again in Dixie," but the coattails were "not the familiar Republican towlines of Dwight Eisenhower. This time they belong to Sen. Barry Goldwater, the new champion of conservatism."[50]

Despite Goldwater's high-flying coattails, though, the trend toward Republicanism beginning with independent support for Eisenhower in 1952 was not based upon personality alone. Even without the attraction of a candidate like Goldwater, growing numbers of South Carolinians were joining with the GOP. The recollections of individuals who began their partisan activity in 1960 help draw out the issues that party members felt were important. J. Drake Edens, briefly introduced above, was a grocery store chain heir and businessman who attended his first precinct meeting in 1960. In a 1974 oral history interview, he noted that he had supported Republican causes and candidates since his high school years, when he watched his father struggle under the onus of New Deal programs that required additional shifts for supermarket workers and changes in labor regulations. While his wife was the more active of the two during the 1960 campaign, his experiences further politicized Edens, and, by 1963, he had taken over from Shorey as chairman of the state party. He went on to serve as the vice chairman of the Republican National Committee from 1965 to 1972. Recalling his reasons for becoming active, he explained, "I was one southern Republican that you can personally attest to the fact that race has never been an issue with me." He was fiscally conservative and believed in strong national defense policies. "Primarily," he concluded, "I was motivated to get active and try to do something about it because I thought the Democrats were going to break the country."[51] Edens' comments demonstrate that many conservatives, even in the South, felt that the Democrats were likely to "break" the country through means other than civil rights measures. Federal spending, labor issues, and national defense concerns were all significant reasons for Republican identification, just as they were for thousands of conservatives elsewhere in the United States.

The Democratic Party's long-standing habit of viewing the South as a lock also contributed to Republicans' growing success in mobilizing Southerners. Roy Turner, who moved to South Carolina from Alabama in 1961, noted that he was impressed by Nixon's statement that "he was not taking any state or region for granted nor 'writing-off' any state or region." In return, Turner made Nixon his first Republican vote.[52]

Diverse motivations aside, race was an important issue in 1960. The paramount importance of economic, foreign policy, and good-government concerns to people like Shorey and Edens does not mean that all new Republicans shared their higher ideals. While Goldwater's appeal was multifaceted, some constituents doubtless recalled their hero's assistance during South Carolina senator Strom Thurmond's 1957 civil rights filibuster.[53] The inclusion of states' rights rhetoric in speeches like Shorey's before the national convention demonstrates GOP aptitude in using the South's traditional, coded language. Workman, the sympathetic journalist, published a 1960 book titled *The Case for the South* that railed against the NAACP, the Supreme Court, and "Northern politicians and propagandists" who were often, he implied, Jewish.[54] He did castigate the Ku Klux Klan but on the grounds of crudity in contrast to "responsible" groups such as White Citizens' Councils.[55] While the South clearly represented a special case, the reaction to Workman's book from around the nation demonstrates the degree to which many Americans from all backgrounds continued to hold racist sentiments. Workman preserved a number of letters that he received from readers, with many words of congratulation coming from citizens of nonsouthern states including Ohio, New York, and Michigan.[56]

As of the book's writing, Workman continued to believe that the only options open to Southerners were to take back the Democratic Party or establish a third party. Scourging Nixon for referring to Earl Warren as a "great Republican chief justice," he bitterly explained that despite growing Democratic hostility, Southerners still "find little incentive to align themselves with a Republican Party which now stands naked and unashamed as the suitor of every Negro and minority bloc vote which is available for love or money."[57] Just two years later, however, Workman ran for the U.S. Senate as a Republican. Something had changed, and it seems safe to say that one key factor was the manner in which Nixon reached out to Southerners during the 1960 campaign.

Shorey maintains that while some might have viewed the party as a "safety net" for those with racist beliefs, legitimate states' rights concerns were wrongfully translated into the "integration issue." However, the doctrine of states' rights in the United States, and especially in the South, has never been separate from issues of race. Even if individuals like Shorey considered states' rights in the more prosaic administrative terms of decentralized government—an entirely legitimate issue, and one long part of the conservative canon—the term continued to serve as code for federal acquiescence in state-level segregation. Shorey acknowledges that integration was "no doubt a factor" for some South Carolinians but maintains that distrust of ever-growing government involvement in all facets of life and the desire for a more responsive two-party system were the larger motivating factors.[58] On balance, the South Carolina Republicans' 1960 platform supports this contention. The platform stated, "We vigorously oppose all attempts to arouse class and race strife for political purposes and firmly believe that such matters can best be handled on a local or sectional basis." The document's primary emphasis, however, was upon smaller government and strident opposition to Communism.[59] The expressed concerns of the platform demonstrate that South Carolina Republicans' goals for the future of their party were far broader than a simple backlash against civil rights. In the subsequent campaign, unfortunately, rhetoric sometimes gave way to racial realities as the GOP strove to mobilize support.

With conservative sentiment mobilizing behind Nixon, the South Carolina Republican Party was faced with two major issues. First, it needed to determine a direction for Republicanism in the state. Second, it needed to continue to assert its importance to the national party and its will upon that party's future. The first issue came to a head at a reconvened session of the state's annual convention, held August 6. National committeeman Wannamaker pointed out that while the GOP in South Carolina was now representative and respectable it was still very much a minority party. Republican Party membership figures in the state were then, as now, difficult to come by because the state of South Carolina does not register voters by party. As of their March convention, 24 of South Carolina's 46 counties had Republican organizations, but nowhere was the party sufficiently developed to contest local elections.[60] To gain viable candidates for Congress, they would need to either "raise them up from pups" or break into the Democratic Party and convert some of its established candidates to Republicanism. Either option, it seemed to Wannamaker, would take a considerable length of time, and as a stopgap alternative he proposed nominating the candidates who had already won the Democratic nomination in their respective districts. In this way, he argued, these representatives could make a claim to represent either party, and perhaps in a closely divided House they might choose to organize with the Republicans. Meanwhile, the measure might improve the position of the GOP in terms of vote percentage and would act as an intermediate step toward turning representatives and voters into Republicans.

Wannamaker's proposal proved highly controversial, with opponents labeling it "me-tooism," and when put to a vote the idea failed.[61] Despite its failure, however, the plan demonstrates South Carolinians' intent to expand beyond "presidential Republicanism" to foster a viable party structure at all levels of government. The delegates' decision meant that despite a few prominent exceptions, Republican Party development would be an organic, bottom-up affair.

In his acceptance speech at the Chicago convention, Nixon declared his intention to "personally . . . carry this campaign into every one of the fifty states of this Nation between now and November the eighth." This declaration marked a significant departure from past party practice. The legacy of the one-party South had, prior to 1960, led the GOP to refrain from active campaigning in most of the former Confederacy under the assumption that such trips would be wasted time. The next paragraph of Nixon's speech, however, indicated that he felt this situation had changed. "I say that just as in 1952 and in 1956 millions of Democrats will join us," he said, latching onto Eisenhower's bipartisan victories, "not just because they are deserting their party, but because their party deserted them at Los Angeles two weeks ago."[62] Nixon was wagering that not only would southern Democrats go for a wildly popular, comparatively nonpartisan army general, but they would consider bolting from a party that had deserted them on such issues as civil rights for a Republican whose identity was far more linked to his party structure.

In addition, Nixon's selection of United Nations ambassador Henry Cabot Lodge served at least initially as a confidence-booster for South Carolinians. Nixon had considered a less conservative running mate, Shorey told the *News and Courier*, but, "Through our efforts the strong conservative attitude of this delegation was expressed." Lodge's record of standing up to the Soviets in the United Nations, he stated, had given him a welcome reputation of "fortitude and competency in a field that is vital to every person in the United States."[63] The *News and Courier* lauded the vice president for his stand against wasteful spending and his emphasis on victory over world Communism, and while its editors hesitated to select a preferred candidate just yet, they concluded that Republicans "have a shrewd, tough leader."[64]

South Carolina Republicans latched onto Nixon's fifty-state pledge, using it both to bolster support for the GOP in their own state and to place pressure on the national party. Nixon had signaled that the South was important to him; in return, South Carolinians expected Nixon to cater to their needs. On September 1, for example, Shorey wrote to Republican National Committee Chairman Thruston Morton, advising Nixon to confine his remarks on civil rights to the statements made in the Republican platform. If the nominee could avoid reference to the sit-in demonstrations underway throughout the South, Shorey advised that it would be prudent for him to do so.[65] Nixon limited his comments on sit-in demonstrations to two question-and-answer sessions, one during a visit to Greenville, N.C., on August 17—prior to Shorey's letter—and one during his national telethon the evening before the election. He expressed support for the objective of the sit-in demonstrations on both occasions, but when he came to the question of protesters' methods, his comments dissolved into a convoluted discussion of legal questions and preference for negotiations between the attorney general and business owners to promote voluntary changes in regulations.[66]

Later in the campaign, formerly desirable vice presidential nominee Lodge made the mistake—in South Carolinians' eyes—of promising, while campaigning in Harlem, that an African American would occupy a cabinet-level position in the Nixon administration. South Carolina Republican leaders were furious, and in a letter to Nixon staffer Charles McWhorter, Shorey requested in a curt postscript that the vice president pass along word to his running mate that "if he does not restrict his commentary on Civil Rights and other such matters to the specifics of the platform that he is going to turn out to be the biggest liability we have."[67] Nixon attempted to minimize the damage Lodge caused, contending that he aimed to select the best men for his cabinet without regard for "race, creed or color." Lodge did modify his statement the next day in campaign visits to Virginia and North Carolina, saying he could not actually pledge anything as the number two man on the ticket and that his statement was an expression of what he felt should be done, not a Republican commitment. Even after a 45-minute campaign meeting with Nixon, Lodge refused to backtrack further, while Nixon continued to equivocate with noncommittal statements. Nixon strategists in both South Carolina and in the national campaign remained frustrated with the way former U.N. ambassador Lodge had undercut the Republican campaign in the South.[68]

Nixon's promise to visit every state in the union was delayed by a knee infection in early September that required his hospitalization. Weather concerns further delayed his plans for a South Carolina visit. Overcoming these setbacks, the vice president doggedly rescheduled every missed trip, despite ending up in Alaska, home to a whopping three electoral votes, the day before the general election. South Carolina did its part to ensure that Nixon's promise to the state was kept, with Shorey leaning on Republican National Committee Director of Planning Activities James Bassett to be sure the trip was rescheduled. Shorey also noted that "South Carolina Democrats for Nixon and Lodge" had not been entirely cooperative with the state Republican Party and pointed out that the GOP was the ongoing organization running Republican candidates. The implication was that Nixon needed to beware of reaching out to dissatisfied Democrats at the expense of Carolinians who were brave enough to actually make the leap to the Republican Party.[69]

Nixon finally made it to Columbia, South Carolina, on November 3, just five days before the election. In a demonstration of the developing trend toward presidential Republicanism, former Democratic Congressman, Senator, Supreme Court Justice, Director of War Mobilization, Secretary of State, and Governor James F. Byrnes introduced the vice president on the steps of the regal, iron-domed statehouse. Byrnes described the frustration of Southerners who had been loyal to the Democratic Party throughout its history and now felt betrayed. "We must put the welfare of the country above the welfare of any political party," he declared. "We must vote for the man and not for the label."[70] Political reporter Workman observed a "good natural crowd" that joined in the singing of songs including the previously mentioned "Dixie Is No Longer in the Bag" and the rousing ditty "Here Comes Nixon" (to the tune of "Good Night Ladies").[71] The University of South Carolina band played "Dixie" to loud cheers, and as Nixon arrived the female element in the audience appeared quite impressed, with one young coed crying to her companion, "I saw him, Jeanne, I saw him. He's beautiful." *The State* reported that the Nixon crowd, estimated at 35,000, was three times as large as Kennedy's a month prior, with superior quantities of ticker tape and streamers—not to mention a large balloon that, cut from its moorings, soared off heralding that "Dixie Is No Longer in the Bag."[72]

Nixon's comments to the crowd combined traditional, states' rights language with specific attention to current economic and foreign policy concerns. Neatly hijacking the Democrats' claim to their own great statesmen, the vice president proclaimed that "the party of Jackson, the party of Jefferson, and the party of Wilson is at opposite ends of the poles from the party of Schlesinger and Galbraith and Reuther and Bowles." Voters wanted "no part" of these men's ideology, "in the South or any part of the country." As in his acceptance speech at Chicago, Nixon asserted that the Democratic Party had abandoned many of its traditional followers by adopting a radical platform at Los Angeles. In South Carolina, however, he carefully used the term "national leadership," which was a traditional southern Democratic code term for Yankees. Unlike Democrats of old, the authors of the current Democratic platform failed to acknowledge the "fundamental principle" of "individual rights and local and State responsibility"—states' rights. In contrast to the "billion dollars worth of progress" South Carolina had made under Eisenhower's leadership, Nixon alleged that Democrats' large spending proposals promised tax hikes and price increases that could mean as much as 25 percent inflation in the cost of staples like groceries. Moving on to foreign policy, Nixon took a hard line, castigating John F. Kennedy for refusing in the past to defend the Chinese Nationalist islands of Quemoy and Matsu and for suggesting that Eisenhower should have apologized to Soviet Premier Nikita Khrushchev for the U-2 incident. Nixon did acknowledge that some members of his audience might disagree with his civil rights positions but quickly returned to more solid ground, touting his extensive travels and advocacy of freedom for all *foreign* peoples.[73]

The vice president targeted Kennedy's stand on the struggling textile industry, a major component of South Carolina's economic structure, more specifically in a prepared statement released to the press before his speech. On October 12 in New York, Nixon claimed, Kennedy had stated that federal funds should be used to retrain unemployed textile and garment workers so they could qualify for other employment. Nixon argued that this program would generally require moving workers and their families to distant communities and curtailment or closure of the textile industry. "I would use the power the President has under existing law," he said, "to minimize the damage to the industry so that textile workers would not be forced out of their jobs." Nixon's pre-speech statement also deplored the "contemptuous cynicism toward the South reflected in putting Senators Kennedy and Johnson on the same ticket."[74] "We have had enough of this attempt to divide America on a regional basis and on a class basis," he told the crowds at the statehouse, touting again his fifty-state pledge.[75]

Nixon's visit also benefited from recent events in Georgia. As described in more detail in chapter 2, Martin Luther King, Jr. was arrested on October 19 at an Atlanta department store sit-in and then transferred to another Georgia jail to serve a four-month sentence based upon charges of driving without a valid license. While Kennedy reached out to Coretta Scott King and his campaign worked behind the scenes to secure King's release, Nixon remained silent—a move many white Southerners no doubt interpreted as acquiescence. By not acting, Nixon campaigned for additional white southern votes.

In light of Byrnes' introduction of Nixon, it is important to note that in at least two important cases, highly prominent South Carolina Democrats either implicitly or explicitly endorsed the vice president's campaign. Byrnes, despite his long and storied history in the Democratic Party, openly supported Eisenhower in 1952 while still serving as the state's Democratic governor. Angry about Eisenhower administration civil rights policies and the *Brown v. Board* court decision, he strayed from Republican presidential allegiance in 1956 and supported instead the independent slate of electors pledged to segregationist Virginia Senator Harry F. Byrd. By 1960, however, he was back in the Republican camp, at least in presidential terms.

On September 23, Byrnes made a statement to the press proclaiming his support for the Nixon-Lodge ticket. He went on to prepare comments for

Nixon regarding the Republican Party's economic record in South Carolina, including a statement on the textile industry almost identical to the one quoted above from Nixon's Columbia pre-speech press release.[76] Byrnes biographer David Robertson has explained Byrnes' tendency to take verbatim notes on conversations using a stylized shorthand only he could read. The existence in Byrnes' files of a telephone conversation transcript between himself and Nixon indicates that he carefully surveyed Nixon's opinions on key issues to be sure he could in good conscience support the vice president. Convinced that Nixon was cautious on civil rights issues and continued to favor the Taft–Hartley labor law, Byrnes evidently felt he could give Nixon his support.[77]

Although he never made a specific endorsement, Thurmond also signaled his support for Nixon throughout the campaign. The maverick Democrat was infuriated by the Democratic Party platform adopted at the national convention in Los Angeles, and he wrote a detailed analysis of the platform, pointing out his many objections on virtually all issues addressed, from national defense policy to domestic programs. His summary of the platform provides a concise analysis of his reaction—and, if the letters he received are any indication, the opinions of many others:

> The 1960 Democratic platform is a blueprint for a welfare state and an end to individual liberty and dignity in the United States of America.
>
> It is a road map for economic collapse and unconditional surrender to the forces of socialism.
>
> It is a chart for amalgamation of the races and a reduction of the individuals of which our country is formed to the lowest common denominator.
>
> It sounds the final death-knell of the Democratic Party known to our forebears and completes the transition to a party dedicated to socialism, welfare statism, conformity, and centralization of power.[78]

Given that ringing lack of endorsement, it was no surprise that by election day, the Columbia *State* reported that Thurmond "talked Monday like a Democrat who will vote Republican Tuesday. . . . he announced he will vote his conscience even if 'this does not suit the party bosses of the national Democratic party.'"[79] In response to a November 3 entreaty to state his position specifically, Thurmond revealed a distinct lack of enthusiasm for either candidate, stating that "whichever candidate wins, the South will ultimately be the loser." His infatuation with electoral college reform following the election indicates, however, where his loyalty ultimately resided.[80]

The reaction Byrnes and Thurmond received from the public indicates both South Carolinians' dissatisfaction with the Democratic Party and, in some cases, their continuing reluctance to break with the party of their fathers. Thurmond's mail was almost entirely supportive of the senator's stands, and Byrnes must have been gratified by letters from admirers such as H.P. North of Columbia, who wrote that "if your support of Mr. Nixon helps to elect him it may be the greatest service you have ever rendered."[81] In contrast to Thurmond, however, Byrnes also received some vitriolic missives from Democratic loyalists like "a woman Democrat," who did not deign to include her name but did mention how sorry she was to "look at your ugly old mug in the paper."[82] Dallas L. Dendy of Laurens wrote to inform the statesman that he reminded him of "a man that signs a bank note and when it comes due forgets about it."[83] Byrnes' outspokenness, as well as his long tradition of Democratic loyalty in contrast to the one-time Dixiecrat Thurmond, likely accounts for the disparity in correspondence.

Electoral Losses and Organizational Gains

Ultimately, South Carolina Republicans—and their sympathetic Democratic friends—fell short of victory in the state, garnering 48.8 percent of the vote in contrast to Kennedy's 51.2 percent.[84] Even the endorsements of several South Carolina newspapers, including the *News and Courier*, *The State*, the Columbia *Record*, the Charleston *Evening Post*, the Beaufort *Gazette*, and the Calhoun *Times* proved insufficient to sway over 50 percent of the South Carolina electorate.[85] The election as a whole, of course, was lost for the Republicans by the smallest of margins, with allegations of voter fraud floating around in Illinois and Texas. Given the closeness of the election in South Carolina, the state party impounded its own state's ballots in response to the suspicious count in Illinois.[86] A successful recount of South Carolina's eight electoral votes plus Illinois' 27 would have still left the vice president 15 electoral votes from victory, but such a switch would have endangered Kennedy's chances of an outright triumph. Nixon chose not to contest the election, however, and Kennedy gained the presidency.

Nixon's loss in 1960 certainly disappointed his South Carolina supporters, but more important than the inevitable frustration that comes with losing a tight election was the foundation 1960 laid for future party development. The pride these early Republican organizers felt in their work is reflected in accounts like "In GOP We Trust," a history of the Anderson County party that was written around 1969. Remembering his work in a Republican Party booth at the Anderson County Fair, author James Duffy wrote, "It was a gallant band that faced the opposition from this bridge head. And bridgehead it was. Although it was touch and go the GOP was not driven back to the sea."[87]

It is important to understand that the development of the state party marked the first time a genuine political party organization had been formed in South Carolina. Southern party development was such a new concept that the manual Edens used to develop the state's GOP organization in the early 1960s was actually produced by the AFL-CIO's Committee on Political Education (COPE).[88] Before the Republican Party entered the scene as a viable second-party option, Democrats had been free to run on individual terms, with candidates of various ideological stripes sharing the same hustings during primary campaigns. While the resulting party was generally, as political scientist V.O. Key, Jr. so eloquently put it, "a holding-company for a congeries of transient squabbling factions," no consolidated structure was needed when there was no interparty competition.[89]

The organizational base established in 1960 provided groundwork for more systematic development during Workman's 1962 Senate run, with organizational efforts coming to fruition in 1964 and 1968. Even before the 1960 campaign ended, party activists were planning for the future. A November 1 letter from Young Republican National Federation co-chair Judy Fernald to Mrs. James Duffy, for example, included material for organizing a local Young Republican club after the campaign.[90] Shorey's home county of Greenville looked ahead even as leaders strove to organize all 105 county precincts by the time of the election. Following the election, the November edition of "G.O.P. News" reported, "it is hoped that efforts will be increased toward the establishment of a real two-party system."[91] South Carolina Republicans also continued their work in party politics at the national level, taking a leading role in the "Draft Goldwater" movement. An initial October 1961 organizational meeting of 22 conservative leaders, for example, included three South Carolinians—greater representation than that of any other state.[92]

Groundwork for the Future

South Carolina Republicans, then, demonstrated their ability to sustain and even increase their organization following two disappointments in 1960: the triumph of a more middle-of-the-road GOP strategy vis-à-vis Goldwater, and then Nixon's loss to Kennedy in November. They were able to do so for two reasons. First, their emphasis was on development of a party organization rather than isolated support for an individual. Their hearts might have belonged to Goldwater, but their actions demonstrated their commitment to the formation of a genuine two-party system. Race was a significant factor for many supporters of the Republican ticket, a reality reflected in South Carolina Republican leaders' reactions to too-strident statements about civil rights by either Nixon or Lodge. South Carolinians' attention to economic and foreign policy concerns, however, indicate that these issues were also important. South Carolinians were willing to compromise and do the legwork necessary to develop a sustainable Republican Party base in the state.

Second, the state party was able to benefit from the increasing power it held over GOP policy. The accelerating breakdown of Democrats' hold on southern states leading up to 1960 made South Carolina Republicans a tantalizing target for the national party. The fight over the GOP platform in Chicago helped the ever-pragmatic Nixon understand where South Carolinians stood along the ideological spectrum, and he catered to their beliefs accordingly. Nixon was not a perfect candidate, but he helped make himself a preferred one for thousands of South Carolinians.

As South Carolina went, so, at varying rates, went the rest of the South. The organizations forged in states like South Carolina in 1960 catalyzed a fundamental transition. With the exception of 1976, when southern evangelical Democrat Jimmy Carter disrupted many developing patterns of partisan affiliation, South Carolina's presidential electors have not voted Democratic since. Indeed, only southern Democratic candidates have had any success in the South post-1968, and in 1968 only one state—Texas—gave its electoral votes to Democratic candidate Hubert Humphrey. Never again would a Republican candidate write off the region as an unattainable electoral prize. The ideological activism of individuals like Shorey and his cohorts in the South Carolina GOP spelled the end of the one-party South.

"Nixon the Freedom Fighter"

American Nationalities for Nixon-Lodge and the Politics of Ethnicity

"... it is urgent that nationality groups having ties to countries suffering from Communist tyranny assist both the United States and these oppressed people by helping to formulate and support imaginative, strong and positive policies which never lose sight of the fundamental goal of freedom and self-determination for all."—John Richardson, Jr., September 13, 1960[1]

Historians have tended to treat white American ethnics' increasingly Republican voting patterns in the late twentieth century as the result of GOP appeals to the politics of whiteness. The turbulence of the 1960s did indeed produce a generation of white Americans with strong ethnic ties who reacted with frustration and resentment when asked to fund government programs targeted at reducing poverty among urban, and often black, Americans. Many argued that despite the immense and varied assistance provided by New Deal–era programs, they had succeeded through their own initiative and should not have to provide "hand-outs" to others. A number of scholars have published both 1960s era and more recent scholarly accounts that provide insights into this transition in ethnic voting patterns.[2]

Long before Richard Nixon reached out to the "Silent Majority" in 1968, however, Republicans had begun attempts to woo ethnic group support. Despite historical ties to the nativist Know-Nothings of the mid-nineteenth century, the Republican Party of the late 1800s garnered significant electoral support from most ethnic groups, and Theodore Roosevelt ran quite well among ethnic Americans in the early 1900s.[3] While support for the Republicans plummeted among white working-class ethnics during the New Deal years, the post–World War II GOP attempted to regain electoral support among these constituencies. From campaign buttons proclaiming "I like Ike" in Slovak ("JA SOM ZA IKE-A") and Czech ("MY RADY IKE") in 1956 to a campaign movie titled *Nixon the Freedom Fighter* in 1960, Republicans strove to situate themselves as the party of choice for American ethnics. They did this not through appeals to race but by situating the GOP as the party of anti-Communism.

To borrow historian Gary Gerstle's analytical framework, rather than offering racial nationalism, these campaigns offered ethnic voters membership in a militantly anti-Communist civic nation. Gerstle has defined civic nationalism as faith in the fundamental equality of all, the individual's inalienable rights to life, liberty, and the pursuit of happiness, and the principles of representative democracy. Political leaders have used this ideology—"the American creed"—to promote freedom and democracy throughout American history, although it has been challenged by frequent recourse to racial ideals.[4] The later 1960s mark just such an episode in the mixed history of American nationalism. In 1960, however, the GOP strove to remold anti-Communism in positive terms, arguing for its necessity if democratic freedoms were to be preserved. Nixon's 1960 presidential campaign offers especially good insight into Republicans' approach toward ethnic Americans before the days of the "Silent Majority." The Republican National Committee had doubled the membership of its Nationalities Division since 1956, and the party used this growth as a jumping-off point for ethnic voter drives. Nixon's campaign leadership established American Nationalities for Nixon-Lodge (ANNL), an organization that sought ethnics' support through such tactics as the above-mentioned Nixon film, meetings with ethnic leaders in Washington, D.C., and a leadership with impeccable anti-Communist credentials. Above all, the 1960 campaign is notable for including Asians among the ethnic groups targeted in the ANNL. Americans with ethnic ties to China or Korea were just as concerned about the Communist menace as Hungarian or Polish Americans, and Nixon's campaign attempted to mobilize these groups using similar appeals. At its most effective, ANNL transformed anti-Communism from a defensive action into a positive program for membership in America's civic nation.

This chapter uses the American Nationalities for Nixon-Lodge to explore the complex politics of anti-Communist nationalism that Republicans of this era used to woo ethnic group support. As ANNL Co-Chairman John

Richardson, Jr. pointed out in his post-election report, the party made significant mistakes. The inability of these 1960-vintage Republicans to mobilize ethnic group support effectively left open the door for the race-based approach taken later in the decade. Their myopia in focusing overwhelmingly upon European issues, despite Asian Americans' inclusion in the organization, squandered a prime opportunity to forge an anti-Communist coalition among Americans of diverse backgrounds. Despite massive growth in the Nationalities Division, the party failed to convert election-time efforts into a permanent organization through which ethnic Republicans could mobilize support. Moreover, despite Republicans' best efforts, Democratic candidate John F. Kennedy often gained the initiative in the struggle over who was most anti-Communist with his denunciations of a hypothetical "missile gap" and advocacy of a hard line against Cuba.[5] Nevertheless, ANNL provides us with a window into how these Republicans tried to respond to and develop ethnics' relationships with the party as exemplar of American identity. This relationship was not to be one of race. Rather, it was a relationship forged upon an American democratic identity in muscular opposition to the Communist foe.

"Ethnicity" and Politics in Historical Context

The definition of "ethnicity" has long been a topic of contentious debate within the academy. A 1974 survey of its usage found that "the majority of those who wrote on the subject avoided defining it altogether." In general, "ethnicity" has incorporated "the features of a perceived shared culture and real or putative common ancestry." For the most part, in academic circles, the term has been used to identify descendants of European immigrants only, although arenas like marketing have used "ethnic" to refer to both descendants of European immigrants and members of what the academy tends to term "minorities"—African, Asian, or Latino Americans.[6] Most scholars argue that the idea of "ethnicity" as a social scientific concept emerged during World War II. Social scientists needed a new term for categorizing groups like Italians or Magyars in an era when the former multiplicity of racial categories had been reduced to a Caucasoid/Mongoloid/Negroid trifecta.[7] Political scientist Victoria Hattam has placed the origins of the concept of "ethnic" as an adjective even earlier, with New York intellectuals in the 1910s and 1920s who were seeking a form of identity that would allow them to preserve their cultural affiliations within a pluralistic ideal of American society. "Ethnicity" for these individuals was configured in contrast to race, with ethnicity constituting a cultural difference while race was an unalterable, bodily difference.[8]

While the term "ethnicity" was in use by 1960, the Republican National Committee and the Nixon campaign used "nationality" instead. Their inclusion of Asian Americans within the ANNL and the national committee's Nationalities Division demonstrates their understanding of "nationality" as pertaining to both European and Asian Americans who maintained the kinds of ties included in the definition of "ethnicity" cited above. "Nationality" also served to highlight American ethnics' ties to actual countries—or subjugated nations—abroad. By contrast, African American outreach was centered in the GOP's Minorities Division and remained separate in the Nixon campaign. Groups like Latino Americans or Jewish Americans were often subjected to split appeals from the Nationalities and Minorities Divisions, or, as in 1956, from an "Ethnic Division" devoted primarily to garnering Jewish votes.

Despite twentieth-century perceptions of the Democratic Party as the party of immigrants, European and Asian ethnic groups have experienced a complex history of political involvement in the United States marked by inter-ethnic rivalries as well as competition and conflict with the dominant political establishment. Resentment of Irish Democratic machine politics in the Northeast led some other Catholic ethnic groups to vote Republican during the 1800s, despite the party's WASP establishmentarianism.[9] Germans and Scandinavians in the 1800s Midwest aligned themselves with the GOP because of its opposition to the expansion of slavery into new territory. Growing fears of eastern industrial capitalism in the late 1800s led some midwestern ethnics into third-party movements, while others, especially Catholics concerned about populist Democrat William Jennings Bryan's evangelical Protestantism, heightened their affiliation with the Republican Party. In places like Ohio, competing ideologies resulted in dual Republican political machines—one establishmentarian and the other populist.[10]

The turn of the century brought new ethnic populations to the United States, as well as new issues around which ethnic political affiliation turned. Midwestern isolationism and the Democratic government's entry into war against Germany pressed Germans and some Scandinavians further into the Republican fold during World War I. The nomination of Al Smith by the Democrats in 1928, however, attracted Catholics and anti-Prohibition ethnics to the Democratic Party. Before the 1930s, newer ethnic groups often remained outside the political arena, either because they intended to return to their home countries or, in the case of Chinese and Japanese Americans, because exclusionary policies prevented them from gaining citizenship and the right to vote. Even Filipino Americans, who were classified as U.S. nationals due to the Philippines' colonial status, were excluded from citizenship.[11] The 1930s, however, brought two key events that fundamentally altered the fabric of ethnic political involvement in the United States. First, the rise of fascist governments in Europe halted many European ethnics' intentions of return to their homelands. Second, the onset of the Great Depression destroyed the Republican Party's credibility among most working Americans.

The success of Franklin Roosevelt and the New Deal in buoying Americans' confidence, if not necessarily in ending the Depression, inaugurated a new period of Democratic Party dominance in American politics that would not end until Richard Nixon's second attempt at the presidency in 1968. Above all, the Roosevelt administration's devotion to labor, agriculture, and the working class cemented a new and lasting relationship between white ethnics, the majority of whom worked as wage laborers or farmers, and the Democratic Party. Asian Americans, many of whom might also have found New Deal policies favorable, continued to suffer from exclusionary government policies. Foreign policy had some impact on the durability of Roosevelt's New Deal coalition, as midwestern isolationists—including many ethnics—opposed entry into World War II. Overall, however, most ethnic groups remained firmly situated in the Democratic column throughout the 1940s.

The 1950s, on the other hand, marked the beginnings of a change in the political alignment of most American ethnic groups. Citizens with ties to Eastern European countries or China were ready targets for anti-Communist appeals, and to at least a limited degree the Republican Party capitalized on these conditions. Wisconsin Senator Joseph McCarthy's red-baiting career benefited immeasurably from his popularity among stridently anti-Communist Catholics, many of whom were members of ethnic communities. Even Irish Catholic Democrats like the Kennedys were McCarthy supporters, reflecting both the strength of religious ties in an era when Catholics retained a sense of distinctiveness from the dominant, Protestant mainstream and the strength of Catholic perceptions of American capitalism as a means to preserve and nurture families. Catholic perceptions of the American way of life were in many ways opposite those of laissez-faire evolutionary capitalism. Believing instead in an underlying moral order and the need for tradition and cumulative wisdom, standing aside and letting Communism chart its own course was inconceivable—it was Americans' moral duty to rescue Captive Nations from "atheistic Communism."[12]

Dwight Eisenhower's status as a nonpartisan hero of World War II made him an easy transitional figure for many Democrats, and GOP strategy in the 1950s catered to the fears and sense of moral imperative that ethnic Americans, and especially Catholic ethnics, held. During the 1952 campaign the Republican Party spoke of Captive Nations and "liberation" of the

Soviet Union's satellite states, a far more exciting program than the containment strategy championed by the Truman administration. Impressed by Truman's outreach to ethnic groups in 1948, the GOP also established an ethnic origins division on both state and national levels. As Joseph Roucek and Bernard Eisenberg put it, "the battle for the hyphenates was on." Some analysts have even claimed that the single most important factor in Eisenhower's 1952 victory was the Polish-American vote—a largely Catholic constituency.[13]

The economic prosperity of the 1950s also brought increasing material prosperity to American ethnics, which accelerated their shift to the GOP. Almost 50 percent of Catholics cast their ballots for Eisenhower in 1956. By 1969, Chinatown had long been the strongest Republican enclave in lower Manhattan. To be sure, part of this devotion had to do with Republicans' long championing of Chiang Kai-Shek and Nationalist China. Just as important, however, the Chinese American population tended to be prosperous during this period, with Chinese Americans' median family income hovering over $500 above that of Americans as a whole.[14] Wealthy Japanese Americans in cities like New York also tended to vote Republican, although in states like Hawaii, Nisei World War II veterans challenged entrenched white Republican rule through the Democratic Party in the 1950s.[15]

Finally, the post–World War II period saw an influx of refugees from newly Communist nations in Asia and Eastern Europe. These new American ethnics were, for obvious reasons, especially anti-Communist and therefore receptive to the GOP's hard line against the Soviets and Chinese Communists. They were often among the more conservative elements in their home populations, making flight from leftist regimes a matter of personal safety and membership in the Republican Party a natural fit.

Despite Eisenhower's success in courting ethnic groups, however, the Democratic Party and its New Deal coalition continued to hold the upper hand. The GOP was tasked with the need for a major organizational effort to sway support, and lack of organization was the most common frustration expressed by ethnic Republican activists to party leaders over the course of the 1950s. In 1955, for example, Robert Agnew of Los Angeles urged John Krehbiel, then the chairman of the Republican Central Committee of Los Angeles County, to make better use of the "nationality" talent Eisenhower's campaign brought to the party in 1952. He cited the success of the "Crusade to Lift the Iron Curtain" committee that functioned during 1952, arguing that this was "a most important effort and we beat the Democrats to the punch that time." Since then, however, the GOP had dropped the ball. Now, Agnew feared, it might be too late: "the nationality groups will no doubt be courted again in 1956 and I would not blame their leaders for negative reactions if, as a johnny-come-lately bunch, we suddenly want their help!" Agnew pressed Krehbiel to avert this catastrophe by appointing a county chairman of the "Republican Nationality Group Committee," appointing a vice-chair from each congressional district to serve on that committee, and organizing nationality groups like the Hungarian-American Republican Club to bring Republicanism to the masses.[16]

Eisenhower's leadership—or lack thereof—had exacerbated tensions between ethnic party activists and the Republican organization. In late 1953, White House spokesmen had advised ethnic leaders that the president opposed the permanent organization of nationality groups. The leaders were told that Eisenhower did not want to differentiate among groups in the electorate. In keeping with Eisenhower's preferences, no permanent organization was established. Recognizing the need for ethnic involvement, however, the Republican National Committee established an advisory group, with eighteen ethnic group representatives assigned to the task of writing the first GOP platform plank renouncing restrictive immigration policies. Efforts to sway the ethnic vote in 1956 were organized through three organizational units within the RNC: Nationalities, Ethnics (a largely Jewish group), and Minorities. Again, however, following the election, the party's organizational structure fell apart.[17]

Advocacy and Ambivalence

Significantly, Agnew sent a copy of his plea to Los Angeles County's native son, Vice President Richard Nixon. Nixon was a leading advocate of expanding the Republican Party's base. A 1960 memo from Republican National Committee Nationalities Division chair A.B. Hermann, for example, cited Nixon and RNC Chairman Thruston Morton as key influences behind a twofold expansion of the Nationalities Division since 1956.[18] During Eisenhower's re-election campaign, the vice president appears to have taken action regarding some of the suggestions Agnew made in his letter to Krehbiel. In October, for example, Nixon staffer Bob Finch arranged for Nixon to have his photograph taken with representatives of Lithuanian and Yugoslavian groups, and he appeared on November 4 before an American-Lithuanians for Eisenhower-Nixon rally in Los Angeles.[19] In May 1959, Italian American GOP activist Blase Bonpane wrote to Nixon of his frustration with the same lack of organization that Agnew pointed out in 1956. The Eisenhower administration had not made a single patronage appointment to reward ethnics' hard work in 1952 and 1956. In both elections, ethnic leaders told their people that the Republican Party was as appreciative of their efforts as the Democrats; "this sort of talk will only be met with complete cynicism and disbelief in 1960, as things are now," Bonpane said.[20] Nixon carefully replied to Bonpane that he appreciated his frank report. There was no question that the Republicans had missed many opportunities, and he hoped to develop a more realistic approach to the problem so ethnics could enthusiastically support the GOP in 1960.[21]

For all his expressions of concern, however, Nixon demonstrated a curiously insufficient understanding of the commitment necessary to garner ethnic groups' support in 1960. Indeed, he turned down early offers of assistance from ethnic group representatives like Nick Nichols, an Ohio florist of Greek descent who advised Nixon in April 1959 that "The man in the street is 'all for Nixon.'" Advocating a Nixon-Rockefeller ticket as unstoppable, Nichols told Nixon that "if there is anything I can do to help let me know." In July, he wrote again, assuring the vice president that Republican leaders "will not take a 'Rockefeller for President' platform—it's all for Richard Nixon" and offering his assistance "if and when you tell me. We can tie up the florists assn., the Greek-American Republican clubs throughout the country, and other numerous organizations I am connected with." Subject to Nixon's approval, Nichols hoped to open an office in Washington "at our own expense . . . to show you we mean business." Nixon discouraged Nichols, telling him that while he appreciated his support and would continue to welcome suggestions and observations, he felt it was too early for organizational steps to be taken. Perhaps he was aware that Nichols was playing the Republican field—in an August 12 letter to Rockefeller, he reminded the governor how his family had handled the Rockefellers' floral orders in Ohio dating back to 1897, offered his support, and proclaimed him "the man for President."[22] Even so, given the tendency of so many politicians to take the pragmatic view, simply consolidating Nichols' support seemed the wiser option.

Despite Nixon's letter, Nichols continued to contact the vice president's office, practically pleading to give thousands to Nixon's campaign in August and October 1959: "I am the head of several organizations who can make so much Nixon-for-President noise—that words can't express. He's the man and the sooner the public knows about it the better." These continued entreaties earned no more than a polite "I certainly agree with you. . . . If you ever get to New York or Washington, please let me hear from you" from campaign director Len Hall.[23] Nichols' enthusiasm might have bordered on overwhelming, but he was not a random eccentric; he was even appointed to the leadership of ANNL the next fall. Nixon's attitude defies imagination but could be attributed to his almost unhealthy desire to maintain complete control over his campaign. This controlling nature, coupled with a lack of openness to suggestions from others, was a source of constant frustration for both ethnic leaders and others who tried to help the Nixon campaign following the vice president's loss.

Organizational ineptitude aside, Republican leaders strove to identify the issues that they felt would be key to the ethnic vote in 1960. First among them, especially as Massachusetts Senator John F. Kennedy gained support among Democrats, was the "Catholic issue." Kennedy was, of course, a Catholic, and so were many of the European ethnics the Republican Party hoped to attract. As explained above, Eisenhower had done relatively well among Catholic voters, but the GOP feared that these new supporters would jump ship to vote for their co-religionist in November. Notably, the political allegiances of Catholics from non-European ethnic groups, such as Filipino Americans, were not a topic of discussion. Also near the top of the agenda were continuing Cold War tensions between the United States and both the Soviet Union and the People's Republic of China. Anti-Communist Republicans had better chances of mobilizing voters on this issue. Events over the past four years, including the Hungarian Uprising of 1956, the Cuban Revolution, ongoing tensions in Vietnam, and continued clashes over the rocky outposts of Quemoy and Matsu in the Straits of Formosa did little to settle concerns about Communist expansion. For ethnic groups sensitized through their personal connections to these regions, politicians' intentions with regard to the Communist threat would be very important.

With these issues in mind, party activists outlined the ways in which the Republican Party could mount a persuasive campaign among ethnic voters. International Rescue Committee President John Richardson, Jr. was to become co-chairman of the ANNL, but even before his appointment he advocated outreach to nationality groups. In late August 1960, he described his proposal for a "Citizen's Advisory Committee on Relations with the Sino-Soviet Bloc" in a memo to campaign staffer Ned Harding. Despite his Catholicism, Richardson argued, Kennedy had a "serious handicap in his efforts to recapture and solidify" the ethnic vote. "This handicap," he explained,

> is compounded of the Democratic Party identification in the minds of many voters with the 'sell-outs' at Yalta and Potsdam, the tardiness of its leaders in arriving at a realistic appreciation of the nature of Communist imperialism, and, most of all, the appointment of [Chester] Bowles and [Adlai] Stevenson as foreign policy advisors.

Bowles and Stevenson, he argued, were "anathema" to many ethnic opinion leaders because of their wishy-washy attitude toward the Soviets. Richardson believed that if Kennedy's weaknesses were "stressed and dramatized" throughout the campaign, the Nixon-Lodge ticket could not only overcome Kennedy's religious-affiliation advantage, but build upon the GOP inroads of 1952 and 1956. As part of this effort, Richardson advocated the establishment of a citizen's advisory committee comprised of international affairs experts, including some prominent figures of Eastern European background, to advise Nixon both during and after the election on Sino-Soviet issues. Including a list of suggested experts, Richardson cautioned that while "to many, names of the type suggested below would seem to be of little political import," to opinion leaders within American ethnic communities "they would speak a most compelling message, especially in contrast to Messrs. Bowles and Kennedy (not to mention Mrs. Roosevelt, the ADA et al)."[24] Richardson's focus on Eastern European ethnic figures and European issues, even as he referred to a "Sino-Soviet Bloc," also provided an early indication of the ANNL leadership's neglect of its Asian American constituents.

All three of the men selected to lead ANNL were well aware of the symbolic importance these efforts could have for American ethnics. Richardson had earned international recognition for his efforts to aid the Hungarian Freedom Fighters in 1956, and he had visited Poland five times in the previous two and one-half years in connection with the Polish Medical Aid Project, which he organized in 1957. He distributed several million dollars of medicine under the auspices of CARE (Cooperation for American Remittances to Europe), and he was a member of the executive committees of the American Friends of the Captive Nations and the Committee for the American Research Hospital for Children in Krakow, Poland. Beyond these many areas of involvement, Richardson's connection to the Eastern Bloc was intensely personal; his adopted daughter had joined his family after escaping from Budapest in 1956. Richardson's counterpart, former Maryland governor Theodore Roosevelt McKeldin, had headed many organizations associated with nationality groups, and he was a favorite in the Jewish community. McKeldin had gained significant national stature in the party by becoming the first Republican to be elected to a second gubernatorial term in his state. He delivered the convention speech nominating Eisenhower to a second term in 1956, and he was mentioned in some circles as a possibility for the vice presidential slot in 1960. ANNL's executive director, Horace E. "Hunky" Henderson, resigned his post as deputy assistant secretary of state for international organization affairs to take the position. He had served as an adviser to the American delegation at the U.N. and head of Hungarian affairs for Radio Free Europe, as well as delegate to two World Health Assemblies, two International Labor Conferences, and a meeting of the U.N. High Commission for Refugees.[25]

Significantly, none of these men were members of the right wing of the Republican Party in 1960. Their affiliations with international organizations, including the United Nations, separated them from go-it-alone factions within the party and placed them firmly within the 1950s' bipartisan, liberal, anti-Communist consensus. Barry Goldwater, for example, referred to the United Nations as "in part a Communist organization" in *Conscience of a Conservative*. While he stopped short of advocating withdrawal from the world body, he warned that unlike the United States, the Communists "do not respect the UN and do not permit their policies to be affected by it." As a result, the United States was placed at a disadvantage in U.N. negotiations.[26] Richardson displayed his commitment to liberal internationalism by dispensing his foreign policy advice not only to Nixon, but also to Nelson Rockefeller as he considered a presidential run in 1959. "There will be no security for anyone until world law replaces the present international anarchy," he told Rockefeller aide Rod Perkins. Richardson advocated declaring that the United States would not "curry favor with despotic rulers anywhere anytime," a principle Nixon was dangerously near breaking with his trip to the Soviet Union. His hesitation to cooperate with non-democratic governments might have given Richardson grounds for discussion with Goldwater, but, in the end, he believed that Americans must work through international organizations with other like-minded nations if the Communist menace were to be successfully challenged.[27]

Beyond their differences with many right-wing Republicans over international cooperation, leaders like McKeldin firmly endorsed a liberal, Modern Republican governmental approach. In 1957, for example, the *New York Herald Tribune* covered a McKeldin speech before the Americans for Democratic Action (ADA), a stridently anti-Communist but firmly liberal organization that was anathema to conservatives. "The liberal," McKeldin stated,

> is chiefly concerned by what may be gained through wise action; the conservative with what may be lost through unwise action. For my part, I feel the hope of gain is more important than the danger of loss, but that gain isn't going to be automatic.[28]

McKeldin had even, it turns out, received an ADA endorsement for the governorship. In August 1959, the Maryland governor had proclaimed himself "tremendously impressed" by Rockefeller following a conference with him, although he cautioned that he believed "either [Nixon or Rockefeller] would make a fine President of the United States" and could beat any Democratic nominee.[29] Through his approval of these men's selection to head ANNL, Nixon signaled his endorsement of their approach. His caution in accepting their counsel, however, could indicate that whatever Nixon's personal agreement with Henderson, McKeldin, and Richardson, he feared aligning himself too thoroughly with the liberal wing of the GOP. Again, the vice president was struggling to balance his preferred policy with his desire to garner support from all sectors.

These advocates of ethnic group outreach, then, were not members of those factions within the GOP that had transitioned from pre–World War II isolationism to a postwar determination to stand alone against the Soviet threat. Neither did they identify with anti-government factions, as would a later generation of white ethnic voters who became frustrated and disillusioned by the events of the 1960s. Rather, ANNL's leadership believed that international cooperation could successfully combat Communist aspirations around the world. Government had a role to play in fighting Communism at home and abroad, as well as in continuing to provide a societal infrastructure that would preserve the United States' domestic strength. Nineteen-sixty, then, marked the last attempt of the Republican Party to mobilize voters on the level of Cold War motivations alone.

Nixon's vice presidential selection further demonstrated his awareness of ethnics' importance in the 1960 campaign. Henry Cabot Lodge had become something of a cult hero for Americans watching televised United Nations debates, and his strident opposition to Communism in the international body was encouraging to citizens with familial or historical ties to Soviet satellite nations. As Harding pointed out in an undated campaign memo, the addition of Lodge to the ticket gave Republicans

> perhaps the best opportunity ever to attract to the Republican ticket a large percentage of the 20,000,000 voters and citizens of foreign origin to whom an effective organized appeal can be made on the basis of the candidate's strong identification with anti-communist action as well as their oft expressed belief to man's right to live in freedom.[30]

Fighting for the "Freedom Fighter"

Despite his selection of Lodge as running mate, Nixon continued to drag his feet on the organizational front. Hermann attempted to impress upon campaign officials the importance of reaching out to nationality groups. In an August 9 memo to Nixon, Leonard Hall, Jim Bassett, Robert Finch, and Thruston Morton, Hermann pointed out, as mentioned above, that despite organizational obstacles the campaign division of the Republican National Committee had managed to increase the membership of the Nationalities Division twofold since 1956. Nixon, he argued, enjoyed a reputation as the "Worlds' number ONE 'Freedom Fighter'" as a result of career triumphs ranging from his prosecution of Alger Hiss to his tough stand against Khrushchev in the Soviet Union in 1959. Nationality leaders had already responded to this reputation by gathering in a nationwide meeting, 600 members strong, at the Conrad Hilton Hotel in Chicago during the nominating convention. These leaders, Hermann noted, had been told by Nixon's handlers that he was not available to appear before them at their meeting, but despite this snub, attendees put plans for a national campaign into action. The Nationalities Division head advocated a series of steps, including personal meetings between leaders and the vice president, photo sessions, special recognition of ethnic contributions during visits to industrial areas, and outreach to the ethnic media. "No stone must be left unturned," he exhorted. "A strong Nationalities vote for the Vice President could be the balance of power in the industrial States."[31]

Campaign staffer Ned Harding also emphasized the dissatisfaction that ethnic leaders had felt when faced with the campaign's non-response to their convention overtures. Seeking to capitalize upon Nixon and Lodge's great anti-Communist stature, the party organization established new names for the Nationalities Division's component programs. Rather than a Polish American Republican Committee, for example, ethnic voters could affiliate with the seemingly nonpartisan "Poles for Nixon." Harding urged the immediate selection of a director, advisory board, special events, bilingual literature, and effective use of National Committee employees already skilled in dealing with ethnic leaders. ". . . This program has not gotten off the ground under the RNC," he pointed out, "and it would seem advisable that this effort be made entirely under the auspices of Volunteers for Nixon-Lodge, during this campaign."[32]

Even so, the Nixon team continued along a procrastination-prone course, preoccupied with Nixon's first southern outreach trip to North Carolina and with plans for his unprecedented fifty-state campaign. On August 27, Nixon aide Stan McCaffrey sent a proposal for the formation of a "Nationality Groups for Nixon and Lodge" organization along with detailed plans for a Labor Day rally in New York with a projected attendance of several thousand ethnic Americans. McCaffrey proposed that Governor Rockefeller preside as host in a venue such as the 5,000-seat Manhattan Center that organizers could easily fill to overflowing. Rockefeller would introduce speeches from the vice president and Ambassador Lodge on freedom, "including the international relations aspect, but with reference, also, it being Labor Day, to free-labor versus slave-labor." Kennedy would speak the same day before a large union gathering in Detroit's Cadillac Square, and McCaffrey reported that Labor Secretary Jim Mitchell felt that the plans constituted a suitable counterpoint, given the absences of large labor audiences or forums in New York State. With Nixon's approval, Mc-Caffrey said, the staff was ready to proceed.[33]

Nixon approved McCaffrey's preliminary proposal, and his campaign proceeded to make plans for a Labor Day gathering. New York State Attorney General Louis Lefkowitz strongly recommended a breakfast or morning meeting with members of the New York State Board of Rabbis. Following the meeting, Secretary Mitchell advised limiting Nixon's schedule to private appointments or staff work, as the campaign wanted to avoid creating conflicts with New York City's Labor Day parade—to which Nixon had not been invited. After a private lunch with Lodge and Rockefeller, Nixon would meet with groups of nationality leaders—Poles, Latvians, Lithuanians, Estonians, French, and Irish at 1:30; Italians, Greeks, Syrians, Lebanese, and Armenians at 1:50; and so on.[34] The vice president would follow up these meetings with a press conference incorporating both regular and foreign language press and an informal reception. Plans for a larger rally appeared to have been abandoned, but McCaffrey noted that he understood "you may wish to have dinner with Jackie Robinson and some of minority group people [sic] at about 6:00."[35] Given the separateness of Nixon's ethnic and minority group appeals, this was probably a coincidence of scheduling, but it does point to the campaign's perception of both groups as "others" to be dealt with outside the mainstream.

While all of this would have no doubt been immensely helpful, there is no record of these meetings actually taking place. The archival record preserves no comment on why the campaign's Labor Day plans fell through, but Nixon's hospitalization for a knee infection was likely the primary cause. The Republicans did not completely abandon ethnic voter outreach over the long weekend. On September 1, for example, Rockefeller's 28-year-old son, Rodman, campaigned in Spanish in the Puerto Rican community in Spanish Harlem.[36] Lodge and Rockefeller kicked off the GOP campaign in New York with a trip through the Catskills, including stops at Jewish resorts, and visited several New York beaches. The public's reaction demonstrated both the ambassador's popularity and possible danger for the GOP's presidential chances. *New York Times* correspondent Harrison Salisbury reported that while still in the Catskills, figures in the crowds were heard commenting that they wished the ticket were reversed.[37] On Coney Island the next day, a woman was overheard asking the candidate's identity. "Lodge, the man at the U.N.," her companion replied. The woman asked who he was running with, was told Nixon, and replied, "oh, that's too bad." Lodge's appeal was evident on a number of levels, not least of which was his adoration by the female population, including a quartet of girls too young to vote but who wished they could, as they found Lodge "cute." On a more serious note, the former ambassador was greeted by a Nicholas Myskiw of Queens, who had escaped from the Ukraine during World War II and thanked Lodge for his good work on the U.N. Security Council.[38]

Lodge's appeal—and the younger Rockefeller's helpful bilingualism—aside, the end result of Nixon's hospitalization was to delay further the beginning of active involvement with nationality groups, but campaign staff forged ahead with plans for an "American Nationalities for Nixon-Lodge" organization, with press secretary Herb Klein announcing formation of the committee at a press conference on September 1. In its first weekly progress report, the ANNL put forth its objective:

> To hold existing Republican strength and to top the 1952 and 1956 Eisenhower inroads into the traditionally Democratic Eastern European, Southern European and Latin American Nationality groups, representing twenty to forty percent of the population of the key industrial states.

Oddly, Richardson, author of the memo, neglected to include Asian Americans in this objective statement, although their presence among the leaders of ANNL indicates that their support was included in the committee's aims. By August 31, the campaign had finalized the selection of 103 ethnic leaders from 22 nationality groups and 18 states, plus the District of Columbia. Of these leaders, three—all from California—had identifiably Asian surnames, although at least one more individual on the list had to have been Filipino American. This representation was below average among the 22 nationalities, with a majority of the remainder possessing surnames that denoted Eastern European ancestry.[39] ANNL organizers clearly regarded Asian representation as a lower priority, even as they strove to bring Asian Americans into the fold. They also neglected to include at least one nationality group that had a significant number of American residents by the late 1950s and would seem immensely logical, given the organization's anti-Communist program: Korean Americans. Plans for ANNL closely paralleled the recommendations of ethnic leaders since Agnew's memo of 1955, but the committee now planned a "Freedom Day" observance on September 19 as a kickoff event for the GOP's ethnic voter campaign.[40]

ANNL's leaders chose the new date for their kickoff carefully. September 19 was the day before the opening of a new United Nations session—one that Khrushchev, satellite nation leaders, and possibly even Castro were scheduled to attend. "Apart from [the program's] direct value in terms of the national interest," Richardson reported, "it is believed that mass public participation with the resulting increased focus on the problem of dealing with international communism will be beneficial to the Nixon-Lodge

cause." Richardson suggested that the Freedom Day observance be organized nationally, with GOP leadership participating in observances in all
key cities.[41] Discussions with Polish leaders, for example, revealed to Richardson that

> even the traditionally Democratic Poles would vote by great majorities for
> Nixon-Lodge if sufficient stress is laid on Yalta, Potsdam, the Bowles-Steven-
> son-Mrs. Roosevelt school of thought, and, affirmatively, on dedication of the
> Vice President to the achievement of peace through the victory of freedom.

He had heard similar reactions, he said, from Italian, Hungarian, and Lithuanian leaders. Emphasizing the crisis of the Captive Nations, Richardson
concluded, was "the one issue which can bring them to our side."[42] Again,
Asian issues were excluded from Richardson's recommendations.

Nixon's knee ailment placed further strain upon his campaign schedule
as the vice president attempted to keep his pledge to visit all fifty states. The
presidential campaigns of Eisenhower, his predecessor, had been the first
to bring mass marketing concepts fully into the American political arena,
appealing to the entire population through short, pithy national television
advertisements and establishing what amounted to a cult of personality
surrounding the former general. Eisenhower's hesitation to appeal to specific subgroups, as described above, was one result of this approach. Given
Eisenhower's success, Nixon planned his fifty-state appeal as a further elaboration of this mass marketing plan for victory.[43] By September 19, he had
checked only about 10 off his list, so ANNL organizers had to share Nixon
with the fine folks of Wilkes-Barre and Scranton, Pennsylvania. He did, however, speak before an assembled audience of ethnic leaders and regional organizers at a morning meeting in the Washington Hotel before heading out on
the campaign trail. Despite the haste of his visit, Nixon's speech beautifully
captured the tenor of the Republicans' campaign in 1960 among nationality
groups. As such, it stands as a paramount example of an appeal to civic nationalism and marks the high point of the ANNL's existence.

Nixon opened his speech with words of thanks to those who sat before him. "I feel very humble," he said, "in the presence of this group in
which are so many who have led the fight for freedom through the years,
long before I ever came into public life." Having acknowledged the dedication of his audience, Nixon went on to speculate upon what might make
America worthy of such hard work and devotion. "Some would say America
is a great country," he explained, "because it is the strongest nation in the
world militarily. It is." Others, he went on, would point to its provision of
the highest standard of living or to the superiority of its natural resources.

All these things were important, Nixon conceded, and "to the Communists that is all that greatness is, but to us greatness is something far more significant." America's greatness was established, he argued, when she was a tiny nation of three million people: "It was great because it stood for something." That something, of course, was freedom and independence, for the United States and for others around the world, but Nixon went beyond these familiar platitudes to bring his audience firmly into this vision:

> Have you ever stopped to consider who are the American people? This is not a master race in the sense that the dictators have used, but the Americans, the people we call the Americans, come from all the nations of the world. We come from all continents, from all countries, from all races and religions and what better evidence of it than here?

Nixon discussed meeting with Herbert Hoover at the time he was working with the former president on Hungarian refugee issues, following the 1956 uprising. He shared with the conference attendees what Hoover said when faced with the question of changing immigration laws to admit more refugees: "every wave of refugees that has come to the United States has strengthened America rather than weakened it."[44]

The ethnic leaders of the ANNL, then, whatever their background, were heirs to the promises of the United States and shared full citizenship with those who came before them. Lest anyone circumscribe this vision, Nixon explicitly denied that some groups might be more equal heirs than others:

> We must do nothing that would weaken this element of greatness. We must do those things that strengthen it. That is why we must fight against hatred and prejudice of any kind, fight against it because it is wrong morally, fight against it because it weakens America wherever it exists in this country in any shape.

Nixon and the Republican Party were offering *all* Americans full citizenship. All were worthy soldiers in the battle against Communism. Nixon noted Khrushchev's coming visit and his own enthusiastic receptions in the Eastern Bloc, reminding the audience of the continuing Communist threat—and his own history of international involvement in the fight against it. Proclaiming himself inspired by the example of his audience members' struggle against the Sino-Soviet menace, Nixon closed by establishing their anti-Communism as synonymous with true Americanism. ". . . You have helped America be true to her ideals," he said, "and I appreciate the opportunity to meet you."[45]

Elsewhere in the campaign, Nixon made comments that cast shadows upon this worthy articulation of the American ideal. While in the South, for example, he alluded to states' rights, the ossified doctrine that would place southern whites firmly in control of race relations in their segregated states. Nixon and the Republicans placed African Americans in a different category from white and Asian ethnic groups both organizationally and in terms of how they formulated their appeals. The vice president desired to build upon Eisenhower's inroads among southern voters, and, as well, Nixon and the party had absorbed the idea of African Americans as a group set apart, while Asian Americans were deemed as having greater potential for assimilation. Nevertheless, his campaign strategy among ethnics brought together Asians and Eastern Europeans, Middle Easterners and Latin Americans, in a common struggle against the Sino-Soviet menace. This configuration differed strongly from the politics of the Silent Majority in the late 1960s.

Nixon's speech marked only the beginning of the ANNL's daylong conference. Following a series of photo ops with the vice president, nationality leaders were ferried to the White House to meet Eisenhower. In typically Eisenhowerian fashion, the president warned of the need to stand for a firm national policy in "these days which seem now to be unusually troublous with at least what seems to be trouble-makers trying to come to our country."[46] Campaign press releases emphasized the participation of yet another Eisenhower administration official: Secretary of Labor James P. Mitchell. Mitchell entered the narrative above as a consultant during abortive planning for a Labor Day event. A New Jersey native who became labor secretary in October 1953, he was a liberal voice within the administration. Nixon liked Mitchell and even considered him as a running mate in 1960, before Mitchell removed himself from contention.[47] He was relatively well perceived by American labor, making him a helpful connection for Republicans trying to reach out to a largely working-class constituency. Finally, and probably most important, Mitchell was a practicing Catholic. As such, he served as a highly visible demonstration that not *all* Catholics were Democrats.

In addition to hearing speeches and posing for pictures, the over 200 representatives present agreed upon a series of "Conclusions" meant to guide their outreach campaign. First, they stated, in these tense times, "American Nationality Groups who have contributed so much to the formation, growth and development of the United States have a tremendous part to play in strengthening America's position of leadership in the free world." Second, given their role as links between the outside world and the United States, nationality leaders must function as "ambassadors of good will." The leaders went on to emphasize their "decisive importance" in the "American strategy for a just peace and the freedom of all people." Citing their interest in challenging the Soviets' supremacy in "educating skillful agents of various national origins," ANNL leaders suggested that in the next administration, a special agency be developed to coordinate directly with organized nationality groups "with the aim of assisting the drive to extend freedom throughout the world as envisioned in Vice President Nixon's acceptance speech." This agency would also be concerned with "the domestic problems of special interest to the Nationality Groups." Finally, the conference endorsed Nixon-Lodge as offering the best hope for carrying out these conclusions, arguing that "the experience, conviction, ability and resourcefulness of these two men must be secured for the leadership of our country and for the struggle for freedom throughout the world in the critical years ahead."[48]

These "Conclusions" served, as did Nixon's speech, to incorporate ethnic leaders into the struggle against world Communism on the part of the United States. Assigning them a specific and significant—even vital—role to fill, Republicans offered American ethnics a unique role in the fabric of civic life. Following the September 19 meeting, a call went out to all "Volunteers for Nixon-Lodge" state chairmen and local representatives to be sure they utilized ANNL leaders "in all such activities where their recognition will be influential on community nationality groups."[49] Meanwhile, Richardson and McKeldin sent out a letter to all nationality group leaders, emphasizing the importance of reaching out to ethnics on a level with which they would be comfortable. Those among them who were already active in the regular Republican Party should certainly continue their efforts, Richardson and McKeldin wrote, but

> it must be emphasized that in 1960 our most effective appeal to a group which normally leans toward the Democratic Party, can and should be made on behalf of Vice President Nixon and Ambassador Lodge and on the basis of their unparalleled experience and leadership in the world struggle against Communism.

In other words, accentuate Nixon the Freedom Fighter and Lodge, Warrior of the U.N.—not the party that so many might continue to associate with white, Anglo-Saxon Protestants.

Following the September 19 meeting, Henderson, McKeldin, and Richardson acknowledged that at the start of the weekend, many ethnic leaders "evidenced acute frustration with their own part in the campaign to date." By the end of the conference, however, all three felt that the attendees had left full of enthusiasm.[50] Indeed, many ethnic activists set out on their own or in concert with the Nixon-Lodge organization to try and sway ethnic opinion. Given the dearth of records dealing with the ANNL outside the scope of Nixon's files, ethnic leaders' own reactions to the ANNL program and their activities on the local level are often obscured. Resources like ethnic publications, however, provide at least some insight into how ethnic leaders and their communities responded to the organization. *Lietuviu Dienos* (Lithuanian Days), a monthly, bilingual magazine published in Hollywood, California, printed a cover photograph of Nixon with two women in traditional Lithuanian garb taken at the ANNL meeting on September 19. Inside the magazine, additional photos featured Mitchell with Lithuanian community leaders in Washington, D.C., and Nixon in Los Angeles with Leonard Valiukas, vice president of the Los Angeles County Republican Assembly—and ANNL member. Back in April, the magazine had reported on the formation of the Richard M. Nixon for President Lithuanian-American National Committee, with Valiukas as one of its founders, and while Kennedy rated a back-cover photo with Lithuanian leaders in June, he never did make the front cover. In the same June issue, which must actually have been published after the Democrats' early July convention, Valiukas criticized the Democratic platform on grounds that it "does not give any hopes of promises of liberation for the captive nations."[51]

Many ethnic newspapers were owned or edited by members of local Democratic machines and urged readers to vote a straight Democratic ticket. Coverage of ANNL was rare, although the Japanese community's *Pacific Citizen* of Los Angeles reported on ANNL leader George Inagaki's drive to organize a statewide Nisei committee for the Republican ticket. The article noted that 1960 marked the first time that the Republican National Committee had actively sought Nisei support, but the article failed to elaborate upon the GOP's tactics and arguments for support of Nixon among Japanese Americans.[52] Back in July, Washington, D.C., correspondent Mike Masaoka noted that many Nisei from Whittier who remembered Nixon as a classmate were pulling for his nomination.[53] The *Pacific Citizen* also printed photographs of both Republican and Democratic activists' activities on behalf of their candidates, including coed Ikuko Kato showing off her Nixonette outfit to UCLA's Nixon representative, Dave Taira.[54]

To counter Democratic machine strength, Republican activists placed ads in both English and foreign languages in publications throughout the nation. For example, the *Novoe Russkoe Slovo* of New York, a Russian-language newspaper, featured ads from the New York State Republican Commission asking, "What happens to America if Kennedy wins?" The ad forecast doom but assured readers that "Russian voters will not fall in the trap—they will vote for Nixon and Lodge!" "You, better than others, understand the dangers of Bolshevism," the Commission proclaimed elsewhere. Vote for Nixon and Lodge, "people of straight thought and strength." The Republican Central Campaign Committee also advertised in *Novoe Russkoe Slovo,* citing a long list of Republican achievements during the last years, including better living conditions, better pay, and peaceful conditions. Nixon and Lodge came highly recommended by Eisenhower, and "their experience helps them see the future with confidence"; they would "build world peace."[55]

A variety of newspapers carried a standard advertisement designed by ANNL and printed in a number of languages. The ad, which generally ran at about four columns wide and seven inches high, featured photos of Nixon poking Khrushchev in the chest during the Kitchen Debate and Nixon and Lodge holding up their hands to the crowd at the nominating convention. Beneath the photo of the vice president's prodding finger ran these lines from his acceptance speech:

> When Mr. Khrushchev says our grandchildren will live under Communism, let us say his grandchildren will live in freedom. When Mr. Khrushchev says the Monroe Doctrine is dead in the Americas, let us say the Doctrine of Freedom lives everywhere in the world.

Advising readers to "Vote for Peace With Freedom and Justice," the ad professed that Nixon and Lodge would stop Communism, inflation, and "the drift to socialism" while protecting readers' freedom, savings, and "the American way of life."[56]

The efforts of one activist, John J. Knezevich, offer an especially interesting insight into ethnic leaders' attempts to motivate members of their communities on their own terms. Knezevich was a journalist, the editor and publisher of the *Palos Verdes* (California) *News,* but he was also an activist in the Serbian community. In a September 13 letter, he shared with Nixon two copies of an advertisement he had placed in the September 7 issue of the *American Srbobran,* a Serbian paper based in Cleveland. Knezevich urged the vice president to "please read it to the very end." The advertisement differed, he said, from the regular format of Nixon's ads, but "the reason is that I have tried to think and write in a manner most appealing to the American Serbs." The ad, a half-page with photos, was addressed "to all Serbians in the United States," and in it Knezevich personally argued the case for Nixon, citing his experience and qualifications and referring specifically to Nixon's superior knowledge of the "TRUE facts concerning Yugoslavia and the Serbian people." "It is taken for granted," he told readers, "that the American Serbians will give at least 98 percent of its total vote to Vice President RICHARD M. NIXON, the republican candidate [*sic*]." This was not, however, enough.

More than that is expected from every one of you. . . .We must immediately begin to actively work for NIXON for President among our friends and acquaintances to convince them that Nixon is the man of the hour. EACH ONE MUST SECURE TEN VOTES FOR NIXON. . . . Never, never, in our history did our Country have a better qualified man for Presidency of the United States than is our Vice President RICHARD M. NIXON. Serbians of the United States, join your hands, hearts, and minds, work day and night for the salvation of our beloved United States and the world, by voting and working for RICHARD M. NIXON, the next president of the United States.

For the contemporary reader, "over the top" would be far too mild a term to apply to such an advertisement. Results seemed to prove, however, that Knezevich knew what he was doing. The newspaperman also enclosed a letter from a family by the last name of Bouvich. "Thank you for the wonderful, direct and valuable information on Nixon," Mrs. Bouvich wrote. "You can be sure my sisters, brothers and relatives will be casting our votes for Nixon, and, we will, in turn, secure ten votes each for him. P.S. We need more Serbs like you!"[57]

Under the surface, however, indications of continuing discontent simmered. Valiukas, the Lithuanian leader from Los Angeles, sent a series of letters to Nixon on "Nixon for President Lithuanian-American National Committee" letterhead, urging him to schedule a get-together with representatives of various nationality groups during his October 13–14 visit to southern California. He emphasized that the meeting would only take 20 to 25 minutes and would provide immensely helpful photo opportunities. Valiukas voiced his frustration that the eight nationality groups affiliated with the California Republican Assembly, a statewide partisan organization, were receiving the cooperation of only one CRA leader. Six other nationality groups had independent Republican clubs, he wrote, and several additional groups were in the process of formation.[58] Receiving no response to his October 2 letter, Valiukas wrote to the campaign again on October 11, this time asking for only ten minutes to take a series of photographs. An October 24 campaign memo indicates that local GOP leader Pat Hillings was called and asked to tell Valiukas that his letter had not reached headquarters until October 15, after Nixon's Los Angeles visit.[59] Either Valiukas' earlier letter had been lost, or the campaign simply chose to ignore him.

Even the ANNL leadership became frustrated with what they felt was Nixon's reluctance to speak forcefully on the issues they felt would sway ethnic support. In an October 26 telegram to Nixon's train, for example, Henderson conveyed Richardson's frustration. It was urgent, he cabled, that Nixon begin taking advantage of the weaknesses of Democratic advisers

Stevenson and Bowles with all the major groups that considered the Communism issue to be of paramount importance. Continuing to press issues he first raised in 1959, Richardson pointed out that Bowles' 1958 book advocated withdrawal of Chinese Nationalist forces from Quemoy and Matsu, as well as a plebiscite on the island of Formosa to determine whether its citizens wanted independence or absorption into a Chinese Communist state. "Why not use this and other quotations from Bowles and Stevenson in answering Kennedy?" he pled.

Nixon made a few final attempts to appeal to ethnic voters in the last weeks of his campaign. The televised candidate debates brought the issues of Quemoy and Matsu and of Cuba into the national discussion. In the second debate, which was devoted to foreign policy, Nixon attacked Kennedy's argument that Quemoy and Matsu were "not strategically defensible" or "essential to the defense of Formosa."[60] In the third debate, Kennedy began to hedge on the issue, enabling Nixon to pound home his own position for the defense of the islands. Nixon biographers have contended that the candidates' exchanges on the issue "generated more heat and headlines than light and insight," with neither getting the issue of legal possession straight.[61] The Nixon campaign's polling service, however, found that by the end of the third debate, Nixon had effectively identified the issue in voters' minds with "stand[ing] up to the Russians."[62]

On the issue of Cuba, Nixon's knowledge of plans that would become the Bay of Pigs invasion gave Kennedy an advantage as the two jockeyed for the toughest stance. Within the Eisenhower administration, Nixon had long argued in favor of a tougher line against Castro, and the administration's current programs of covert exile training and overt quarantine were due at least in part to his efforts. Kennedy, however, spoke publicly in favor of just such actions. Faced with the possibility of betraying the administration's plans, Nixon felt forced into attacking Kennedy's own hard-line proposal as "dangerously irresponsible."[63] The Massachusetts senator, on the other hand, could speak from his outsider's position without such restraints.[64]

But Nixon did use Richardson's frequently urged advice in a telegram sent to a Nixon-Lodge Freedom Rally held by Hungarian Americans in New York City on October 30. Emphasizing America's need to use every political, economic, and psychological weapon at its command, he cited the nation's moral obligation "because of the responsibility we share for the ignoble retreat of the West before Soviet bluff and bluster during and after World War II. No American can ever hear the name Yalta without a deep sense of shame."[65] October 30 also marked a minor triumph for ANNL as the *New York Times* announced that Mario C. Remo, formerly chair of the Italian division and finance committee for the Democratic National Committee's Nationalities Division, had defected to the Republicans.[66]

Finally, on November 4, McCaffrey passed along to the Nixon-Lodge Committee of northern California a Nixon statement, made in Philadelphia, "for possible use in Chinese newspapers." This episode marked the only instance, beyond his attention to the Quemoy and Matsu issue, when the vice president specifically reached out to Asian voters. The statement proclaimed that "many of the most glorious chapters in American history have been written by those immigrants who came here with a strong yearning to share in the American ideal of opportunity and freedom." Accordingly, "there can be no question but that our immigration laws should and must be liberalized." The vice president pointed out that Eisenhower had urged extensive amendment of the nation's immigration laws in the last legislative session, but Congress, "controlled by Mr. Kennedy and his followers," declined to take action. Nixon sought a substantial increase in the number of immigrants allowed into the country each year, as well as a pooling of the national quotas and the abandonment of an outdated census as the immigration quota base.[67] He also argued that attention must be paid to the special plight of relatives of American citizens. Finally, "further amendments to the immigration laws must be enacted to give greater recognition to immigrants from the newly-emerging nations of the world."[68] Nixon's statement drew upon themes of outreach to the world through elimination of racist vestiges at home that were also prominent among proponents of African American civil rights. Despite his attempts to link Kennedy to immigration reform opponents, however, Nixon could not erase the Massachusetts senator's 1958 book *A Nation of Immigrants*, described by historian Erika Lee as an "unabashed celebration of America's immigrant heritage and a call for immigration reform."[69] Once again, Kennedy had triumphed in the politics of symbolism.

Electoral Aftermath

Of course the election returns of November 8, 1960, brought news of Nixon's narrow defeat. They also brought evidence that despite the efforts of nationality group activists, most ethnic Americans chose to cast their votes for Kennedy. While Eisenhower had been able to build a substantial base of support within the Polish community, for example, earning almost half its 1956 vote, Polish Americans returned to the Democratic Party, awarding Kennedy 78 percent of their ballots.[70] Nixon's level of support also fell by 20 to 25 percent among Irish and Italian urban voters in the Great Lakes region.[71] Kennedy recorded substantial wins in Jewish and

Italian communities, and among Puerto Rican and Mexican ethnics, he recorded a nine-to-one margin.[72] Some scholars have argued that religion was the primary factor determining ethnics' voting behavior in 1960, Kennedy having made identification with religio-ethnic groups respectable.[73] Overall, Kennedy gained 20 to 25 percentage points of the Catholic vote over Stevenson's 1956 totals.[74] Studies of Polish voting patterns and analyses of the ethnic vote in Boston, Cincinatti, and Providence provide further evidence of this Catholic voting trend.[75]

While all statistical indications show religious affinity as being the strongest factor propelling ethnics into Kennedy's column, it is important to note that some observers and scholars have placed blame for Nixon's loss elsewhere. Activist Roma Lipsky, who worked with Democratic nationality groups in 1960, contended in 1961 that Democrats' success came more from their newly formulated approach of appealing to "communities of interest" rather than traditional nationality blocs.[76] Contemporary historian Lizabeth Cohen elaborated further upon this idea of "communities of interest," explaining how the Kennedy campaign used the new marketing strategy of market segmentation—successor to Eisenhower and Nixon's mass-market appeals—to reach out effectively to ethnics and other groups. The Massachusetts senator's Catholicism and physical attractiveness provided easy entry to two market segments: Catholics and women. Following the Democratic National Convention, however, the Kennedy team developed a laundry list of affinity groups using nationality, work, and age as means of mobilizing voters. They went on to target doubtful states and areas of high population, in contrast to Nixon's broad-brush strategy. The Republicans' efforts at cultivating specialized interest groups simply could not compete, given Nixon's overriding interest in appealing to the masses.[77] Kennedy's successful exploitation of fears about declining American prestige and a nonexistent "missile gap" also served to stoke his popularity among voters concerned about the Communist menace.[78]

Richardson compiled his own list of reasons for Nixon's ineffectiveness among ethnic Americans. While he attributed ANNL's problems in part to the religious issue and to economic uncertainties, more important for the co-director were "basic mistakes made prior to and during the campaign." These mistakes were the result, he concluded, of "the failure of Administration and Party leadership to appreciate the importance of the special concerns of these groups, comprising probably 12 to 14 million voters." For the past eight years, the party had made patronage appointments with such homogeneity that it appeared "an Anglo-Saxon background and name is a requirement for success in the GOP." In terms of foreign policy, Richardson argued that Republicans had talked the talk of liberation but had failed to convince voters that they meant what they said. Ethnic voters had eight years of the Eisenhower administration to review as they made their decision. During those eight years, Eisenhower had demonstrated the limits of "liberation" with such moves as his pragmatic refusal to involve American troops in the Soviets' crushing of the Hungarian Uprising in 1956.[79] The party had failed to provide a permanent organization for mobilizing nationality leaders and neglected to construct a good working relationship between the RNC campaign director and the leadership of ANNL during the fall campaign. As a result, experienced personnel were isolated on obscure projects, and responsibility for direction of ethnic outreach was left, as described above, until the last week of August. ANNL suffered from inadequate funding, and no one had been able to impress upon the candidates the importance of issues like immigration, which was not addressed until the last ten days of the campaign. "The almost continuous efforts by the undersigned and others to impress these matters on the campaign leadership and the candidates were not effective," Richardson lamented. "We simply failed, as far as we could see, to 'get through.'" He contrasted ANNL's frustrations with the experiences of Michel Cieplinski, the Democratic Party's nationalities director, who "was regularly a member of the Kennedy staff and it appears that both he and Governor Williams, the Nationalities Chairman, had Kennedy's 'ear.'"[80]

Perhaps most revealing, however, are the reactions expressed by ethnic leaders. These activists remained largely unconvinced of the all-encompassing power of Kennedy's Catholicism—and, like Richardson, extremely frustrated by what they deemed severe lapses in the organization and strategy of the Nixon-Lodge campaign. Significantly, their criticisms often mirrored those expressed long before the fall campaign got underway. RNC Nationalities Director Hermann evidently sought out the reaction of ethnic leaders following Nixon's loss, as Nixon's files include several copies of letters citing questions Hermann had asked.

Valiukas, the Lithuanian leader from California, sent copies of his response to Hermann to Nixon, Rockefeller, Arizona Senator Barry Goldwater, and Senator Styles Bridges. This list would have sent a message to Nixon of Valiukas' awareness of and interest in exploiting intraparty tensions to ethnics' benefit. Valiukas agreed 100 percent, he said, with Bridges' recent comment that Nixon had thrown away a won election, pulling his punches when he should have gone on the offensive. "Vice President Nixon, according to Bridges, had plenty of convictions—and not enough courage to fight for them." The Republicans lost the November election, Valiukas argued, because they lacked good party leadership, because Eisenhower had done nothing during his two terms to build up the party, and because Nixon and Lodge had neglected both minority groups and nationalities.

Valiukas told of numerous attempts to secure the support of California Republican leaders in a state where 20 percent of citizens were first- or second-generation Americans. "They did not do one single thing about it," he bitterly reported. Nationality leaders were in a position to give the campaign nationwide publicity in ethnic newspapers, but again, "we were denied this. . . . the Republican Party did very little, if anything, to win the nationalities." Furthermore, Eisenhower, while a "very fine American," was a "very poor Party leader." Since 1953, the president had been "too busy" to meet with Lithuanian American leaders, and Valiukas believed that other nationality groups had met with similar problems. The Democrats exploited this situation in the last election, with the result that many Lithuanian Americans Valiukas spoke with were reasoning, "'Well, if the Republican President does not want to give us several minutes of his time a year, why should we vote for this party . . .'"

Finally, he reported, "we were breaking our necks in trying to help Dick and Cabot, but we did not get any cooperation from the Vice President's office." Valiukas and his fellow ethnic leaders had attempted to portray Nixon and Lodge as "great fighters for the freedom of the enslaved nations"; the Republican Party's program for ethnics made it as far as the leadership level. Unfortunately, when Valiukas acted on this program, writing to Nixon and urging him to mention the names of the Captive Nations in his talks, "he never did one single time." Every time Nixon and Lodge stopped in California during the campaign, they were "'too busy'" to meet with nationality groups—and Valiukas had experienced no luck in scheduling a meeting between Nixon and ethnic leaders in attempts dating back to 1956. Valiukas had suggested to Nixon, he explained, that both Nixon and Lodge should have had able advisers from ethnic backgrounds. "Probably he thought he did not need any. This was a big mistake." He urged the Republican National Committee to immediately hire a nationalities expert so this long litany of mistakes could be avoided in the future.[81]

Colonel Leon Nicolai, a Russian community leader in San Francisco who had worked with the RNC Nationalities Division throughout the 1950s, expressed more optimism about Nixon and his future in the party, urging him to take control over the GOP machinery in 1961 and reorganize. "When I read how happy Communistic Moscow is over our election," he wrote, "I realized they expect the return of the Roosevelt Era." In the face of such Soviet glee, continuing the good fight was essential. Nicolai laid the blame for the lost election on Eisenhower, albeit on slightly different terms than Valiukas. He wrote to Nixon of his surprise that at Eisenhower's speech before the ANNL organizing meeting in September, the president made no mention of Nixon's candidacy. "We were very discouraged," he wrote, "and many members of our committee expected from the President talk about your campaign for the Presidency. We feel that the President started campaigning for you much too late."[82] If Eisenhower had been a more enthusiastic party man, or at least a Nixon man, perhaps some of his support among American ethnics could have been transferred to the vice president.

The plethora of concerns ANNL committeemen raised about the conduct of the election did not, of course, wholly exclude the Catholic issue. George E.K. Borshy, president of the Hungarian Reformed Federation of America,[83] mentioned Catholicism several times in his own letter to Hermann bewailing the electoral loss. His comments, however, are more a reflection of anti-Catholic prejudice than of Catholicism as a primary issue:

> . . . you must not forget the fact that the great majority of these groups . . . consist of simple Roman Catholic workers who were greatly influenced by the rosy promises of the Democratic candidate concerning minimum wages and social security and also by the union terror and their Catholic loyalty.

Borshy also expressed concern about the television debates, arguing that they gave the lesser-known Kennedy valuable publicity, and he implied that the lack of Nixon-Lodge coverage in Hungarian American newspapers was largely due to Communist ownership or editorship.[84] More significant, perhaps, than his slightly paranoid explanation of the electoral defeat was the cover letter Borshy sent to Nixon with a copy of his Hermann composition. Borshy was Hungarian-born and became an American citizen in about 1940. He had not previously been active in politics, he wrote, but in 1960 he took on the duty because

> I felt that I had to work for the success of the Party which, beginning with Lincoln and continuing through Theodore Roosevelt, Senator Borah, you and Mr. Lodge, with its progressive conservatism and global vision, could best understand the tragic history, destiny and present miserable situation of my native land.

He contrasted this Republican vision with the Democratic Party, which he condemned for its "narrow vision" post–World War I, arguing that it "upset the equilibrium and thus sowed the seeds of a new war." Furthermore, following World War II, the Democrats had won the victory but lost the peace—a clear, if implicit, reference to Yalta and Potsdam.

The Demise of Civic Nationalism

The civic nationalist program of the Nixon-Lodge campaign had, then, been effective in mobilizing ethnic leaders like Valiukas, Nicolai, and Borshy—men who were members of the ANNL committee. Many of these individuals had already been active in the Republican Party for years, although Borshy is a strong example of someone attracted to the party through the ideology of civic nationalism. Perhaps the "Catholic issue" would have been insurmountable among such predominantly Catholic constituencies in 1960. Beyond this problem, however—an issue beyond Nixon's control—lay a more fundamental problem of organization. Nixon and the Republican Party were simply unable, or perhaps unwilling, to put forth sufficient time and personal effort to reach out to this important segment of the American public. As a result, the civic nationalist position was doomed not on its own merits, but because its possibilities were never fulfilled.

Nixon wanted ethnics' support, and he believed he had the anti-Communist reputation necessary to mobilize this support. The vice president failed to realize, however, that ethnics wanted more than an image of "Nixon the Freedom Fighter"; they required a candidate who would show—through his presence and his cooperation—his respect for their growing role in American life. Mere rhetoric was insufficient to sway the majority of American ethnics, and even the rhetorical groundwork of the ANNL campaign failed to incorporate all the citizens it purported to serve—notably, Asian Americans. In contrast, Kennedy's Nationalities Divisions developed special committees to serve thirty different ethnic groups. Republicans would regain the initiative in marketing innovation by 1964, when conservative activist and direct-mail pioneer Richard Viguerie began to develop his methods of reaching out to millions of people through personalized appeals.

In 1968, Nixon altered his strategy, making use of advanced polling and market research techniques and even going so far as to craft specialized campaign songs for specific target audiences.[85] Using the language of "law and order," Nixon mobilized white ethnic voters concerned about civil unrest and opposed to taxes that funded inner-city social programs—despite the many benefits these voters had gained through New Deal institutions and other, earlier government activity. Unfortunately, by the time Nixon grew sufficiently aware of ethnics' prominence to reach out more fully, the frustrations and concerns of the 1960s had created the conditions for a new program of outreach—one based upon racial fear and division rather than a united America against the Communist foe. While civic nationalism was not necessarily incompatible with the other components of the new conservative order, Nixon's 1960 experience led him to embrace a different, and much more polarizing, method of reaching ethnic voters. Here again, then, 1960 played a fundamentally transitional role.

Conclusion

Rightward into the Future

"Those who believe in the traditional American philosophy of government, which is clearly identified with the conservative cause, might
very well decide the nation would benefit from a realignment of the
parties and a more frankdisclosure of the philosophy of each group."
—Barry Goldwater, November 9, 1960[1]

November 9, 1960, brought with it all the recriminations catalogued in
previous chapters as various constituencies strove to explain Nixon's loss in
their own terms. It also brought a wave of predictions about the future of
the Republican Party. Liberals like Nelson Rockefeller and his team believed
that they held the keys to victory for the GOP in 1964, while conservatives
continued to mobilize behind the scenes, building upon the organizations
and networks they established in 1960 to develop a well-funded and cohesive movement to draft Barry Goldwater as nominee four years hence. Ultimately, conservatives demonstrated their capacity to successfully consolidate their efforts and build a dominant presence in the Republican Party,
taking advantage along the way of favorably changing demographics and
issue orientations within the American electorate.

By 1964, even as liberals like Rockefeller continued to enjoy personal-
ity-based individual success in local and state elections, conservatives held
the reins of the Republican Party at the national level. Goldwater's campaign, tinged as it was with extremist rhetoric and the never-repudiated
loyalty of fringe groups like the John Birch Society, was a spectacular failure. Goldwater's loss, though, offered lessons—among them, how to deal

with extremists. Having captured control of the party machinery, conservatives could then stand against extremism—legitimizing their own ideological framework in the end as "responsible" Republicanism. Former actor and General Electric representative Ronald Reagan successfully united party conservatives and independent conservative organizations and excluded extremism from the equation in his 1966 California gubernatorial victory.[2] From this point forward, conservatism has been the dominant ideology within the Republican Party.

The benefits of historical hindsight, of course, were unavailable in 1960, and Republicans of all ideological stripes planned for the future under the assumption that their programs marked the way toward GOP victory in four years. Nixon's crushingly narrow defeat afforded him the luxury of imagining that he might be able to regain the party leadership and try again in 1964. To his credit, he declined to force a recount in regions of Illinois and Texas where indications of electoral fraud were rife, thereby avoiding a lengthy interregnum without a president-elect and delays in the orderly transfer of power. Rather, Nixon quietly returned to private life for a time, taking a position with a prominent law firm in Los Angeles and writing his first volume of memoirs, *Six Crises*. In the book, Nixon listed three factors he viewed as important in his defeat following a year's reflection. First, the campaign was too long, in terms of distance, time, and volume of speeches and appearances. Second, he had failed to save his strength for major events. Finally, Nixon believed he had spent too much time "in the last campaign"—a key to his thoughts about the future—on substance and too little time on his appearance, going into the first televised debate, for example, while underweight and sickly-looking from his recent knee infection.[3]

In other words, Nixon had tried to be too much to too many—to reach too many campaign stops, speak personally to too many voters, and address too many issues. His efforts to walk the fences of American politics exhausted him and diluted his message to all constituent groups. While he initially professed no further ambitions beyond entering a private law practice, in 1962 he decided to run for governor of his home state of California. Nixon skeptics and political insiders alike speculated that this electoral run was simply a stepping-stone by which the former vice president could reenter public life and reach for the brass ring of the presidency again in 1964. Nixon was never captivated by the minutiae of state-level politics, and this lack of interest, combined with concerns that he would abandon the state in two years, resulted in an easy 1962 reelection for incumbent Democrat Edmund G. "Pat" Brown. Following his second defeat in two years, Nixon made his famous "you won't have Nixon to kick around anymore, gentlemen" speech to a gathering of reporters at the Ambassador Hotel and moved to New York, seemingly signaling his political retirement. New York was, after all, Rockefeller country.

Rockefeller's troops viewed Nixon's defeat as proof that he had waged a bland campaign lacking in ideas—and the governor could have done much better. Accordingly, soon after the election New York State GOP Chair Jud Morhouse laid out a framework for "How to Win in 1964," beginning with winning reelection as governor in 1962. Rockefeller successfully completed this component of the plan, but in other areas the governor and his staff continued to display the same reticence and lack of attention to detail that plagued them leading up to and during 1960. Morhouse recommended, for example, that Rockefeller supporters establish a paper called something like "The Progressive Republican" to counter the influence of the conservative periodical *Human Events*. He urged the governor to make a fuss about the necessity of the Republican Party regaining its strength in big cities and causing "attention to be paid by top leaders to the philosophical area itself to which the arch Conservatives are blind,—civil rights, minority groups, labor, urban development, health insurance, etc." Finally, Morhouse encouraged Rockefeller's staff to develop a network of devoted people to educate Republican officials at all levels, from state and local officers to major donors and RNC members, as well as to consolidate New York's position within the national committee.[4]

Unfortunately for the future of liberal or "modern" Republicanism, Rockefeller and his staff failed in most of these areas, and no other major liberal Republican emerged to lead the liberal wing of the party. No publication was established, and while leaders like Ohio State Chairman Ray Bliss created a "Big Cities" program adopted by the RNC, programs such as this and two extra-party committees created in the early 1960s, the All Republican Conference and National Republican Citizens' Committee, neglected tensions within the party structure. Despite memberships including such luminaries as Dwight Eisenhower, the committees attempted to reconstruct liberal Republicanism from outside rather than working within Republican ranks to take back power. In so doing, liberals tended to ignore or belittle conservatives as constituting a "lunatic fringe." Rockefeller himself serves as a prime example of liberals' focus on experts and studies in guiding political decisions, rather than outreach to the people. While Rockefeller commissioned studies, conservatives worked to consolidate their own ranks and continued to develop a remarkable framework of grassroots organizations. Rockefeller neglected to build the kinds of connections Morhouse recommended and made matters worse by divorcing his wife of thirty years to marry a recent divorcée on his staff, causing a scandal. Rockefeller stumbled his way through the 1964 primary season with limited support from party regulars, planning to make California his campaign's litmus test. Unfortunately, his new wife delivered their first son the day before the primary. The arrival of Nelson, Jr. reawakened questions about his father's personal ethics, and his loss in California put an end to his campaign.[5]

As Nixon and Rockefeller torpedoed their chances through ill-timed gubernatorial races and offspring, as well as lack of attention to changing trends in the country, conservatives mobilized their newly strengthened grassroots organizations to work for the nomination of Barry Goldwater in 1964. In October 1961, less than a year after Nixon's defeat, 22 men gathered in Chicago to form a behind-the-scenes organization dedicated to drafting Goldwater. As mentioned in chapter 5, this group included three men from South Carolina, in addition to such individuals as the chairman of the Young Republicans in 1960, Ned Cushing; *National Review* publisher Bill Rusher; enthusiastic young Ohio congressman John Ashbrook; and GOP organizational guru Clif White.[6] The assembled conservatives developed a plan that, in White's words, "amounted to nothing less than a long-term guerrilla operation," dedicated to getting the hearts and minds of the rank and file devoted to Goldwater. White demonstrated the kind of foresight Rockefeller lacked, pointing out that most delegates to the Republican National Convention were chosen by precinct committeemen who were themselves selected as early as two years before a presidential election.[7]

By mid-1963, the Draft Goldwater movement had gone public, and an Independence Day Draft Goldwater rally at the National Guard Armory in Washington, D.C., drew almost 9,000 people from 44 states. Rockefeller's New York sent two busloads of supporters. Although the Arizona senator was reluctant to enter the race—following John F. Kennedy's assassination, Goldwater knew the GOP's chances in 1964 were very slim—he finally acceded to supporters, declaring his candidacy in January 1964. Despite the largest civil rights rally ever in San Francisco—whose assembled protesters included none other than Jackie Robinson—and a strongly worded condemnation of extremism by keynote speaker and Oregon Governor Mark Hatfield, Goldwater won the Republican nomination on the first ballot. Goldwaterites' dedication stemmed from two factors. First, they had felt excluded for years from the party machinery, which had been dominated by eastern establishment Republicans. Second, Goldwater stood head and shoulders above the rest in conservatives' search for a candidate who understood them and whom they themselves could understand.[8] In other words, conservatives at all levels of the political process, from Goldwater down to the grassroots, were on the same page. In the early 1960s, this marked the most significant factor underlying conservative success and liberal failure on a national level.

   Conservatives went on to benefit, moreover, from the eruption of several divides in American life over the course of the 1960s. Goldwater's refusal to vote for the landmark civil rights bill of 1964 on supposedly procedural grounds mobilized large numbers of Southerners. Five of six states supporting the senator in 1964 were located in the Deep South.[9] By 1968, however, the civil rights movement had spread from the South to the rest of the nation, with cities like Los Angeles, Detroit, and Chicago exploding in riots and the less overt institutionalized racism of residential redlining coming under fire. African Americans began to believe that enforcement of basic legal rights and access to the vote would not eliminate entrenched economic problems, and some young people turned to confrontational or separatist tactics. White Americans were faced with the realities of race relations in the United States as they never had been before. Many responded with anger and frustration that they were being asked to fund social programs to help "violent" urbanites—conveniently ignoring the massive federal assistance most middle-class whites had received through programs like government-backed home loans and federal funding for road infrastructure that connected their sheltered suburban neighborhoods to urban workplaces. Furthermore, the Vietnam War exposed major fissures in American society. The black-and-white Cold War world fractured into confusing shades of gray as Americans debated the justice, motivation, and pragmatism of such a Third-World struggle. While most conservatives continued their strident support of South Vietnam and all fights against Communism, domestic issues like civil unrest, leftist student movements, and liberal judicial activism began to win increasing amounts of attention. Mere articulation of an anti-Communist philosophy no longer sufficed to win conservative support. Finally, the rising costs of war and a legacy of government borrowing to fund economic expansion had combined to place the U.S. economy on increasingly tottery legs.

   Into this maelstrom sprang none other than Richard Nixon, who capitalized on white Americans' discontent to win the 1968 presidential election on a platform of "law and order" and an undefined plan to gain "peace with honor" in Vietnam. Here again Nixon stood in the middle, between the liberal Democratic Vice President Hubert H. Humphrey and the racist Alabama Governor George Wallace, who won the electoral votes of several southern states.[10] By this point, however, the political center had shifted sufficiently rightward, at least among the majority of Americans, that Nixon could situate himself comfortably on the conservative side of the spectrum and gain sufficient votes to win the election. Indeed, combining votes for Wallace, who could best be defined as a racially conservative populist, and votes for Nixon, voters comfortable with conservative candidate platforms cast 56.9 percent of 1968 ballots.[11]

Four of the states casting their votes for Wallace were among Goldwater's supporters in 1964. Nixon, then, did not simply step into Goldwater's shoes, but instead articulated a conservative platform more broadly accepted by Americans facing the tumult of the latter 1960s. Nixon's actual policies while in office were often far more liberal than his statements, and progressive goals like school integration were actually furthered under his administration.[12] The president's centrist policies infuriated some leading conservatives, but given his incumbent status, Nixon remained in control of the GOP. By 1972, with Wallace eliminated from contention by the paralyzing bullets of a would-be assassin, the Alabama governor's racially conservative voter base joined forces with Republicans and others concerned about the Democrats' extremely liberal candidate, South Dakota Senator George McGovern, to reelect Nixon with 60.7 percent of the vote.[13] Had Nixon finished his second term, perhaps a more progressive conservatism would have become established practice within the GOP. As it was, his administration was shortly taken down by the Watergate scandal. Republicans purged any vestiges of his reign, turning instead to Ronald Reagan's sunny-faced conservative "populism of the new middle class."[14]

Nineteen-sixty, then, marked the first step of a two-step process through which conservatives gained control over the Republican Party. The Reagan Revolution of 1980 marked the second step: the ascendancy of 'one of their own' to the presidency. The first step, however, was accomplished through the groundwork that eager conservatives laid in 1960. By the end of that year, the key elements of a network of grassroots operatives among several constituencies, most notably youth and Southerners, were in place. These conservative constituencies successfully articulated their goals, connected to their chosen leadership, and created organizations that would move conservative politics forward from 1960. Conservative intellectuals, emboldened by the opportunity that Nixon's failed presidential run offered to alter the course of Republican Party politics, would continue to develop the ideology of conservatism and work to foster change in the political realm. Meanwhile, traditional Republican constituencies like liberals and African Americans were alienated by Nixon's—and earlier, Rockefeller's—failure to adequately address their needs. Their alienation left the party in organizational disarray. Conservatives' success in promoting Goldwater as Nixon's successor was the straw that broke the liberals' back, eliminating them from leading positions of influence within the Republican Party to date. Nineteen-sixty would have been liberals' last chance to hold their ground; this opportunity was squandered. Finally, Nixon and the Republican Party failed to consolidate support by using a program of Cold War civic nationalism, marking the last attempt to articulate a big-tent appeal that would have special resonance for ethnic Americans. The turmoil of the 1960s would serve to move constituencies like white ethnics, who felt underserved by the liberal establishment, into the conservative realm.

The degree to which these pioneers of the conservative movement were successful has been evident in recent decades. The idea of a conservative government is no longer a mere idea; it has been Americans' reality. Its continued success depends on conservatives' ability to continually revive and reshape their message to an ever-changing electorate—and on liberals' capacity to formulate a philosophy and movement capable of fostering a new realignment in American political life. The outcome of the 2008 election may signal a new direction. Future elections will signal whether 2008 represents a specific reaction to perceived excess or a general trend toward a new political order. Meanwhile, Americans continue to live in a world that the conservatives of 1960 created.

Notes

Introduction

1. Robert Humphreys to Leonard Hall, Dec. 31, 1958: Richard M. Nixon Pre-Presidential Papers, Series 320, Box 361, "Humphreys, Bob," National Archives and Records Administration, Pacific Southwest Branch, Laguna Niguel, CA (hereafter NALN).

2. Memo, Brent [Bozell] from Edna [of Goldwater office staff], July 29, 1959, Barry M. Goldwater Papers, Arizona Historical Society, Tempe, AZ (hereafter AHF).

3. Paul F. Boller, Jr., *Presidential Campaigns from George Washington to George W. Bush* (New York: Oxford University Press, 2004), 295.

4. Certainly some Democrats in government were more liberal than the mainstream—the conservative media often cited individuals such as Representative James Roosevelt (D-CA) and his mother, Eleanor—but by and large, left-wing activism in the 1950s United States was sidelined, given the dangers of being tarred as Communist.

5. *U.S. News and World Report*, Nov. 14, 1958, 29–30. *U.S. News* went so far as to point out that Goldwater's victory was one of the few important ones for Republicans in 1958 but proceeded to focus entirely on Rockefeller as Nixon's main competition well into 1960.

6. Joan Hoff, *Nixon Reconsidered* (New York: Basic Books, 1994).

7. Walter Dean Burnham, "Party Systems and the Political Process," in William Nisbet Chambers and Burnham, eds., *The American Party Systems: Stages of Political Development* (New York: Oxford University Press, 1967), 289–301. Burnham believed the country had experience of five national party systems since the development of the American state: an experimental system from 1789–1820; a democratizing system from 1828–1854 or 1860; a Civil War system from 1860–1893; an industrialist system from 1894–1932; and a New Deal system from 1932 into the 1960s. Burnham built upon the work of V.O. Key, Jr. and E.E. Schattschneider. James L. Sundquist, another scholar credited with providing principal arguments in support of realignment theory, makes a detailed and somewhat more cautious argument for periods of fundamental realignment in the 1850s, 1890s, and 1930s (David R. Mayhew, *Electoral Realignments: A Critique of an American Genre* [New Haven, CT: Yale University Press, 2002], 2; James L. Sundquist, *Dynamics of the Party System: Alignment and Realignment of Political Parties in the United States* [Washington, D.C.: The Brookings Institution, 1973], 3).

8. Walter Dean Burnham, *Critical Elections and the Mainsprings of American Politics* (New York: W.W. Norton and Co., 1970), 27.

9. Ibid., 10.

10. Ibid., 118, 191.

11. For the former, see Byron Shafer, ed., *The End of Realignment? Interpreting American Electoral Eras* (Madison: University of Wisconsin Press, 1991); for the latter, see Mayhew.

12. It remains to be seen whether Barack Obama's November 2008 election to

the presidency and large congressional majorities for the Democrats might constitute a new shift in party alignment.

13. Thomas Byrne Edsall and Mary D. Edsall, *Chain Reaction: The Impact of Race, Rights and Taxes on American Politics* (New York: W.W. Norton and Co., 1991), 4.

14. E.J. Dionne, Jr., *Why Americans Hate Politics* (New York: Simon and Schuster, 1991), 11.

15. Nicol C. Rae, *The Decline and Fall of the Liberal Republicans from 1952 to the Present* (New York: Oxford University Press, 1989), 3.

16. Barry M. Goldwater, *The Conscience of a Conservative* (New York: Victor, 1960), 13.

17. Nelson A. Rockefeller, *The Future of Federalism* (Cambridge, MA: Harvard University Press, 1962), 59.

18. Arthur M. Schlesinger, Jr., *The Vital Center*, revised ed. (New York: Da Capo Press, 1988), 255–256.

19. Cary Reich, *The Life of Nelson A. Rockefeller: Worlds to Conquer, 1908–1958* (New York: Doubleday, 1996), 689.

20. Stephen Skowronek, *The Politics Presidents Make: Leadership from John Adams to Bill Clinton* (Cambridge, MA: Belknap Press, 2nd ed. 1997), 46.

21. Rae, 156.

22. Tom Reiss, "The First Conservative: How Peter Viereck Inspired—and Lost—a Movement," *The New Yorker* (Oct. 24, 2005), 38.

23. The genesis of conservative thought is discussed in more detail in chapter 3.

24. For discussion of liberal anti-Communism, see Richard H. Pells, *The Liberal Mind in a Conservative Age: American Intellectuals in the 1940s and 1950s* (New York: Harper and Row, 1985).

25. Daniel Bell, "Interpretations of American Politics," in *The Radical Right: The New American Right, Expanded and Updated*, Daniel Bell, ed. (Garden City, NY: Anchor Books, 1963; revised ed.), 58.

26. Richard Hofstadter, "The Pseudo-Conservative Revolt," in *The Radical Right*, 94.

27. Seymour Martin Lipset, "The Sources of the 'Radical Right,'" in *The Radical Right*, 369.

28. Godfrey Hodgson, *The World Turned Right Side Up: A History of the Conservative Ascendancy in America* (Boston: Hougton Mifflin Co., 1996), 56.

29. Hofstadter, *The Radical Right*, 77; Lipset, *The Radical Right*, 344–45.

30. Clinton Rossiter, *Parties and Politics in America* (Ithaca, NY: Cornell University Press, 1960), 163. The writings of Bell, Hofstadter, et al. provide additional examples.

31. Arthur Larson, *A Republican Looks at His Party* (New York: Harper and Brothers, 1956), 10–16. For more on Arthur Larson, see David L. Stebenne, *Modern Republican: Arthur Larson and the Eisenhower Years* (Bloomington: Indiana University Press, 2006). Steven Wagner evaluates Eisenhower's political philosophy in *Eisenhower Republicanism: Pursuing the Middle Way* (DeKalb: Northern Illinois University Press, 2006).

32. Alan Brinkley, "The Problem of American Conservatism," *American Historical Review* 99 (Apr. 1994): 409–429.

33. George H. Nash, *The Conservative Intellectual Movement in America Since 1945* (New York: Basic Books, 1976), xiii.

34. Whitney Strub, *Perversion for Profit: The Politics of Obscenity and Pornography in the Postwar United States* (New York: Columbia University Press, forthcoming 2010).

35. Nash, 256.

36. Hodgson, *The World Turned Right Side Up*; Jerome L. Himmelstein, *To the Right: The Transformation of American Conservatism* (Berkeley: University of California Press, 1990); Donald T. Critchlow, *The Conservative Ascendancy: How the GOP Right Made Political History* (Cambridge, MA: Harvard University Press, 2007); Mary C. Brennan, *Turning*

Right in the Sixties: The Conservative Capture of the GOP (Chapel Hill: University of North Carolina Press, 1995); William C. Berman, *America's Right Turn: From Nixon to Clinton* (Baltimore, MD.: The Johns Hopkins University Press, 2nd ed. 1998); Lisa McGirr, *Suburban Warriors: The Origins of the New American Right* (Princeton, NJ: Princeton University Press, 2001); Jonathan M. Schoenwald, *A Time For Choosing: The Rise of Modern American Conservatism* (Oxford: Oxford University Press, 2001). In addition to these more general works on the development of the conservative movement, a series of books addressing more specific elements are helpful in developing an understanding of conservatism in the late 1950s and early 1960s. Among these are Rebecca E. Klatch's *Women of the New Right* (Philadelphia: Temple University Press, 1987); Patrick Allitt's *Catholic Intellectuals and Conservative Politics in America, 1950–1985* (Ithaca, NY: Cornell University Press, 1993); Dan T. Carter's *The Politics of Rage: George Wallace, the Origins of the New Conservatism, and the Transformation of American Politics,* 2nd ed. (Baton Rouge: Louisiana State University Press, 1995, 2000); John A. Andrew's *The Other Side of the Sixties: Young Americans for Freedom and the Rise of Conservative Politics* (New Brunswick, NJ: Rutgers University Press, 1997); Kurt Schuparra's *Triumph of the Right: The Rise of the California Conservative Movement, 1945–1966* (Armonk, NY: M.E. Sharpe, 1998); Matthew Dallek's *The Right Moment: Ronald Reagan's First Victory and the Decisive Turning Point in American Politics* (New York: The Free Press, 2000) and Rick Perlstein's *Before the Storm: Barry Goldwater and the Unmaking of the American Consensus* (New York: Hill and Wang, 2001).

37. Critchlow, 285–86.

38. Hodgson, 19.

39. McGirr, 4.

40. Schoenwald, 6, 11.

41. Social movement theorists have tended to be concentrated in the fields of political science and sociology, with historians using the term in more concrete context to describe specific groups and their actions. Scholars have often described social movements in purely political terms, especially Marxist theorists who argue that social movements necessarily involve a conflict between an oppressed proletariat and a privileged ruling and/or economic class. More recent scholarship has placed social movements within a historical context and argued that they can have political, economic, or cultural goals. Even so, social movement theorists such as Daniel A. Foss, Ralph Larkin, Christine A. Kelly, Bob Edwards, and John D. McCarthy have tended to assume that these movements must necessarily be progressive or even leftist (Daniel A. Foss and Ralph Larkin, *Beyond Revolution: A New Theory of Social Movements* [South Hadley, MA: Bergin and Garvey Pub., Inc., 1986], 1–2; Christine A. Kelly, *Tangled Up in Red, White and Blue: New Social Movements in America* [Lanham, MD.: Rowman and Littlefield Publishers, Inc., 2001], 3–5; Bob Edwards and John D. McCarthy, "Resources and Social Movement Mobilization," in David A. Snow, et al., *The Blackwell Companion to Social Movements* [Malden, MA: Blackwell Publishing, Ltd., 2004], 124). David A. Snow, Sarah A. Soule, and Hanspeter Kriesi have developed a more satisfactory and inclusive definition of "social movement," postulating that social movements are ". . . collectivities acting with some degree of organization and continuity outside of institutional or organizational channels for the purpose of challenging or defending extant authority, whether it is institutionally or culturally based, in the group, organization, society, culture, or world order of which they are a part" (David A. Snow, et al., "Mapping the Terrain," in Snow, et al., 11).

42. Snow in Snow, et al., 7–8.

43. Sociologists studying the history of American political development provide additional theoretical assistance. Theda Skocpol, for example, argues in *Protecting Soldiers and Mothers: The Political Origins of Social Policy in the United States* (Cambridge, MA: Belknap Press, 1992) that the structure of American politics has historically allowed

"unusual leverage to social groups that can, with a degree of discipline and consistency of purpose, associate across many local political districts." This "structured polity" approach, which takes into account the importance of both political actors and institutional configurations, proves applicable to conservative networks of the 1950s and 1960s just as Skocpol used it to analyze the development of maternalist social welfare policies in the Progressive Era (55, 41). Skocpol emphasizes the importance of the historical moment in conditioning the success or failure of political activities, a reality that helps account for the importance of individual and party actions at given points in time in determining the future of political alignments.

44. Rae, 42.

45. Ibid., 9.

46. Gary A. Donaldson argues that 1960 marked the first "modern campaign"—the first election in which image was a deciding factor (*The First Modern Campaign: Kennedy, Nixon, and the Election of 1960* [Lanham, MD: Rowman and Littlefield Publishers, Inc., 2007], viii). Ironically, Eisenhower was well aware throughout his presidency of the importance of image and mass marketing—see, for example, chapter 5.

47. Wagner, 115–16.

48. *Congressional Quarterly Weekly Report*, Aug. 26, 1960, 1495.

49. Richard M. Nixon, *Six Crises* (Garden City, NY: Doubleday and Co., Inc., 1962), 418.

1—A Rocky Course for Liberalism

1. "Rocking with Rockefeller" sheet music, copyright 1958, Johnny Carriger, Alexandria, VA: Nelson A. Rockefeller Papers Collection, Record Group 15, Series 22, Subseries 5, Box 56, Folder 1309, Rockefeller Archive Center, Sleepy Hollow, NY (hereafter Rockefeller Archives).

2. Larson, *A Republican Looks at His Party*, ix–10.

3. Piers Brendon, *Ike: His Life and Times* (New York: Harper and Row, 1986), 294. Steven Wagner also discusses Eisenhower's flirtation with the idea of a third party; see, for example, *Eisenhower Republicanism*, 114–15.

4. Skowronek, 46.

5. *U.S. News and World Report*, Jan.Jan. 2, 1959, 21; *Newsweek*, Nov. 10, 1958, 19; *New York Times*, Mar.Mar. 15, 1959.

6. Romney was elected governor of Michigan in 1962, and Scranton was elected to a term as congressman in 1960 before winning the Pennsylvania gubernatorial election in 1962.

7. Rae, 5.

8. Ibid., 41.

9. Pells, ix.

10. *U.S. News and World Report*, Jan. 23, 1959, 33.

11. Reich, 675, 684. Tragically, Reich was killed in an automobile accident before he could complete the second volume of his highly detailed biography.

12. William M. Bush to Nelson A. Rockefeller, Dec. 23, 1958; Bartley C. Crum to NAR, Nov. 20, 1958: Record Group 4, Series J.1, Subseries 2, Box 14, Folder 109, Rockefeller Archives.

13. Joanne Collins to NAR, Aug. 4, 1959: Record Group 4, Series J.1, Subseries 2, Box 14, Folder 109, Rockefeller Archives.

14. Mrs. F.R. Edwards to NAR, Nov. 5, 1958; A.C. Harlander to NAR, Oct. 30, 1958; Eve Berkowitz to NAR, Sept. 19, 1958: Record Group 4, Series J.1, Subseries 2, Box 14, Folder 109, Rockefeller Archives; Dec. 8, 1958 clipping from Richard B. Kay: Record Group 4, Series J.1, Subseries 2, Box 14, Folder 110, Rockefeller Archives.

15. Finding aid notes: Record Group 15, Series 22, Subseries 5, Rockefeller Archives.

16. RFPCIC Press Release, Oct. 6, 1959: Record Group 15, Series 22, Subseries 5, Box 54, Folder 1250, Rockefeller Archives.

17. Memo, Dick Amper to Rod Perkins, Sept. 22, 1959: Record Group 15, Series 22, Subseries 5, Box 55, Folder 1275, Rockefeller Archives. The two offices eventually worked out a process for passing letters on to RFPCIC.

18. F. Clinton Murphy to NAR, Nov. 20, 1959; Hunter and Staples, Inc. report: Record Group 15, Series 22, Subseries 5, Box 54, Folder 1266, Rockefeller Archives.

19. Albert Otis to NAR, Sept. 26, 1959: Record Group 15, Series 22, Subseries 5, Box 54, Folder 1266, Rockefeller Archives; Memo of telephone call, Ilene Slater to George Hinman, Oct. 26, 1959: Record Group 15, Series 22, Subseries 5, Box 54, Folder 1267, Rockefeller Archives.

20. Ray Bengert to Alexander Halpern, Oct. 20, 1959: Record Group 15, Series 22, Subseries 5, Box 55, Folder 1268, Rockefeller Archives.

21. Adair County Citizens for Rockefeller "Proclamation," Nov. 18, 1959: Record Group 15, Series 22, Box 55, Folder 1279, Rockefeller Archives.

22. Memo, Mrs. NAR to George Hinman, Dec. 10, 1959; Caroline K. Simon to Hinman, Dec. 21, 1959: Record Group 15, Series 22, Subseries 5, Box 56, Folder 1294, Rockefeller Archives.

23. Memo, Halpern to NAR, undated: Record Group 15, Series 22, Subseries 5, Box 54, Folder 1257, Rockefeller Archives.

24. Handwritten, undated replies to undated RFPCIC mass mailing: Record Group 15, Series 22, Box 54, Folder 1253, Rockefeller Archives.

25. Illegible of Fort Wayne, IN, to Halpern, undated: Record Group 15, Series 22, Subseries 5, Box 54, Folder 1253, Rockefeller Archives.

26. Geo. S. Cluff to Halpern, Dec. 10, 1959: Record Group 15, Series 22, Subseries 5, Box 54, Folder 1253, Rockefeller Archives.

27. Memo, Rod Perkins to Dick Amper and Martha Dalrymple, Aug. 24, 1959: Record Group 15, Series 22, Subseries 5, Box 54, Folder 1260, Rockefeller Archives.

28. "The Rockefeller Record": Record Group 15, Series 22, Subseries 4, Box 49, Folder 1189, Rockefeller Archives. Not quoted but also present in same folder: "Nelson Rockefeller: Man With a Mission."

29. *U.S. News and World Report*, Feb. 29, 1960, 82–83. The 16 states, in order of voting, were New Hampshire, Wisconsin, Illinois, New Jersey, Massachusetts, Pennsylvania, Indiana, Ohio, West Virginia, Nebraska, Maryland, Oregon, Florida, California, New York, and South Dakota. Illinois, Pennsylvania, and New York voted only on district delegates, with at-large delegates chosen later by either the state convention or party committees. In Indiana and Maryland, the primary was an indirect election, with delegates chosen for state conventions that would then elect national delegates.

30. *U.S. News and World Report*, July 20, 1959, 29; Sept. 28, 1959, 16; Oct. 12, 1959, 25.

31. *U.S. News and World Report*, Oct. 19, 1959, 29.

32. Nixon, 302.

33. Memo, Harry O'Donnell, Sept. 1, 1959: Record Group 15, Series 22, Subseries 4, Box 50, Folder 1209, Rockefeller Archives.

34. Memo, Morhouse to Hinman, Perkins, Bixby, and Hornbeck, Sept. 15, 1959: Record Group 15, Series 22, Subseries 4, Box 51, Folder 1217, Rockefeller Archives.

35. Strategy Outline, Oct. 14, 1959, Morhouse to Bixby, Hornbeck, Hinman, Happy Murphy, Perkins: Record Group 15, Series 22, Subseries 4, Box 50, Folder 1210, Rockefeller Archives; Press Release, Sept. 12, 1959: Record Group 15, Series 22, Subseries 5, Box 55, Folder 1286, Rockefeller Archives.

36. "Intelligence Summary as of Aug. 17 [1959]": Record Group 15, Series 22, Subseries 4, Box 50, Folder 1201, Rockefeller Archives. ·

37. "DNA" might have stood for "Definitive News Analysis," but the Rockefeller Archive Center staff has found no corroboration in the written record. The staff of DNA was on Rockefeller's personal payroll.

38. Twenty-five percent of respondents, for example, said they could not rank his potential performance, while only 6 percent declined to rank Nixon.

39. Six State Survey on Presidential Images, J.E. Bachelder, Hadley Cantril, and Lloyd A. Free, Oct. 15, 1959: Record Group 15, Series 22, Subseries 4, Box 51, Folder 1222, Rockefeller Archives.

40. Memo, Bill Brinton, Nov. 16, 1959: Record Group 15, Series 22, Subseries 4, Box 48, Folder 1186, Rockefeller Archives.

41. Support for a Rockefeller presidential run among New Yorkers was overwhelmingly confined to downstate residents and especially those living in the vicinity of New York City. *All* the members of the New York Draft Rockefeller Executive Committee, for example, which formed in 1960, were from Westchester County south (Member list: Record Group 15, Series 22, Subseries 5, Box 56, Folder 1295, Rockefeller Archives). Upstate New Yorkers tended to be more conservative than their downstate neighbors, and gubernatorial policies like Rockefeller's 1959 tax hikes to balance the state budget left a sour taste in upstate mouths.

42. "Citizens Groups" Card Files: Record Group 15, Series 22, Subseries 5, Box 57, Rockefeller Archives.

43. Bill Brinton to Hinman, Dec. 9, 1959; Thomas P. Losee to Hinman, Dec. 18, 1959: Record Grup 15, Series 22, Subseries 5, Box 48, Folder 1186, Rockefeller Archives.

44. "List of Contributors": Record Group 15, Series 22, Subseries 5, Box 54, Folder 1251, Rockefeller Archives.

45. *U.S. News and World Report*, Nov. 23, 1959, 59.

46. Memo, Victor Borella to Hinman, Dec. 7, 1959: Record Group 4, Series J.1, Subseries 2, Box 111, Folder 96, Rockefeller Archives.

47. "Confidential—for NAR only," Dec. 8, 1959: Record Group 4, Series J.1, Subseries 2, Box 111, Folder 96, Rockefeller Archives.

48. Press Release, Dec. 26, 1959: Record Group 4, Series J.1, Subseries 2, Box 11, Folder 94, Rockefeller Archives.

49. Halpern to NAR, Jan. 5, 1960: Record Group 15, Series 22, Subseries 5, Box 54, Folder 1250, Rockefeller Archives.

50. Seymour Blum to RFPCIC, Jan. 5, 1950: Record Group 15, Series 22, Subseries 5, Box 55, Folder 1287, Rockefeller Archives.

51. Memo, Mary K. Boland to Political and Public Relations Group, Jan. 11, 1960: Record Group 4, Series G, Subseries 3, Box 25, Folder 302, Rockefeller Archives. Nixon's first congressional campaign, against incumbent Democrat Jerry Voorhis, and his senate campaign, against incumbent Democrat Helen Gahagan Douglas, were often condemned as examples of dirty campaigning. Historical reactions to these charges have differed; see, for example, Irwin F. Gellman, *The Contender: Richard Nixon, The Congress Years* (New York: The Free Press, 1999), who presents a favorable viewpoint, versus Greg Mitchell, *Tricky Dick and the Pink Lady: Richard Nixon vs. Helen Gahagan Douglas—Sexual Politics and the Red Scare, 1950* (New York: Random House, 1998), who is far more critical of Nixon.

52. Memo, Boland to Hinman, Dec. 30, 1959: Record Group 15, Series 22, Subseries 4, Box 50, Folder 1212, Rockefeller Archives.

53. Memo, Hinman to Oren Root, Jan. 7, 1960: Record Group 15, Series 22, Subseries 4, Box 50, Folder 1211, Rockefeller Archives. Root was the grandnephew of Elihu Root, a former senator who had held the positions of Secretary of War and Secretary of

State in the Theodore Roosevelt Administration. His dedication to liberal Republican candidates had a long history; in 1940, he was chairman of the Associated Willkie Clubs of America.

54. Memo, Hinman to Root, Jan. 6, 1960: Record Group 15, Series 22, Subseries 4, Box 50, Folder 1211, Rockefeller Archives.

55. *New York Times*, Apr. 15, 1960, 1.

56. Ibid., Mar. 10, 1960, 22; Apr. 7, 1960, 28; May 21, 1960, 1.

57. John F. Carter to Jud Morhouse, Feb. 29, 1960 and Apr. 17, 1960: Record Group 15, Series 22, Subseries 4, Box 49, Folder 1191, Rockefeller Archives.

58. *U.S. News and World Report*, May 9, 1960, 47.

59. Memo, Hinman to NAR, May 12, 1960: Record Group 4, Series J.2, Subseries 4, Box 92, Folder 635, Rockefeller Archives.

60. *Congressional Quarterly* XVIII (May 20, 1960): 890.

61. Press Release, May 23, 1960: Record Group 15, Gubernatorial Speeches, Box 3, Folder 165, Rockefeller Archives.

62. *Congressional Quarterly Weekly Report* XVIII (May 27, 1960): 929.

63. Ibid., (June 3, 1960): 964.

64. June 3, 1960 News Summary: PPS 69.85, Richard M. Nixon Papers, Richard M. Nixon Presidential Library and Birthplace, Yorba Linda, CA (hereafter Nixon Library).

65. Glennoirre Blough to NAR, May 25, 1960: Record Group 15, Series 22, Subseries 5, Box 55, Folder 1270, Rockefeller Archives.

66. Telegram, Samuel Walker to NAR, May 31, 1960: Record Group 15, Series 22, Subseries 5, Box 56, Folder 1295, Rockefeller Archives.

67. *New York Herald Tribune*, June 9, 1960.

68. Ibid., June 9, 1960.

69. Ibid., June 10, 1960.

70. Memo, Emmet Hughes to NAR, May 31, 1960: Record Group 4, Series G, Subseries 3, Box 26, Folder 308, Rockefeller Archives.

71. Campaign 1960 Position Papers and Statements, Box 2, various folders, Nixon Library.

72. *Philadelphia Inquirer* clipping, June 10, 1960: Series 320, Box 44, "Annenberg, Walter H.," Nixon Papers, NALN.

73. Celia P. Fay to NAR, June 11, 1960: Record Group 15, Series 22, Subseries 5, Box 55, Folder 1276, Rockefeller Archives.

74. R.R. Greenbaum to NAR, June 16, 1960: Record Group 15, Series 22, Subseries 5, Box 55, Folder 1278, Rockefeller Archives.

75. NAR to Ernest Shupstick, July 18, 1960: Record Group 15, Series 22, Subseries 5, Box 54, Folder 1267, Rockefeller Archives.

76. Press Release, July 6, 1960: Record Group 15, Series 22, Subseries 4, Box 48, Folder 1186, Rockefeller Archives.

77. Perkins to Hinman, May 2, 1960: Record Group 4, Series J.1, Subseries 2, Box 12, Folder 102, Rockefeller Archives.

78. Memo, GLH-PFH, June 17, 1960: Record Group 4, Series J.1, Subseries 2, Box 12, Folder 102, Rockefeller Archives.

79. Memo, GLH-PFH, June 17, 1960: Record Group 4, Series J.1, Subseries 2, Box 12, Folder 102, Rockefeller Archives.

80. Jack Barnes to Malcolm Wilson, July 5, 1960: Record Group 15, Series 22, Subseries 5, Box 56, Folder 1295, Rockefeller Archives.

81. "A Republican Approach to the Great Issues": Record Group 4, Series J.1, Subseries 2, Box 14, Folder 115, Rockefeller Archives.

82. "Let Freedom Ring: A Centennial Memorandum for the 1960 Republican Party Platform": Record Group 4, Series J.1, Subseries 2, Box 14, Folder 115, Rockefeller Archives.

83. Press release, July 21, 1960: Record Group 15, Series 22, Subseries 4, Box 48, Folder 1186, Rockefeller Archives.

84. "Rockefeller Roll Call," July 23, 1960: Record Group 4, Series J.1, Subseries 2, Box 11, Folder 94, Rockefeller Archives.

85. Memo, "MDH" to unstated, undated: Record Group 15, Series 22, Subseries 4, Box 50, Folder 1200, Rockefeller Archives.

86. Nixon, 315–16.

87. See, for example, *U.S. News and World Report*, June 29, 1960, 35.

88. Hinman to NAR, Sept. 27, 1960: Record Group 4, Series J.1, Subseries 2, Box 11, Folder 96, Rockefeller Archives.

89. Hughes to NAR, Oct. 6, 1960: Record Group 4, Series J.1, Subseries 2, Box 11, Folder 97, Rockefeller Archives.

90. Press release, Oct. 23, 1960: Record Group 15, Series 22, Subseries 4, Box 52, Folder 1230, Rockefeller Archives.

91. Memo, Perkins to NAR, Oct. 26, 1960: Record Group 15, Series 22, Subseries 4, Box 49, Folder 1188, Rockefeller Archives.

92. New York State Republican Committee Comparative Vote Statistics: Record Group 4, Series G, Subseries 3, Box 25, Folder 301, Rockefeller Archives.

93. Memo, Hinman to NAR, Nov. 11, 1960: Record Group 4, Series J.1, Subseries 4, Box 92, Folder 635, Rockefeller Archives.

94. RNC Research Division "Preliminary Analysis of the 1960 Presidential Vote," Record Group 4, Series J.1, Subseries 2, Box 11, Folder 96, Rockefeller Archives.

95. Memo, Hugh Morrow to NAR, Dec. 2, 1960: Record Group 4, Series J.1, Subseries 2, Box 111, Folder 96, Rockefeller Archives.

96. Rae, 9.

2—Elephant on a Tightrope

1. The interrelationship between the American civil rights movement and U.S. foreign policy, especially with regard to African and Asian nations, has become a fertile field in recent historiography. Examples include Thomas Borstelmann, *The Cold War and the Color Line: American Race Relations in the Global Arena* (Cambridge, MA: Harvard University Press, 2001); Mary L. Dudziak, *Cold War Civil Rights: Race and the Image of American Democracy* (Princeton, NJ: Princeton University Press, 2000); James H. Meriwether, *Proudly We Can Be Africans: Black Americans and Africa, 1935–1961* (Chapel Hill: University of North Carolina Press, 2002); Brenda Gayle Plummer, *Rising Wind: Black Americans and U.S. Foreign Affairs, 1935–1960* (Chapel Hill: University of North Carolina Press, 1996); Brenda Gayle Plummer, ed., *Window on Freedom: Race, Civil Rights, and Foreign Affairs, 1945–1988* (Chapel Hill: University of North Carolina Press, 2003); and Penny Von Eschen, *Race Against Empire: Black Americans and Anticolonialism, 1937–1957* (Ithaca, NY: Cornell University Press, 1997).

2. Lewis L. Gould, *Grand Old Party: A History of the Republicans* (New York: Random House, 2003), 252.

3. Steven F. Lawson, *Running for Freedom: Civil Rights and Black Politics in America Since 1941* (New York: McGraw-Hill, Inc., 1991), 14, 38–39.

4. Ibid., 40–41; Robert Fredrick Burk, *The Eisenhower Administration and Black Civil Rights* (Knoxville: University of Tennessee Press, 1984), 15, 18.

5. Burk, vi; David A. Nichols, *A Matter of Justice: Eisenhower and the Beginning of the Civil Rights Revolution* (New York: Simon and Schuster, 2007), 273.

6. Burk, vi, 93, 98, 113.

7. Lawson, 54–55.

8. Ibid., 56–58.

9. AP Wire, 8/8/57: Series 320, Box 153, "Civil Rights," Nixon Papers, NALN.

10. Martin Luther King, Jr., to RN, Aug. 30, 1957: PPS 320.107.12, Richard M. Nixon Pre-Presidential Papers, Nixon Library).

11. Memorandum, Aug. 13, 1957: Series 320, Box 153, "Civil Rights," Nixon Papers, NALN.

12. Memo from McWhorter to RN, Oct. 4, 1957: Series 320, Box 153, "Civil Rights," Nixon Papers, NALN.

13. E. Frederic Morrow, *Way Down South Up North* (Philadelphia: Pilgrim Press, 1973), 25–26.

14. E. Frederic Morrow, *Forty Years a Guinea Pig* (New York: The Pilgrim Press, 1980), 87, 90, 92, 156.

15. Memo from E. Frederic Morrow to RN, Nov. 10, 1958: Series 320, Box 532, "Morrow, Fred," Nixon Papers, NALN.

16. Val Washington to RN, Mar. 3, 1958; Memo from CKMcW to RN, Mar. 4, 1958: Series 320, Box 801, "Washington, Val," Nixon Papers, NALN.

17. Roy Wilkins to RN, Apr. 21, 1959: Series 320, Box 820, "Wilkins, Roy," Nixon Papers, NALN.

18. RN to Chuck Percy, Mar. 21, 1959: Series 320, Box 630, "Republican Committee on Program and Progress," Nixon Papers, NALN.

19. Morrow to Rose Mary Woods, Dec. 1, 1959; handwritten, undated note on U.S. Senate memo paper: Series 320, Box 532, "Morrow," Nixon Papers, NALN.

20. Draft, RN to John A. Morsell; memo, RN to CSP, AW, DSH, July 2, 1959; RN to Morsell, July 8, 1959: Series 320, Box 546, "National Association for the Advancement of Colored People," Nixon Papers, NALN.

21. Multiple copies of form letter: Series 320, Box 546, "NAACP," Nixon Papers, NALN.

22. Telegram from Wilkins to RN, Jan. 22, 1960: Series 320, Box 820, "Wilkins," Nixon Papers, NALN.

23. Memo from Finch to Agnes Waldron, Feb. 3, 1960: Series 320, Box 820, "Wilkins," Nixon Papers, NALN.

24. Lester Granger to George L. Hinman, Sept. 2, 1959; Louis E. Martin to Granger, Aug. 28, 1959: Record Group 15, Series 22, Subseries 4, Box 50, Folder 1211, Rockefeller Archives.

25. *Baltimore Afro-American*, Sept. 12, 1959; Chicago *Defender*, Sept. 9, 1959, 7; *Pittsburgh Courier*, Sept. 19, 1959.

26. *Baltimore Afro-American*, Sept. 19, 1959.

27. Press release, Nov. 13, 1959: Record Group 15, Box 1, Folder 66, Rockefeller Archives. "Brotherhood of man and fatherhood of God" was one of Rockefeller's favorite stock phrases—longtime associates came to refer to it as his "BOMFOG" routine.

28. *Baltimore Afro-American*, Nov. 7, 1959.

29. Danny Ryan to NAR, Nov. 20, 1959: Record Group 15, Series 22, Subseries 5, Box 56, Folder 1294, Rockefeller Archives.

30. Walter Hiles to NAR, Dec. 10, 1959: Record Group 15, Series 22, Subseries 5, Box 54, Folder 1267, Rockefeller Archives.

31. *New York Post*, Nov. 25, 1959.

32. *Baltimore Afro-American*, Jan. 9, 1960.

33. *Chicago Daily Defender*, Jan. 4, 1960, 10.

34. Arnold Rampersad, *Jackie Robinson: A Biography* (New York: Alfred A. Knopf, 1997), 324–25, 334, 340–41.

35. *New York Post*, Dec. 30, 1959.

36. H.S. Craig memo, Jan. 11, 1960; Horace S. Craig blanket memo, Jan. 20, 1960: Record Group F., Series 3, Box 27, Folder 314, Rockefeller Archives.

37. Position Paper M-8 (Preliminary), Apr. 8, 1960: Record Group 4, Series G, Subseries 3, Box 27, Folder 317, Rockefeller Archives.

38. Feb. 5, 1960 News Summary, PPS 69/25, Nixon Library.

39. *Baltimore Afro-American*, Mar. 5, 1960.

40. Mar. 12–14, 1960 News Summary: PPS 69/42, Nixon Library; Apr. 15–18, 1960 News Summary: PPS 69/65, Nixon Library.

41. Apr. 23–25, 1960 News Summary: PPS 69/70, Nixon Library.

42. Memo to Bob Finch of Val Washington phone call, 4/8: Series 320, Box 801, "Washington," Nixon Papers, NALN.

43. Laura Jane Gifford, "Washington, Valores J. (Val)," in *African American National Biography* (New York: Oxford University Press, 2008).

44. Emmett S. Cunningham to RN, Apr. 25, 1960: Series 320, Box 801, "Washington," Nixon Papers, NALN.

45. Memo, McWhorter to RN, Mar. 8, 1960: Series 320, Box 520, "Mitchell, Clarence," Nixon Papers, NALN.

46. Jackie Robinson to RN, May 11, 1960: Series 320, Box 649, "Robinson, Jackie," Nixon Papers, NALN. The only Nixon vote unfavorable to civil rights that the NAACP noted in its compendium of the candidates' positions up to 1950 came in Feb. 1950, when then-Congressman Nixon voted against a strong FEPC ("Congressional Civil Rights Record of Presidential and Vice Presidential Candidates": Series 320, Box 546, "NAACP," Nixon Papers, NALN).

47. *Baltimore Afro-American*, May 28, 1960, 4.

48. John Temple Graves to RN, June 17, 1959; RN memo, July 2, 1959; Graves to RN, Mar. 29, 1960: Series 320, Box 301, "Graves, John Temple," Nixon Papers, NALN.

49. *Amsterdam News* (New York), May 14, 1960, two clippings: Series 320, Box 554, "Negro Press," Nixon Papers, NALN.

50. *New York Herald Tribune*, June 9, 1960.

51. William J. Davenport to NAR, June 10, 1960: Record Group 15, Series 22, Subseries 5, Box 56, Folder 1295, Rockefeller Archives.

52. *Pittsburgh Courier*, June 18, 1960.

53. *Chicago Daily Defender*, June 16, 1960, 12.

54. June 18–20, 1960 News Summary: PPS 69/93, Nixon Library.

55. *New York Post*, June 10, 1960, 96.

56. Memo to Finch of Washington phone call, June 14, 1960: Series 320, Box 801, "Washington," Nixon Papers, NALN.

57. *Amsterdam News* (New York), June 25, 1960: Series 320, Box 554, "Negro Press," Nixon Papers, NALN; *Baltimore Afro-American*, July 2, 1960.

58. Governor's office press release, July 23, 1960: Record Group 15, Series 25, Box 6, Folder 109, Rockefeller Archives.

59. Theodore H. White, *The Making of the President 1960* (New York: Signet, 1961), 234.

60. Herbert S. Parmet, *Richard Nixon and His America* (Boston: Little, Brown and Co., 1990), 388–389.

61. *Official Report of the Proceedings of the Twenty-Seventh Republican National Convention* (Washington, D.C.: Republican National Committee, 1960), 255.

62. For example, White, 234; Roscoe Drummond column, July 26, 1960 News Summary, PPS 69/120, Nixon Library; *Chicago Tribune* editorial, July 27, 1960 News Summary: PPS/69/121, Nixon Library.

63. The plank stated, "We reaffirm the constitutional right to peaceable assembly to protest discrimination by private business establishments. We applaud the action of the businessmen who have abandoned discriminatory practices in retail establishments, and we urge others to follow their example" (*Official Proceedings*, 256).

64. *Chicago Daily Defender*, July 25, 28, Aug. 1, 1960—all p. 12.

65. *Baltimore Afro-American*, Aug. 6, 1960.

66. *New York Post*, July 29, 1960.

67. Ibid., July 18, 1960.

68. Henry Cabot Lodge, *The Storm Has Many Eyes: A Personal Narrative* (New York: W.W. Norton and Co., 1973), 184; Anne E. Blair, *Lodge in Vietnam: A Patriot Abroad* (New Haven, CT: Yale University Press, 1995), xi.

69. Lodge, 184; William J. Miller, *Henry Cabot Lodge* (New York: James H. Heineman, Inc., 1967), 325.

70. *Battle Line*, Aug. 24, 1960: Series 320, Box 67, "Battle Line," Nixon Papers, NALN.

71. *Pittsburgh Courier*, Sept. 10, 1960, 3.

72. *Chicago Defender*, Aug. 4, 1960, 3.

73. *Baltimore Afro American*, July 23, 1960, 2.

74. New York State Republican Party press release, Aug. 10, 1960: Series 320, Box 445, "Lefkowitz, Louis J.," Nixon Papers, NALN.

75. Republican National Committee press release, Aug. 12, 1960: Series 320, Box 801, "Washington," Nixon Papers, NALN.

76. Press conference transcript, Aug. 17, 1960: Series 207, Box 142, Folder 1, Nixon Papers, NALN.

77. Aug. 21–22, 1960 News Summary: PPS 69/142, Nixon Library; Aug. 19, 1960 News Summary: PPS 69/140, Nixon Library.

78. Undated memo signed "dbean": Series 207, Box 142, Folder 1, Nixon Papers, NALN.

79. Aug. 24, 1960 News Summary: PPS 69/144, Nixon Library.

80. Memo, Don Hughes to McWhorter, Aug. 23, 1960: Series 320, Box 820, "Wilkins," Nixon Papers, NALN.

81. Aug. 24, 1960 News Summary: PPS 69/144, Nixon Library.

82. *Baltimore Afro-American*, Sept. 3, 1960, 9.

83. Rampersad, 346–47.

84. Memo to Stan McCaffrey of Washington phone call, Aug. 31, 1960: Series 320, Box 801, "Washington," Nixon Papers, NALN.

85. Press release, Sept. 9, 1960: Series 320, Box 532, "Morrow," Nixon Papers, NALN; Memo from Bill Safire and Charlie Sigety to Len Hall, et al., Oct. 24, 1960: Series 320, Box 666, "Safire, William," Nixon Papers, NALN.

86. RN to S.B. Fuller, Aug. 18, 1960: Series 320, Box 277, "Fuller, S.B.," Nixon Papers, NALN; RN to George Sevelle, Aug. 18, 1960: Series 320, Box 686, "Sevelle, George," Nixon Papers, NALN; RN to William O. Walker, Aug. 18, 1960: Series 320, Box 794, "Walker, William O.," Nixon Papers, NALN.

87. Sevelle to RN, Sept. 2, 1960: Series 320, Box 686, "Sevelle," Nixon Papers, NALN.

88. *California Eagle*, Sept. 8, 1960.

89. Burk, 258.

90. Morrow, *Forty Years*, 205.

91. "State and National Polls": PPS 71/1, Nixon Library.

92. "Herald-Dispatch poll in 43 states": PPS 71/1, Nixon Library. Nixon's support sat right at 50 percent in Washington, but Kennedy only garnered 47 percent of black support.

93. *Chicago Daily Defender*, Sept. 15, 1960, 3.

94. Morrow, *Forty Years*, 205.

95. *Pittsburgh Courier*, Sept. 17–Nov. 5, 1960. Note that several of the endorsement ads ran multiple times and were counted only once in the tally.

96. *Chicago Daily Defender*, Sept. 14, 1960, 2; Sept. 19, 1960, 12.

97. Pat Hillings to RN, Sept. 30, 1960: Series 320, Box 341, "Hillings, Patrick," Nixon Papers, NALN.

98. *New York Times*, Oct. 13, 1960, 1; Oct. 14, 1960, 1; Oct. 17, 1960, 1.

99. *Chicago Daily Defender*, Oct. 20, 1960, 12.

100. *Baltimore Afro-American*, Oct. 22, 1960, 1–2.

101. "State and National Polls": PPS 71/1, Nixon Library.

102. Nixon, 362.

103. David Nichols, for example, cites Irwin F. Gellman, author of *The Contender: Richard Nixon, The Congress Years, 1946–1952* (New York: Free Press, 1999), as stating that research for his planned multi-volume biography indicates that the impact of the King incident on the election's outcome was exaggerated in the years after 1960 (Nichols, 332).

104. Taylor Branch, *Parting the Waters: America in the King Years, 1954–63* (New York: Touchstone, 1988), 366–68.

105. Morrow, *Forty Years*, 206–208.

106. Rampersad, 351.

107. *Pittsburgh Courier*, Nov. 5, 1960, 6.

108. Preliminary Analysis of the 1960 Presidential Vote: Record Group 4, Series J, Subseries 2, Box 11, Folder 96, Rockefeller Archives. The survey's sample area in the South included Kentucky, Mississippi, Louisiana, and Texas, states that in many cases offered little or no opportunity for African Americans to vote. The RNC research staff alluded to this, stating, "low turnout makes the change less impressive in terms of votes."

109. Morrow, 206; Clifford M. Kuhn, "'There's a Footnote to History!': Memory and the History of Martin Luther King's Oct. 1960 Arrest and Its Aftermath" *Journal of American History* 84 (Sept. 1997), 586.

110. *The Young Republican News*, Mar./Apr. 1961; Robinson to RN, May 25, 1961: Series 320, Box 649, "Robinson," Nixon Papers, NALN.

111. Morrow to RN, Apr. 18, 1961: Series 320, Box 532, "Morrow," Nixon Papers, NALN.

112. Elaine Jenkins to RN, Oct. 1, 1962: Series 320, Box 382, "Jenkins, Elaine B.," Nixon Papers, NALN.

113. Rampersad, 353–54.

114. See, for example, Nick Bryant, *The Bystander: John F. Kennedy and the Struggle for Black Equality* (New York: Basic Books, 2006).

3—"Nixonfeller" and the Remnant

1. *National Review*, Aug. 13, 1960, 69.

2. Reiss, 38.

3. William F. Buckley, Jr., *God and Man at Yale* (Washington, D.C.: Regnery Publishing, Inc., 1952, 1977, 1986), xii.

4. Nash, 14–15; 39.

5. Ibid., 144.

6. William A. Rusher, *The Rise of the Right* (New York: William Morrow and Co., 1984), 17, 27–28.

7. Ibid., 36–37.

8. Nash, 145–46.

9. William F. Buckley, Jr., *Miles Gone By: A Literary Autobiography* (Washington, D.C.: Regnery Publishing, Inc., 2004), 283–84.

10. Rusher argues that *God and Man at Yale* represented the first joining of conservatism's three strands (39).

11. Nash, 153.

12. Ibid., 155–59.

13. Rusher, 55.

14. Nash, 174.

15. Ibid., 178, 184.

16. Rusher, 16; John B. Judis, *William F. Buckley, Jr.: Patron Saint of the Conservatives* (New York: Simon and Schuster, 1988), 44–46.

17. Russell Kirk, *The Conservative Mind*, 4th ed. (New York: Avon Books, 1968), 17–18.

18. Allitt, ix–x.

19. Dionne, 25.

20. Ibid., 160–61.

21. William F. Buckley, Jr., *Up From Liberalism* (Bantam Books: 1959, 1968, 2nd ed.), xv.

22. Ibid., 77, 84.

23. Ibid., 86.

24. Ibid., 163.

25. Ibid., 173, 175.

26. *NR*, Sept. 11, 1958.

27. Ibid., Oct. 11, 1958.

28. Ibid., Oct. 25, 1958.

29. Ibid., Nov. 8, 1958.

30. Ibid., Nov. 22, 1958.

31. McGirr.

32. *NR*, Dec. 20, 1958.

33. Ibid., Jan. 31, 1959.

34. Robert M. Collins, *More: The Politics of Economic Growth in Postwar America* (Oxford: Oxford University Press, 2000) provides an engaging overview of the post–World War II political economy, arguing that the pursuit of economic growth was the central and defining feature of U.S. public policy post–World War II.

35. *NR*, Jan. 17, 1959.

36. Ibid., June 6, 1959.

37. Ibid., July 18, 1959.

38. Ibid., Jan. 31, 1959.

39. Ibid., Jan. 17, 1959.

40. Ibid., May 5, 1959. An article by Whittaker Chambers and an editorial both opposed travel restrictions.

41. Ibid., Apr. 25, 1959.

42. Ibid., Aug. 15, 1959.

43. Ibid., Oct. 10, 1959.

44. Ibid., Oct. 24, 1959.

45. Ibid., Nov. 7, 1959. Bozell's article, reflecting the befuddlement with which *NR* greeted Rockefeller's surprisingly attractive stand, was titled "What Gives With Rocky?"

46. Ibid., Mar. 14, 1959.

47. Buckley, *Miles Gone By*, 51–52; Judis, 30.

48. *NR*, Mar. 14, 1959.

49. Ibid., July 4, 1959.

50. William F. Buckley, Jr., to Charles K. McWhorter, July 6, 1959: Series 320, Box 551, "National Review," Nixon Papers, NALN.

51. Memo for file from McWhorter, Apr. 6, 1959: Series 320, Box 551, "National Review," NALN.

52. Buckley to Nixon, Dec. 26, 1957: Series 320, Box 110, Buckley, "William F., Jr.," NALN.

53. *NR*, Nov. 21, 1959.

54. Ibid., Dec. 5, 1959.

55. Ibid., Dec. 19, 1959.

56. Ibid., Aug. 27, 1960; Sept. 10, 1960.

57. See, for example, Barry Goldwater to Clarence Budington Kelland, July 13, 1959: Barry Goldwater Papers, Arizona Historical Foundation. In his letter, Goldwater

maintained he had "no interest in the Presidency nor the Vice Presidency, and I am not seeking either of them." He told Kelland that he believed he could not stop Manion and his group from proceeding if they so desired, but he did not feel they would get very far—if for no other reason than that he thought "the country might accept a Catholic, but I don't think they are ready to take a person who is Jewish, or half Jewish." Goldwater's mother baptized him as an Episcopalian, but his father was Jewish.

58. Goldwater to Eugene Pulliam, Aug. 15, 1959: Barry Goldwater Papers, AHF.

59. "Abstract of Minutes Taken at Goldwater Meeting," Jan. 23, 1960, Chicago, IL: Barry Goldwater Papers, AHF.

60. *NR,* Jan. 16, 1960.

61. Ibid., Feb. 13, 1960.

62. Ibid., Mar. 12, 1960.

63. Ibid., Mar. 26, 1960.

64. Ibid., Apr. 9, 1960. Stassen tried to develop a "dump Nixon" campaign in 1956, only to see it completely dissolve and witness his own vice presidential selection, Massachusetts Governor Christian Herter, himself offer Nixon up for re-nomination at the Republican National Convention in San Francisco.

65. Ibid., Apr. 9, 1960; Apr. 23, 1960.

66. Ibid., May 7, 1960.

67. Goldwater, 11–12.

68. *NR,* May 21, 1960.

69. Ibid., June 18, 1960.

70. Ibid., July 30, 1960.

71. Ibid., July 30, 1960.

72. Ibid.

73. Ibid.

74. Ibid., Oct. 22, 1960.

75. Ibid., Aug. 27, 1960.

76. Ibid., Sept. 24, 1960.

77. Ibid., Oct. 8, 1960.

78. Ibid., Oct. 22, 1960.

79. Inter-Office Memo, Frank Meyer to Wm. Buckley, Bozell, Burnham, John Chamberlain, Rusher, Priscilla Buckley, May 10, 1960: William F. Buckley, Jr. Papers, Manuscript Group 576, Correspondence, 1960, Box 10, Yale University Archives and Manuscripts Collections, New Haven, CT (hereafter Buckley Papers, Yale).

80. Inter-Office Memo, William Rusher to Buckley, Sept. 14, 1960: Buckley Papers, Yale.

81. Inter-Office Memo, PLB to WFB, undated: Buckley Papers, Yale.

82. Inter-Office Memo, Jim Burnham to Buckley, Oct. 9, 1960: Buckley Papers, Yale.

83. Inter-Office Memo, Rusher to Buckley, Oct. 10, 1960: Buckley Papers, Yale.

84. Inter-Office Memo, Buckley to Burnham, Oct. 11, 1960: Buckley Papers, Yale.

85. *NR,* Nov. 19, 1960.

86. Ibid., Dec. 3, 1960.

87. Ibid., Jan. 14, 1960.

4—Buttoned-down Rebels

1. Andrew, 2–3. William F. Rorabaugh also discusses the 1960s as an optimistic time in *Kennedy and the Promise of the Sixties* (New York: Cambridge University Press, 2002).

2. Gregory L. Schneider, *Cadres for Conservatism: Young Americans for Freedom and the Rise of the Contemporary Right* (New York: New York University Press, 1999), 1.

3. Bob Edwards and John D. McCarthy in Snow, et al., 142.

4. Skocpol, 55, 57.

5. *Wall Street Journal*, Nov. 3, 1960, 14.

6. *Harvard Crimson*, Apr. 17, 1959.

7. The five Democratic possibilities listed were Lyndon Johnson, John F. Kennedy, Hubert Humphrey, Adlai Stevenson, and Stuart Symington.

8. "Harvard Students Presidential Preference Poll," May 1959: Record Group 15, Series 22, Subseries 4, Box 49, Folder 1193, Rockefeller Archives.

9. Undated flier, Harvard Students for Rockefeller: Record Group 15, Series 22, Subseries 4, Box 49, Folder 1193, Rockefeller Archives.

10. Personal Report on National Students for Rockefeller, Feb. 9, 1960 (hereafter Personal Report): Record Group 15, Series 22, Subseries 4, Box 49, Folder 1193, Rockefeller Archives.

11. *Harvard Crimson*, May 15, 1959.

12. Rusher, 79.

13. Bruce Chapman to Alexander Halpern, Oct. 13, 1959: Record Group 15, Series 22, Subseries 5, Box 54, Folder 1252, Rockefeller Archives.

14. Jack Wilson to George Hinman, Nov. 16, 1959: Record Group 4, Series J.1, Subseries 2, Box 11, Folder 96, Rockefeller Archives.

15. Camden M. Hall to Halpern, Oct. 13, 1959: Record Group 15, Series 22, Subseries 5, Box 54, Folder 1252, Rockefeller Archives.

16. Personal Report: Record Group 15, Series 22, Subseries 4, Box 49, Folder 1193, Rockefeller Archives.

17. *Harvard Crimson*, Nov. 3, 1959.

18. Personal Report: Record Group 15, Series 22, Subseries 4, Box 49, Folder 1193, Rockefeller Archives.

19. "College Groups" card file: Record Group 15, Series 22, Subseries 5, Box 57, Rockefeller Archives. The states listed were California, Colorado, Connecticut, the District of Columbia, Illinois, Indiana, Maryland, Massachusetts, New York, Michigan, Minnesota, Missouri, New Hampshire, Ohio, Pennsylvania, Rhode Island, Texas, Virginia, Washington, and Wyoming.

20. Chapman to William J. Walsh, Dec. 12, 1959: Record Group 15, Series 22, Subseries 5, Box 54, Folder 1252, Rockefeller Archives.

21. *Harvard Crimson*, Jan. 29, 1960.

22. Philip G. Altbach and Patti Peterson, "Before Berkeley: Historical Perspectives on American Student Activism," *Annals of the American Academy of Political and Social Science* 395 (May 1971): 10–11.

23. Schneider, 16.

24. Andrew, 25.

25. The Student Committee for the Loyalty Oath countered widespread opposition in the academic world to a provision in the National Defense of Education Act of 1958 calling for recipients of federal funds through the program to sign loyalty oaths.

26. M. Stanton Evans, *Revolt on the Campus* (Chicago : Henry Regnery Company, 1961), 20, 22, 27, 40, 42, 44.

27. *U.S. News and World Report*, Apr. 25, 1960, 80–83.

28. Evans, 88.

29. Ibid., 89.

30. Schneider, 27.

31. Ibid., 28.

32. *Madison Capital Times* (Wisconsin), May 3, 1960: Scrapbook 83, Barry Goldwater Papers, AHF.

33. *Chicago Daily News*, June 9, 1960: Scrapbook 96, Barry Goldwater Papers, AHF; *Sunnyslope News* (Phoenix, Arizona), July 21, 1960: Scrapbook 90, Barry Goldwater Papers, AHF.

34. *Yuma Daily Sun*, July 17, 1960: Scrapbook 90, Barry Goldwater Papers, AHF.

35. Evans, 91–92.

36. *Chicago Daily News*, June 9, 1960: Scrapbook 96, Barry Goldwater Papers, AHF.

37. *Phoenix Gazette*, Dec. 16, 1959: Scrapbook 76, Barry Goldwater Papers, AHF.

38. Barry Goldwater to Stephen Shadegg, Jan. 20, 1960: Barry Goldwater Papers, AHF.

39. Evans, 94–95.

40. Ibid., 99.

41. The South Carolinians' position is outlined in more detail in chapter 5.

42. Perlstein, 91–92.

43. Evans, 101.

44. *Baltimore Sun*, Aug. 15, 1960: Series 320, Box 424, "Kolbe, James," Nixon Papers, NALN.

45. "Remarks of Honorable Barry M. Goldwater, United States Senator from Arizona," in *Official Report of the Proceedings of the Twenty-Seventh Republican National Convention* (Washington, D.C.: Republican National Committee, 1960), 289–91 (hereafter *Official Proceedings*).

46. *Arizona Republic* (Phoenix), Dec. 17, 1959: Scrapbook 76, Barry Goldwater Papers, AHF.

47. Schneider, 30–34.

48. See comments regarding Allitt's work in chapters 2 and 6.

49. Schneider, 32–33. In 1956, Soviet troops quashed an uprising by Hungarian reformers. Many conservatives believed that the Eisenhower administration should have more forcefully supported the uprising.

50. Evans, 48–50.

51. Ibid., 113.

52. Andrew, 71.

53. College Youth for Nixon Newsletter, May 1960: Series 320, Box 162, "College Youth for Nixon," Nixon Papers, NALN.

54. Ibid.

55. Goldwater, 9.

56. College Youth for Nixon Newsletter, July 1960: Series 320, Box 162, "College Youth for Nixon," Nixon Papers, NALN.

57. The Connally Amendment, sponsored by Senator Tom Connally (D-Texas), exempted the United States from the jurisdiction of the International Court of Justice in matters "essentially within the domestic jurisdiction of the United States of America as determined by the United States of America." Nixon supported some level of American independence but felt that the Connally Amendment went too far.

58. James Abstine to Mid-West Volunteers for Nixon, May 21, 1960: Series 320, Box 18, "Abstine, James," Nixon Papers, NALN.

59. Evans, 121.

60. "What the Republicans Can Do to Win in 1958 and 1960," Feb. 1, 1957: Series 320, Box 647, "Robinson," Nixon Papers, NALN.

61. Press Release, Mar. 1, 1959: Series 320, Box 680, "Scott, Hugh," Nixon Papers, NALN.

62. *Daily Emerald* (University of Oregon), Sept. 26, 1960, 7.

63. Ibid., Nov. 2, 1960, 3.

64. Memo, Bill Stricklin to Stan McCaffrey, Aug. 22, 1960: Series 320, Box 162, "College Youth for Nixon," Nixon Papers, NALN.

65. Memo, Carol Dawson to Bob Finch, Aug. 16, 1960: Series 320, Box 597, "Pike, Thomas," Nixon Papers, NALN.

66. RNC Research Report, "The 1960 Elections," Apr. 1961: Record Group 4, Series G, Subseries 3, Box 27, Folder 316, Rockefeller Archives.

67. Ibid.
68. Andrew, 73.
69. Ibid., 78.
70. Schneider, 39.
71. *Harvard Crimson*, Nov. 23, 1960.
72. Ibid., Apr. 29, 1964.
73. Rae, 5.
74. *Harvard Crimson*, Jan. 21, 1960.
75. Ibid., Feb. 14, 1961.
76. Ibid., Mar. 30, 1961; Apr. 15, 1961; Apr. 25, 1961; May 24, 1961.
77. Ibid., May 31, 1961; Sept. 25, 1961.
78. Blair, 112; Perlstein, 374.
79. Andrew, 75.

5 — "Dixie Is No Longer in the Bag"

1. "Here Comes Nixon": William D. Workman, Jr., Papers, South Caroliniana Library, University of South Carolina, Columbia, SC (hereafter SCL). The song was to be played and sung after Vice President Richard Nixon spoke at Columbia, SC, on Nov. 3, 1960. Subsequent verses proclaimed, among other things, that "In a minute we'll be fixin' everything just right with Nixon."

2. Jack Bass and Walter DeVries, *The Transformation of Southern Politics: Social Change and Political Consequence Since 1945* (New York: Basic Books, 1976), 27.

3. Scholars like Cole Blease Graham, Jr. and William Moore have argued that political trends in the South do not resemble realignment so much as they represent dealignment, with issues and specific personalities taking preference over an established party order (Cole Blease Graham, Jr., and William V. Moore, *South Carolina Politics and Government* [Lincoln: University of Nebraska Press, 1994], 73). This argument does have some validity in explaining what has transpired in Southern states post–World War II, but it seems apparent that despite a sizable decline in party loyalty, political affiliation does still matter. Harold Stanley, for example, has pointed out that despite growing tendencies toward candidate-based voting since 1952, Southerners continue to perceive important party differences, and while white Southerners increasingly choose to identify as Republican, partisan identification continues to be important (Harold W. Stanley, "Southern Partisan Changes: Dealignment, Realignment, or Both?" *Journal of Politics* 50 [Feb. 1988], 85).

4. David Robertson, *Sly and Able: A Political Biography of James F. Byrnes* (New York: W.W. Norton and Co., 1994), 82, 98.

5. Kevin Phillips, *The Emerging Republican Majority* (New Rochelle, NY: Arlington House, 1969), 195.

6. David Lublin, *The Republican South: Democratization and Partisan Change* (Princeton, NJ: Princeton University Press, 2004), 34; Robertson, 247. South Carolina Senator James F. Byrnes did not sign the manifesto.

7. More recent scholarship generally agrees with the conclusions reached by scholars contemporary to the period: Donald S. Strong, *Urban Republicanism in the South* (University of Alabama: Bureau of Public Administration, 1960); Donald S. Strong, *The 1952 Presidential Election in the South* (University of Alabama: Bureau of Public Administration, 1955); Bernard Cosman, "Presidential Republicanism in the South, 1960," *Journal of Politics* 24 (May 1962): 303–22.

8. As previously mentioned, *Brown v. Board* caused problems for Eisenhower among some Southern constituencies, even as his overall position improved. South Carolina was one of these problematic regions, with Charlestonian voters largely favoring an independent slate of electors pledged to Virginia Senator Harry F. Byrd.

Black belt support for Eisenhower declined as well (Strong, *Urban Republicanism in the South*, 20, 29). Here, race and tradition would seem to be the factors dictating lower support for Eisenhower than in other parts of the South. Race had been contested less flamboyantly in South Carolina than in other states, but the absence of boycotts and marches did not indicate any less of a problem. In 1960, for example, the state was one of three in the Deep South in which no public schools had been integrated. Palmetto State whites were angrily aware that one of the test cases composing *Brown* came from their own Clarendon County. South Carolina stood second only to Mississippi in the size of its black population, and Charleston was a much older and more demographically stable city than others in the fast-growing South.

9. Dewey W. Grantham, *The Life and Death of the Solid South* (Lexington: University Press of Kentucky, 1988), 140.

10. Graham and Moore, 81.

11. Strong, *Urban Republicanism in the South*, 1.

12. Rossiter, 141.

13. Hodgson, 97.

14. Graham and Moore, 80. See note 8 for further discussion of the 1956 vote in South Carolina.

15. Samuel DuBois Cook, "Political Movements and Organizations," in *The American South in the 1960s*, Avery Leiserson, ed. (New York: Frederick A. Praeger, 1964), 148. While the presence of a third party in 1948 complicated the election, the Dixiecrat movement began precisely because Southerners were angry with Democratic policies but were not yet willing to vote Republican. Most historians of southern politics consider 1948 to be a turning point in southern support for the national Democratic Party. See, for example, Graham and Moore 66; Grantham, 123–124; Bass and DeVries, 4.

16. Cosman, 306.

17. Earl Black and Merle Black, *Politics and Society in the South* (Cambridge, MA : Harvard University Press, 1987), 265.

18. Gregory D. Shorey, Jr., to author, Nov. 26, 2004.

19. Bass and DeVries, 25–26.

20. Shorey to author, Nov. 26, 2004.

21. 1960 Delegate List; Mar. 26, 1960. List of State Officers, County Chairmen and State Committeemen: Gregory D. Shorey Papers, SCL.

22. Shorey to author, Nov. 26, 2004.

23. Greg Shorey to Hon. George Wahr Ballade, Mar. 9, 1959: Series 320, Box 693, "Shorey, G.D. Jr.," Nixon Papers, NALN.

24. Shorey to author, Nov. 26, 2004; Hodgson, 97. This Jesse Helms, who later became mayor of Greenville, was no relation to the former North Carolina senator.

25. Book review draft, Mar. 1960: Workman Papers, SCL.

26. Press release draft, Mar. 12, 1960; T.R. Waring to Workman, Mar. 21, 1960: Workman Papers, SCL.

27. (Columbia, SC) *State*, Mar.Mar. 27, 1960, 1.

28. Robert Alan Goldberg, *Barry Goldwater* (New Haven, CT: Yale University Press, 1995), 135.

29. "1960 Platform of the Republican Party of South Carolina," *Columbia* (SC) *State*, Mar. 28, 1960.

30. *Columbia* (SC) *State*, Mar. 27, 1960, 1.

31. (Charleston, SC) *News and Courier*, Mar. 29, 1960, A6.

32. Minutes of the 1960 Republican State Convention, held at Hotel Jefferson, Columbia, SC, Mar. 26, 1960: Workman Papers, SCL.

33. Michael S. Lottman, "The GOP and the South," *Ripon Forum* VI (July–Aug. 1970), 62.

34. Shorey and Barker to M. Jeff Watts, Jr., June 24, 1960: Series 320, Box 693, "Shorey," Nixon Papers, NALN.

35. Undated Workman column clipping: Series 320, Box 693, "Shorey," Nixon Papers, NALN.

36. James T. Patterson, *Mr. Republican: A Biography of Robert A. Taft* (Boston: Houghton Mifflin, 1972), 260, 304, 329–30.

37. Perlstein, 85.

38. Shorey to author, Nov. 26, 2004. As confirmation of his suspicions, Shorey cited an incident in which he personally viewed Rockefeller at work on another attempt at behind-the-scenes influence on party direction. In 1964, at an out-of-the-way bistro in Sausalito, CA, Shorey ran into Rockefeller dining with Pennsylvania Governor William Scranton—the leading candidate of liberal Republicans by the time of the San Francisco convention.

39. *Charleston News and Courier*, July 25, 1960, A1.

40. *Columbia State*, July 25, 1960.

41. Perlstein, 86.

42. Wannamaker to Workman, July 21, 1960: Workman Papers, SCL.

43. Wannamaker to Workman, July 24, 1960: Workman Papers, SCL.

44. Perlstein, 89.

45. *Charleston News and Courier*, July 26, 1960, A1.

46. Ibid.

47. "Mr. Gregory D. Shorey, Jr. of South Carolina, Seconding the Nomination of Honorable Barry M. Goldwater for President," *Official Proceedings*, 286–87.

48. Undated memo to "those attending 'Goldwater Speaks' Luncheon" from Richland Country Republican Clubs and Citizens for Nixon-Lodge: Workman Papers, SCL.

49. (Douglas, AZ) *Daily Dispatch*, Oct. 7, 1960: Scrapbook 98, Barry Goldwater Papers, AHF.

50. Madison *Wisconsin State Journal*, n.d.: Scrapbook 194, Barry Goldwater Papers, AHF.

51. "Interview with J. Drake Edens," 13 Feb. 1974: Southern Oral History Program, in the Southern Historical Collection, Manuscripts Department, Wilson Library, University of North Carolina at Chapel Hill.

52. Morgan Ruppe, Robert Scott, and Roy Turner, "Personal Experiences During the Growth Days of the Republican Party in York County, SC," no date: Gregory D. Shorey Papers, SCL.

53. Nadine Cohodas, *Strom Thurmond and the Politics of Southern Change* (New York: Simon and Schuster, 1993), 295. Goldwater gave the South Carolina senator some relief—and indicated his sympathy—during his 24-hour, 18-minute filibuster by asking permission to insert some material into the record at 1:30 a.m. (Thurmond began his tirade at 8:54 the previous evening).

54. William D. Workman, Jr., *The Case for the South* (New York: The Devin-Adair Co., 1960), 94.

55. Ibid., 19.

56. "Reaction, Readers, Outside South, 1959–1960 (Jan.)": Workman Papers, SCL.

57. Workman, 258, 254.

58. Shorey to author, Nov. 26, 2004.

59. Paid Political Advertisement in the Columbia *State*, Mar. 28, 1960.

60. "Minutes of the1960 Republican State Convention," held at Hotel Jefferson, Columbia, SC, Mar. 26, 1960: Workman Papers, SCL.

61. "Minutes of the Reconvened Session of the 1960 Annual Convention of the South Carolina Republican Party," held at Hotel Jefferson, Columbia, SC, Aug. 6, 1960: Workman Papers, SCL.

62. "The Honorable Richard M. Nixon Accepts the Nomination for President of

the United States," *Official Proceedings*, 348.

63. Charleston *News and Courier*, July 29, 1960.

64. Ibid., July 30, 1960, A6.

65. Shorey to Thruston Morton, Sept. 1, 1960: Series 320, Box 693, "Shorey," Nixon Papers, NALN.

66. *The Speeches of Vice President Richard M. Nixon, Presidential Campaign of 1960* (Washington, D.C.: U.S. Government Printing Office, 1961), 1096–1097, 1193.

67. Shorey to Charles McWhorter, Oct. 17, 1960: Series 320, Box 693, "Shorey," Nixon Papers, NALN.

68. *New York Times*, Oct. 13, 1960, 1; Oct. 14, 1960, 1; Oct. 17, 1960, 1.

69. Shorey to James Bassett, Oct. 3, 1960: Series 320, Box 693, "Shorey," Nixon Papers, NALN.

70. James F. Byrne's Introduction of Vice President Richard M. Nixon, Nov. 3, 1960, at Statehouse, Columbia, SC: Workman Papers, SCL.

71. Notes on Nov. 3 Nixon visit: Workman Papers, SCL.

72. *Columbia State*, Nov. 4, 1960, 1.

73. *The Speeches*, 973–978.

74. Statement of the vice president of the United States upon arrival in South Carolina, Nov. 3, 1960: Workman Papers, SCL.

75. *The Speeches*, 974.

76. "Byrnes Backs Nixon and Lodge: His Statement" (brochure); Notes "Prepared by Governor Byrnes": MSS 90, James F. Byrnes Papers, Clemson (Clemson, SC) University (hereafter Byrnes Papers, Clemson).

77. "Tele-call, Nixon to JFB": Byrnes Papers, Clemson.

78. Analysis of 1960 Democratic Platform by Senator Strom Thurmond, July 24, 1960: MSS 100, Strom Thurmond Collection, Clemson (Clemson, SC) University (hereafter Thurmond Collection, Clemson).

79. Columbia *State*, Nov. 8, 1960: Series 320, Box 756, "Thurmond, Strom," Nixon Papers, NALN.

80. Thurmond to constituent, Nov. 3, 1960: Thurmond Collection, Clemson.

81. H.P. North to Byrnes, Sept. 23, 1960: Byrnes Papers, Clemson.

82. "A woman Democrat" to Byrnes, Sept. 26, 1960: Byrnes Papers, Clemson.

83. Dallas L. Dendy to Byrnes, Nov. 10, 1960: Byrnes Papers, Clemson.

84. Graham and Moore, 80.

85. Campaign 1960 News Summaries: PPS 69/143, 69/165, 69/171, 69/200, 69/207, Nixon Library; *Charleston News and Courier*, Nov. 6, 1960, A6.

86. Shorey to author, Nov. 26, 2004.

87. "In GOP We Trust": MSS 69, James E. Duffy Papers, Clemson (Clemson, SC) University (hereafter Duffy Papers, Clemson).

88. Bass and DeVries, 24.

89. V.O. Key, Jr., *Southern Politics in State and Nation* (New York: Vintage Books, 1949), 16.

90. Fernald to Duffy, Nov. 1, 1960: Duffy Papers, Clemson.

91. "G.O.P. News," Nov. 1960: Gregory D. Shorey, Jr. Papers, SCL.

92. The three men were Robert F. Chapman, Roger Milliken, and Greg Shorey. Milliken's brother, Connecticut resident Gerrish Milliken, was also present (Rusher, 101).

6—"Nixon the Freedom Fighter"

1. John J. Richardson, Jr. to American Nationalities for Nixon-Lodge leaders, Sept. 13, 1960: Nixon Papers, Series 207, Box 144, Folder 3, NALN.

2. See, for example, Carter; Nathan Glazer and Daniel Patrick Moynihan, *Beyond the Melting Pot: The Negroes, Puerto Ricans, Jews, Italians, and Irish of New York City*, 2nd

ed. (Cambridge, MA: MIT Press, 1970); Michael Novak, *The Rise of the Unmeltable Ethnics* (New York: MacMillan, 1971); Phillips; and Perry L. Weed, *The White Ethnic Movement and Ethnic Politics* (New York: Praeger Publishers, 1973). In addition, Samuel Lubell provided a prescient forecast in *The Future of American Politics,* 2nd ed. (Garden City, NY: Doubleday and Co., Inc. 1956). Weed concisely lays forth the basic thrust of Republican appeals to white ethnics by 1968.First, through the language of the Silent Majority, the GOP appealed to fears and resentments brought on by urban riots and special programs to help minority citizens. On this level, the party attempted to create commonalities of class and race—of a generation of white ethnics who had pulled themselves up by their bootstraps in opposition to a violent, undeserving underbelly in American society. This ideal overlooks, of course, the vast assortment of New Deal programs that had aided so many white ethnics in their climb out of immigrant poverty. Secondly, the Republicans promoted fears of job competition and inflation that helped them sell their more conservative economic platform to a constituency with working-class roots (Weed, 157–58).

3. Gould, 127, 151.

4. Gary Gerstle, *American Crucible: Race and Nation in the Twentieth Century* (Princeton, NJ: Princeton University Press, 2001), 4.

5. For a detailed account of Kennedy's use of the (imaginary) missile gap in 1960, see Christopher A. Preble, *John F. Kennedy and the Missile Gap* (DeKalb, IL: Northern Illinois University Press, 2004).

6. Marilyn Halter, *Shopping for Identity: The Marketing of Ethnicity* (New York: Schocken Books, 2000), 199.

7. Thomas A. Guglielmo and Earl Lewis, "Changing Racial Meanings: Race and Ethnicity in the United States, 1930–1964," in Ronald H. Bayor, ed., *Race and Ethnicity in America: A Concise History* (New York: Columbia University Press, 2003), 170.

8. Victoria Hattam, "Ethnicity: An American Genealogy," in Nancy Foner and George M. Fredrickson, eds., *Not Just Black and White: Historical and Contemporary Perspectives on Immigration, Race, and Ethnicity in the United States* (New York: Russell Sage Foundation, 2004), 44–52.

9. Phillips, 144–47.

10. Ibid., 336.

11. Concordia R. Borja-Mamaril and Tyrone Lin, *Filipino Americans: Pioneers to the Present* (Portland, OR: Filipino American National Historical Society—Oregon Chapter, 2000), 132.

12. Allitt, x, 2.

13. Joseph S. Roucek and Bernard Eisenberg, "Introduction: The New Awareness," in Roucek and Eisenberg, eds., 16.

14. The median family income among Chinese Americans in 1959 was $6,207; among all Americans, the figure was $5,660 (Iris Chang, *The Chinese in America* [New York: Viking, 2003], 258).

15. Phillips, 110; Vincent N. Parrillo, "Asian Americans in American Politics," in Roucek and Eisenberg, eds., 97.

16. Robert T. Agnew to John Krehbiel, Mar. 18, 1955: Series 320, Box 22, "Agnew, Robert T.," Nixon Papers, NALN.

17. Weed, 143.

18. Memorandum, A.B. Hermann to Vice President Nixon, et al., Aug. 9, 1960: Series 320, Box 37, "American Nationalities for Nixon-Lodge," Nixon Papers, NALN.

19. American-Lithuanian Republicans of California to Agnew, Sept. 27, 1956; Agnew to Nixon, Oct. 2, 1956: Series 320, Box 22, "Agnew, Robert T.," Nixon Papers, NALN.

20. Blase A. Bonpane to Nixon, May 22, 1959: Series 320, Box 93, "Bonpane, Blase A.," Nixon Papers, NALN.

21. Nixon to Bonpane, June 17, 1959: Series 320, Box 93, "Bonpane, Blase A.," Nixon Papers, NALN.

22. Nichols to NAR, Aug. 12, 1959: Record Group 15, Series 22, Subseries 5, Box 56, Folder 1298, Rockefeller Archives.

23. Nick Nichols to Nixon, Apr. 16, 1959; Nichols to Nixon, July 11, 1959; Nixon to Nichols, Aug. 6, 1959; Nichols to Don Hughes, undated; Nichols to Bob Finch, Oct. 1, 1959; Len Hall to Nichols, Nov. 2, 1959: Series 320, Box 561, "Nichols, Nick," Nixon Papers, NALN.

24. "Proposal for a Citizens' Advisory Committee on Relations with the Sino-Soviet Bloc," John Richardson, Jr., Aug. 24, 1960: Series 320, Box 37, "ANNL," Nixon Papers, NALN.

25. Press Release, Sept. 19, 1960: Series 320, Box 332, "Henderson, Horace E.," Nixon Papers, NALN; various newspaper clippings dated late 1957: Series 320, Box 501, "McKeldin, Theodore Roosevelt," Nixon Papers, NALN.

26. Goldwater, 114–17.

27. John Richardson, Jr. to Rod Perkins, Aug. 24, 1959: Record Group 15, Series 22, Subseries 4, Box 52, Folder 1227, Rockefeller Archives.

28. New York Herald Tribune clipping, Mar. 31, 1957: Series 320, Box 501, "McKeldin, Theodore Roosevelt," Nixon Papers, NALN.

29. *Baltimore Sun*, Aug. 25, 1959: Series 320, Box 501, "McKeldin," Nixon Papers, NALN.

30. Memo, Ned Harding to Finch, undated: Series 320, Box 37, "ANNL," Nixon Papers, NALN.

31. Memo, A.B. Hermann to Nixon, et al., Aug. 9, 1960: Series 320, Box 37, "ANNL," Nixon Papers, NALN.

32. Memo, Ned Harding to Finch, undated: Series 320, Box 37, "ANNL," Nixon Papers, NALN.

33. Memo, Stan McCaffrey to Nixon, Aug. 22, 1960: Series 320, Box 37, "ANNL," Nixon Papers, NALN.

34. The complete list also included a 2:10 group of Hungarians, Ukrainians, Slovaks, Carpathian-Ruthenians, and Croatians; a 2:30 group of Puerto Ricans, Filipinos, "Other Spanish speaking" and Chinese; and a 2:50 session with Germans, Scandinavians, Finns, Czechs, Russians, and Yugoslavs.

35. Memo, McCaffrey to Nixon, Aug. 27, 1960: Series 320, Box 37, "ANNL," Nixon Papers, NALN.

36. *New York Times*, Sept. 2, 1960, 8.

37. Ibid., Sept. 4, 1960, 1.

38. Ibid., Sept. 6, 1960, 1.

39. The 22 nationalities represented were listed as Armenian, Carpatho-Russian, Chinese, Croatian, Czech, Filipino, German, Greek, Hungarian, Irish, Italian, Japanese, Latvian, Lebanese, Lithuanian, Polish, Puerto Rican, Russian, Serbian, Slovak, Slovenian, Syrian, and Ukrainian. These leaders came from California, Connecticut, Florida, Illinois, Indiana, Maryland, Massachusetts, Michigan, Minnesota, New Hampshire, New Jersey, New York, Ohio, Oregon, Pennsylvania, South Carolina, Virginia, Washington, D.C., and West Virginia ("American Nationalities for Nixon-Lodge," Aug. 31, 1960: Series 320, Box 501, "McKeldin, Theodore Roosevelt," Nixon Papers, NALN).

40. American Nationalities for Nixon-Lodge Confidential Weekly Progress Report #1, 9/3/60: Series 320, Box 37, "ANNL," Nixon Papers, NALN.

41. ANNL Confidential Weekly Progress Report #1, 9/3/60: Series 320, Box 37, "ANNL," Nixon Papers, NALN.

42. Memo, Richardson to Hardin, Sept. 12, 1960: Series 207, Box 144, Folder 3, Nixon Papers, NALN.

43. Lizabeth Cohen, *A Consumer's Republic: The Politics of Mass Consumption in*

Postwar America (New York: Alfred A. Knopf, 2003), 333; Craig Allen discusses Eisenhower's use of the media and adeptness at public relations in *Eisenhower and the Mass Media: Peace, Prosperity and Prime-Time TV* (Chapel Hill: University of North Carolina Press, 1993).

44. *The Speeches*, 174–75.

45. Ibid., 175–78.

46. "Conference Conclusions," Sept. 19, 1960: Series 320, Box 37, "ANNL," Nixon Papers, NALN.

47. Nixon records in his 1962 memoir that Mitchell felt his presence on the ticket "would be attacked as a crude attempt to cater to the Catholic vote simply because the Democrats had nominated a Catholic for President" (Nixon, 317).

48. "Conference Conclusions," Sept. 19, 1960: Series 320, Box 37, "ANNL," Nixon Papers, NALN.

49. Memo, Sept. 23, 1960: Series 320, Box 37, "ANNL," Nixon Papers, NALN.

50. Progress Report #3, 9/24/60: Series 320, Box 37, "ANNL," Nixon Papers, NALN.

51. *Lithuanian Days* (Hollywood,), Oct. 1960; Apr. 1960; June 1960.

52. *Pacific Citizen* (Los Angeles), Sept. 30, 1960, 16.

53. Ibid., July 15, 1960.

54. Ibid., Oct. 14, 1960.

55. *Novoe Russkoe Slovo* (New York), Nov. 6, 1960; Nov. 5, 1960; Nov. 4, 1960. Translation from Russian by Max Kravtsov.

56. Ibid., Nov. 3, 1960. Curiously, the ad ran in English in this all Russian-language newspaper. By contrast, in the all Lithuanian Chicago newspaper *Draugas* almost all the text was in Lithuanian (Oct. 29, 1960), and in the bilingual Slovenian paper *Ameriska Domovina* out of Cleveland, most of the text was in Slovenian (Nov. 3, 1960). The ad also ran in the Japanese *Pacific Citizen* of Los Angeles (Oct. 28, 1960), among other newspapers.

57. John J. Knezevich to Nixon, Sept. 13, 1960, with attachments: Series 320, Box 419, "Knezevich, John J.," Nixon Papers, NALN.

58. Leonard Valiukas to Nixon, Oct. 2, 1960: Series 320, Box 778, "Valiukas, Leonard," Nixon Papers, NALN.

59. Valiukas to Nixon, Oct. 11, 1960; Memo, "gp," Oct. 24, 1960: Series 320, Box 778, "Valiukas," Nixon Papers, NALN.

60. Nixon, 345.

61. Stephen Ambrose, *Nixon: The Education of a Politician, 1913–1962* (New York: Touchstone, 1987), 588.

62. Claude Robinson Polling Data, Oct. 21, 1960: PPS 61, Nixon Library.

63. Nixon, 354–55.

64. Nixon, however, alleged that Kennedy knew of the administration's plans, having received a full CIA briefing on July 23, 1960 (Nixon, 354).

65. Telegram, Nixon to Nixon-Lodge Freedom Rally, Oct. 30, 1960: Series 320, Box 641, "Richardson, John," Nixon Papers, NALN.

66. *New York Times*, Oct. 30, 1960, 58.

67. On this point, Nixon—or his speechwriter—was confused. Nixon cited the 1920 census as the base for U.S. immigration quotas. But the National Origins Act of 1924 set the 1890 census as the baseline in an effort to exclude additional numbers of Eastern and southern European migrants. Asian immigration, of course, was more or less halted with the 1882 Chinese Exclusion Act and the 1907 Gentleman's Agreement with Japan.

68. Telegram, McCaffrey to Robert G. Alderman, Nov. 4, 1960: Series 320, Box 37, "ANNL," Nixon Papers, NALN.

69. Erika Lee, "American Gatekeeping: Race and Immigration Law in the

Twentieth Century," in Nancy Foner and George M. Fredrickson, eds., *Not Just Black and White: Historical and Contemporary Perspectives on Immigration, Race, and Ethnicity in the United States* (New York: Russell Sage Foundation, 2004), 127.

70. Donald Pienkos, "Polish-American Ethnicity in the Political Life of the United States," in Roucek and Eisenberg, eds., 287–89.

71. Phillips, 345.

72. Roma Lipsky, "Electioneering Among the Minorities," *Commentary* 31 (May 1961): 432.

73. Weed, 125.

74. Phillips, 163.

75. Pienkos observed that only in 1960 and 1964 did postwar Polish Americans support the Democratic Party in numbers similar to those of the New Deal years. In 1960, Catholicism was the leading factor; he credits the 1964 aberration to GOP candidate Barry Goldwater's extremism. Dawidowicz and Goldstein demonstrate that well-off Irish districts in Boston abandoned their 1956 support for Eisenhower to vote 69.9 percent for Kennedy. In Cincinnati, one of a few traditionally Republican American cities and home to a large German population, Kennedy managed to eke out a 50.4 percent victory. In Irish and Italian-dominated Providence, Kennedy sailed through with 72 percent of the vote in contrast to Adlai Stevenson's squeaker margin in 1956 (Pienkos, 288; Lucy S. Dawidowicz and Leon J. Goldstein, *Politics in a Pluralist Democracy: Studies of Voting in the 1960 Election* [New York: Institute of Human Relations Press, 1963], 10, 22–24, 28).

76. Lipsky, 429.

77. Cohen, 336–38.

78. See, for example, Preble.

79. For more on the Eisenhower administration's reaction to the uprising, see Csaba Békés, "The 1956 Hungarian Revolution and World Politics," Working Papers No. 16, Cold War International History Project, Woodrow Wilson Center for Scholars, Sept. 1996.

80. Preliminary Report (Summary of Conclusions and Recommendations), Dec. 22, 1960: Series 320, Box 37, "ANNL," Nixon Papers, NALN.

81. Valiukas to Hermann, Jan. 1, 1961: Series 320, Box 778, "Valiukas," Nixon Papers, NALN.

82. Col. Leon Nicolai to Nixon, Nov. 19, 1960: Series 320, Box 561, "Nicolai, Col. Leon," Nixon Papers, NALN.

83. A Protestant organization.

84. George E.K. Borshy to Hermann, Mar. 15, 1961: Series 320, Box 94, "Borshy, George E.K.," Nixon Papers, NALN.

85. Cohen, 338–39.

Conclusion

1. "Post-Election Statement by Barry Goldwater," Nov. 9, 1960: Speeches Vol. II, Barry Goldwater Papers, AHF.

2. Schoenwald, 6–7, 11.

3. Nixon, 422.

4. "How to Win in 1964": Record Group 4, Series J.1, Subseries 2, Box 11, Folder 96, Rockefeller Archives.

5. Brennan, 55–59, 73.

6. Rusher, 101.

7. F. Clifton White with Jerome Tuccille, *Politics as a Noble Calling: The Memoirs of F. Clifton White* (Ottawa, IL: Jameson Books, Inc., 1994), 140–42.

8. Schoenwald makes a very convincing argument to this effect (130, 135, 143).

9. Alabama, Georgia, Louisiana, Mississippi, and South Carolina. Goldwater's home state of Arizona also voted for him.

10. Wallace won Alabama, Arkansas, Georgia, Louisiana, and Mississippi.

11. *Congressional Quarterly's Guide to U.S. Elections*, 3rd ed. (Washington, D.C.: Congressional Quarterly, Inc., 1994), 462.

12. Hoff.

13. Ibid., 463.

14. Gil Troy, *Morning in America: How Ronald Reagan Invented the 1980s* (Princeton, NJ: Princeton University Press, 2005), 43.

Bibliography

Archival Collections

William F. Buckley, Jr. Papers, Yale University Archives and Manuscripts Collections, New Haven, CT (cited as Buckley Papers, Yale).

James F. Byrnes Papers, MSS 90, Clemson University, Clemson, SC (cited as Byrnes Papers, Clemson).

James F. Duffy Papers, MSS 69, Clemson (cited as Duffy Papers, Clemson).

Barry M. Goldwater Papers, Arizona Historical Foundation, Tempe, AZ (cited as AHF).

Richard M. Nixon Papers, Richard M. Nixon Presidential Library and Birthplace, Yorba Linda, CA (cited as Nixon Library).

Richard M. Nixon Pre-Presidential Papers, National Archives and Records Administration, Pacific Southwest Branch, Laguna Niguel, CA (cited as NALN).

Nelson A. Rockefeller Papers Collection, Rockefeller Archives Center, Sleepy Hollow, NY (cited as Rockefeller Archives).

Gregory D. Shorey Papers, South Caroliniana Library, University of South Carolina, Columbia, SC (cited as SCL).

Strom Thurmond Collection, MSS 100, Clemson University, Clemson, SC (cited as Thurmond Collection, Clemson).

William D. Workman, Jr., Papers, South Caroliniana Library, University of South Carolina, Columbia, SC (cited as SCL).

Correspondence

Gregory D. Shorey

Oral History

"Interview with J. Drake Edens," Feb. 13, 1974: Southern Oral History Program, in the Southern Historical Collection, Manuscripts Department, Wilson Library, University of North Carolina at Chapel Hill.

Periodicals

Ameriska Domovina (Cleveland)
Baltimore Afro-American
California Eagle
[Charleston] *News and Courier* (SC)
Chicago Defender
Columbia State
Congressional Quarterly Weekly Report

Daily Emerald (University of Oregon, Eugene, OR)
Draugus (Chicago)
Harvard Crimson
Lietuviu Dienos (Hollywood, CA)
National Review
New York Herald Tribune
New York Post
New York Times
Newsweek
Novoe Russkoe Slovo (New York)
Pacific Citizen (Los Angeles)
Pittsburgh Courier
The State (Columbia, SC)
U.S. News and World Report
Wall Street Journal

Published Works

Allen, Craig. *Eisenhower and the Mass Media: Peace, Prosperity and Prime-Time TV*. Chapel Hill: University of North Carolina Press, 1993.

Allitt, Patrick. *Catholic Intellectuals and Conservative Politics in America, 1950–1985*. Ithaca, NY: Cornell University Press, 1993.

Altbach, Philip G., and Patti Peterson. "Before Berkeley: Historical Perspectives on American Student Activism." *Annals of the American Academy of Political and Social Science* 395 (May 1971): 1–14.

Ambrose, Stephen. *Nixon: The Education of a Politician, 1913–1962*. New York: Touchstone, 1987.

Andrew, John A., III. *The Other Side of the Sixties: Young Americans for Freedom and The Rise of Conservative Politics*. New Brunswick, NJ: Rutgers University Press, 1997.

Bass, Jack, and Walter DeVries. *The Transformation of Southern Politics: Social Change and Political Consequence Since 1945*. New York: Basic Books, 1976.

Bayor Ronald H., ed. *Race and Ethnicity in America: A Concise History*. New York: Columbia University Press, 2003.

Békés, Csaba. "The 1956 Hungarian Revolution and World Politics." Working Paper No. 16, Cold War International History Project. Washington, D.C.: Woodrow Wilson International Center for Scholars, Sept. 1996.

Bell, Daniel, ed. *The Radical Right: The New American Right, Expanded and Updated*. Garden City, NY: Anchor Books, 1963, revised ed.

Berman, William C. *America's Right Turn: From Nixon to Clinton*. Second edition. Baltimore, MD.: The Johns Hopkins University Press, 1998.

Black, Earl, and Merle Black. *Politics and Society in the South*. Cambridge. MA: Harvard University Press, 1987.

Blair, Anne E. *Lodge in Vietnam: A Patriot Abroad*. New Haven, CT: Yale University Press, 1995.

Boller, Paul F., Jr. *Presidential Campaigns from George Washington to George W. Bush*. New York: Oxford University Press, 2004.

Borja-Mamaril, Concordia R., and Tyrone Lin. *Filipino Americans: Pioneers to the Present*. Portland, OR: Filipino American National Historical Society—Oregon Chapter, 2000.

Borstelmann, Thomas. *The Cold War and the Color Line: American Race Relations in the Global Arena*. Cambridge, MA: Harvard University Press, 2001.

Branch, Taylor. *Parting the Waters: America in the King Years, 1954–63*. New York: Touchstone, 1988.

Brendon, Piers. *Ike: His Life and Times*. New York: Harper and Row, 1986.

Brennan, Mary C. *Turning Right in the Sixties: The Conservative Capture of the GOP*. Chapel Hill: University of North Carolina Press, 1995.

Brinkley, Alan. "The Problem of American Conservatism." *American Historical Review* 99 (Apr. 1994): 409–29.

Bryant, Nick. *The Bystander: John F. Kennedy and the Struggle for Black Equality*. New York: Basic Books, 2006.

Buckley, William F., Jr. *God and Man at Yale*. Washington, D.C.: Regnery Publishing, Inc., 1952, 1977, 1986.

———. *Miles Gone By: A Literary Autobiography*. Washington, D.C.: Regnery Publishing, Inc., 2004.

———. *Up From Liberalism*. Second edition. New York: Bantam Books, 1959, 1968.

Burk, Robert Fredrick. *The Eisenhower Administration and Black Civil Rights*. Knoxville: University of Tennessee Press, 1984.

Burnham, Walter Dean. *Critical Elections and the Mainsprings of American Politics*. New York: W.W. Norton and Co., 1970.

Carter, Dan T. *The Politics of Rage: George Wallace, the Origins of the New Conservatism, and the Transformation of American Politics*. Second edition. Baton Rouge: Louisiana State University Press, 1995, 2000.

Chambers, William Nisbet, and Walter Dean Burnham. *The American Party Systems: Stages of Political Development*. New York: Oxford University Press, 1967.

Chang, Iris. *The Chinese in America*. New York: Viking, 2003.

Cohen, Lizabeth. *A Consumer's Republic: The Politics of Mass Consumption in Postwar America*. New York: Alfred A. Knopf, 2003.

Cohodas, Nadine. *Strom Thurmond and the Politics of Southern Change*. New York: Simon and Schuster, 1993.

Collins, Robert M. *More: The Politics of Economic Growth in Postwar America*. Oxford: Oxford University Press, 2000.

Congressional Quarterly's Guide to U.S. Elections. Third edition. Washington, D.C.: Congressional Quarterly, Inc., 1994.

Cosman, Bernard. "Presidential Republicanism in the South, 1960." *Journal of Politics* 24 (May 1962): 303–22.

Critchlow, Donald T. *The Conservative Ascendancy: How the GOP Right Made Political History*. Cambridge, MA: Harvard University Press, 2007.

Dallek, Matthew. *The Right Moment: Ronald Reagan's First Victory and the Decisive Turning Point in American Politics*. New York: The Free Press, 2000.

Dawidowicz, Lucy S., and Leon J. Goldstein. *Politics in a Pluralist Democracy: Studies of Voting in the 1960 Election*. New York: Institute of Human Relations Press, 1963.

Dionne, E.J., Jr. *Why Americans Hate Politics*. New York: Simon and Schuster, 1991.

Donaldson, Gary A. *The First Modern Campaign: Kennedy, Nixon, and the Election of 1960*. Lanham, MD: Rowman and Littlefield Publishers, Inc., 2007.

Dudziak, Mary L. *Cold War Civil Rights: Race and the Image of American Democracy*. Princeton, NJ: Princeton University Press, 2000.

Edsall, Thomas Byrne and Mary D. *Chain Reaction: The Impact of Race, Rights and Taxes on American Politics*. New York: W.W. Norton and Co., 1991.

Evans, M. Stanton. *Revolt on the Campus*. Chicago: Henry Regnery Company, 1961.

Foner, Nancy, and George M. Fredrickson, eds. *Not Just Black and White: Historical and Contemporary Perspectives on Immigration, Race, and Ethnicity in the United States*. New York: Russell Sage Foundation, 2004.

Foss, Daniel A., and Ralph Larkin. *Beyond Revolution: A New Theory of Social Movements*. South Hadley, MA: Bergin and Garvey Pub., Inc., 1986.

Gellman, Irwin F. *The Contender: Richard Nixon, The Congress Years, 1946–1952*. New York: The Free Press, 1999.

Gerstle, Gary. *American Crucible: Race and Nation in the Twentieth Century*. Princeton, NJ: Princeton University Press, 2001.

Gifford, Laura J. "Washington, Valores J. (Val)." *African American National Biography*. New York: Oxford University Press, 2008.

Glazer, Nathan, and Daniel Patrick Moynihan. *Beyond the Melting Pot: The Negroes, Puerto Ricans, Jews, Italians, and Irish of New York City*. Second edition. Cambridge, MA: MIT Press, 1970.

Goldberg, Robert Alan. *Barry Goldwater*. New Haven, CT: Yale University Press, 1995.

Goldwater, Barry M. *The Conscience of a Conservative*. New York: Victor, 1960.

Gould, Lewis L. *Grand Old Party: A History of the Republicans*. New York: Random House, 2003.

Graham, Cole Blease, Jr., and William V. Moore. *South Carolina Politics and Government*. Lincoln: University of Nebraska Press, 1994.

Grantham, Dewey W. *The Life and Death of the Solid South*. Lexington: University Press of Kentucky, 1988.

Halter, Marilyn. *Shopping for Identity: The Marketing of Ethnicity*. New York: Schocken Books, 2000.

Himmelstein, Jerome L. *To the Right: The Transformation of American Conservatism*. Berkeley: University of California Press, 1990.

Hodgson, Godfrey. *The World Turned Right Side Up: A History of the Conservative Ascendancy in America*. Boston: Houghton Mifflin Co., 1996.

Hoff, Joan. *Nixon Reconsidered*. New York: Basic Books, 1994.

Judis, John B. *William F. Buckley, Jr.: Patron Saint of the Conservatives*. New York: Simon and Schuster, 1988.

Kelly, Christine A. *Tangled Up in Red, White and Blue: New Social Movements in America*. Lanham, MD: Rowman and Littlefield Publishers, Inc., 2001.

Key, V.O., Jr. *Southern Politics in State and Nation*. New York: Vintage Books, 1949.

Kirk, Russell. *The Conservative Mind*. Fourth edition. New York: Avon Books, 1968.

Klatch, Rebecca E. *Women of the New Right*. Philadelphia: Temple University Press, 1987.

Kuhn, Clifford M. "'There's a Footnote to History!': Memory and the History of Martin Luther King's Oct. 1960 Arrest and Its Aftermath." *Journal of American History* 84 (Sept. 1997): 583–95.

Larson, Arthur. *A Republican Looks at His Party*. New York: Harper and Brothers, 1956.

Lawson, Steven F. *Running for Freedom: Civil Rights and Black Politics in America Since 1941*. New York: McGraw-Hill, Inc., 1991.

Leiserson, Avery, ed. *The American South in the 1960s*. New York: Frederick A. Praeger, 1964.

Lipsky, Roma. "Electioneering Among the Minorities." *Commentary* 31 (May 1961): 428–32.

Lodge, Henry Cabot. *The Storm Has Many Eyes: A Personal Narrative*. New York: W.W. Norton and Co., 1973.

Lottman, Michael S. "The GOP and the South." *Ripon Forum* VI (July–Aug. 1970): 9–86.

Lubell, Samuel. *The Future of American Politics*. Second edition. Garden City, NY: Doubleday and Co., 1956.

Lublin, David. *The Republican South: Democratization and Partisan Change*. Princeton, NJ: Princeton University Press, 2004.

Mayhew, David R. *Electoral Realignments: A Critique of an American Genre*. New Haven, CT: Yale University Press, 2002.

McGirr, Lisa. *Suburban Warriors: The Origins of the New American Right*. Princeton, NJ: Princeton University Press, 2001.

Meriwether, James H. *Proudly We Can Be Africans: Black Americans and Africa, 1935–1961*.

Chapel Hill: University of North Carolina Press, 2002.

Miller, William J. *Henry Cabot Lodge*. New York: James H. Heineman, Inc., 1967.

Mitchell, Greg. *Tricky Dick and the Pink Lady: Richard Nixon vs. Helen Gahagan Douglas— Sexual Politics and the Red Scare, 1950*. New York: Random House, 1998.

Morrow, E. Frederic, *Forty Years a Guinea Pig*. New York: The Pilgrim Press, 1980.

———. *Way Down South Up North*. Philadelphia: Pilgrim Press, 1973.

Nash, George H. *The Conservative Intellectual Movement in America Since 1945*. New York: Basic Books, 1976.

Nichols, David A. *A Matter of Justice: Eisenhower and the Beginning of the Civil Rights Revolution*. New York: Simon and Schuster, 2007.

Nixon, Richard M. *Six Crises*. Garden City, NY: Doubleday and Co., 1962.

Novak, Michael. *The Rise of the Unmeltable Ethnics*. New York: MacMillan, 1971.

Official Report of the Proceedings of the Twenty-Seventh Republican National Convention. Washington, D.C.: Republican National Committee, 1960.

Parmet, Herbert S. *Richard Nixon and His America*. Boston: Little, Brown and Co., 1990.

Patterson, James T. *Mr. Republican: A Biography of Robert A. Taft*. Boston: Houghton Mifflin, 1972.

Pells, Richard H. *The Liberal Mind in a Conservative Age: American Intellectuals in the 1940s and 1950s*. New York: Harper and Row, 1985.

Perlstein, Rick. *Before the Storm: Barry Goldwater and the Unmaking of the American Consensus*. New York: Hill and Wang, 2001.

Phillips, Kevin. *The Emerging Republican Majority*. New Rochelle, NY: Arlington House, 1969.

Pienkos, Donald E. *For Your Freedom Through Ours: Polish American Efforts on Poland's Behalf, 1863–1991*. Boulder, CO: East European Monographs, 1991.

Plummer, Brenda Gayle. *Rising Wind: Black Americans and U.S. Foreign Affairs, 1935–1960*. Chapel Hill: University of North Carolina Press, 1996.

———, ed. *Window on Freedom: Race, Civil Rights, and Foreign Affairs, 1945–1988*. Chapel Hill: University of North Carolina Press, 2003.

Preble, Christopher A. *John F. Kennedy and the Missile Gap*. DeKalb, IL: Northern Illinois University Press, 2004.

Rae, Nicol C. *The Decline and Fall of the Liberal Republicans from 1952 to the Present*. New York: Oxford University Press, 1989.

Rampersad, Arnold. *Jackie Robinson: A Biography*. New York: Alfred A. Knopf, 1997.

Reich, Cary. *The Life of Nelson A. Rockefeller: Worlds to Conquer, 1908–1958*. New York: Doubleday, 1996.

Reiss, Tom. "The First Conservative: How Peter Viereck Inspired—and Lost—a Movement," *The New Yorker* (Oct. 24, 2005): 38–47.

Robertson, David. *Sly and Able: A Political Biography of James F. Byrnes*. New York: W.W. Norton and Co., 1994.

Rockefeller, Nelson A. *The Future of Federalism*. Cambridge, MA: Harvard University Press, 1962.

Rorabaugh, William. J. *Kennedy and the Promise of the Sixties*. New York: Cambridge University Press, 2002.

Rossiter, Clinton. *Parties and Politics in America*. Ithaca, NY: Cornell University Press, 1960.

Roucek, Joseph S., and Bernard Eisenberg, eds. *America's Ethnic Politics*. Westport, CT: Greenwood Press, 1982.

Rusher, William A. *The Rise of the Right*. New York: William Morrow and Co., 1984.

Schlesinger, Arthur M., Jr. *The Vital Center*. Revised edition. New York: DaCapo Press, 1988.

Schneider, Gregory L. *Cadres for Conservatism: Young Americans for Freedom and the Rise of the Contemporary Right*. New York: New York University Press, 1999.

Schoenwald, Jonathan M. *A Time for Choosing: The Rise of Modern American Conservatism*. Oxford: Oxford University Press, 2001.

Schuparra, Kurt. *Triumph of the Right: The Rise of the California Conservative Movement, 1945–1966* Armonk, NY: M.E. Sharpe, 1998.

Shafer, Byron, ed. *The End of Realignment? Interpreting American Electoral Eras*. Madison: University of Wisconsin Press, 1991.

Skocpol, Theda. *Protecting Soldiers and Mothers: The Political Origins of Social Policy in the United States*. Cambridge, MA: Belknap Press, 1992.

Skowronek, Stephen. *The Politics Presidents Make: Leadership from John Adams to Bill Clinton*. Second edition. Cambridge, MA: Belknap Press, 1997.

Snow, David A., et al. *The Blackwell Companion to Social Movements*. Malden, MA: Blackwell Publishing, Ltd., 2004.

The Speeches of Vice President Richard M. Nixon, Presidential Campaign of 1960. Washington, D.C.: U.S. Government Printing Office, 1961.

Stanley, Harold W. "Southern Partisan Changes: Dealignment, Realignment, or Both?" *Journal of Politics* 50 (Feb. 1988): 64–88.

Stebenne, David L. *Modern Republican: Arthur Larson and the Eisenhower Years*. Bloomington: Indiana University Press, 2006.

Strong, Donald S. *The 1952 Presidential Election in the South*. University of Alabama: Bureau of Public Administration, 1955.

———. *Urban Republicanism in the South*. University of Alabama: Bureau of Public Administration, 1960.

Strub, Whitney. *Perversion for Profit: The Politics of Obscenity and Pornography in the Postwar United States*. New York: Columbia University Press, forthcoming 2010.

Sundquist, James L. *Dynamics of the Party System: Alignment and Realignment of Political Parties in the United States*. Washington, D.C.: The Brookings Institution, 1973.

Troy, Gil. *Morning in America: How Ronald Reagan Invented the 1980s*. Princeton, NJ: Princeton University Press, 2005.

Von Eschen, Penny. *Race Against Empire: Black Americans and Anticolonialism, 1937–1957*. Ithaca, NY: Cornell University Press, 1997.

Wagner, Steven. *Eisenhower Republicanism: Pursuing the Middle Way*. DeKalb, IL: Northern Illinois University Press, 2006.

Weed, Perry L. *The White Ethnic Movement and Ethnic Politics*. New York: Praeger Publishers, 1973.

White, F. Clifton, with Jerome Tuccille. *Politics as a Noble Calling: The Memoirs of F. Clifton White*. Ottawa, IL: Jameson Books, Inc., 1994.

White, Theodore H. *The Making of the President, 1960*. New York: Signet, 1961.

Workman, Jr., William D. *The Case for the South*. New York: The Devin-Adair Co., 1960.

Index